Peter Moore is an itinerant hobo who is lucky enough to be able to support his insatiable travel habit (he has visited 92 countries so far) through writing. He is the author of *The Wrong Way Home*, *The Full Montezuma*, *Swahili for the Broken-Hearted* (shortlisted for the WHSmith People's Choice Travel Book Award), *Vroom with a View* and the classic alternative travel guide, *No Shitting in the Toilet*. When he is not on the road, you'll find Peter in either London or Sydney watching 'Neighbours'. Sad, really.

Praise for Peter Moore's travel writing:

'Peter Moore is the genuine article, a traveller's traveller . . . Thoroughly enjoyable . . . Inspirational stuff'
FHM

'Moore's a sharp observer of the bizarre . . . Read, enjoy, escape'
Maxim

'Moore writes in a racy, witty style that has no pretensions or self-censorship . . . this book is a hilarious read and fits snugly into any pack'
TNT Magazine

'Moore has a parched dry wit, the solid brass *cojones* of a true traveller and a rare eye for the madness of the wider world'
John Birmingham

Also by Peter Moore

The Wrong Way Home
No Shitting in the Toilet
Swahili for the Broken-Hearted
Vroom with a View

and available from Bantam Books

The Full Montezuma

Around Central America and the Caribbean
with the Girl Next Door

PETER MOORE

BANTAM BOOKS

LONDON • TORONTO • SYDNEY • AUCKLAND • JOHANNESBURG

THE FULL MONTEZUMA
A BANTAM BOOK : 0553 81701 9

First published in Australia and New Zealand in 2000 by Bantam

PRINTING HISTORY
Bantam Books edition published 2001

7 9 10 8 6

Bantam Books are published by Transworld Publishers,
61–63 Uxbridge Road, London W5 5SA,
a division of The Random House Group Ltd,
in Australia by Random House Australia (Pty) Ltd,
20 Alfred Street, Milsons Point, Sydney, NSW 2061, Australia,
in New Zealand by Random House New Zealand Ltd,
18 Poland Road, Glenfield, Auckland 10, New Zealand
and in South Africa by Random House (Pty) Ltd,
Endulini, 5a Jubilee Road, Parktown 2193, South Africa.

Printed and bound in Great Britain by
Cox & Wyman Ltd, Reading, Berkshire

Papers used by Random House
are natural, recyclable products made from wood grown in
sustainable forests. The manufacturing processes conform to
the environmental regulations of the country of origin

Contents

Acknowledgements

First of all, thanks to all the people who have e-mailed me about the first two books. It can be a long, lonely slog writing a book and your e-mails brightened my day and motivated me to keep going. Thanks heaps.

Thanks to Ronald Tierney, who I should have thanked in *The Wrong Way Home*, but forgot. Always a good person to dream up exotic journeys with.

To all my family, especially my nieces and nephews Jessica, Taylor, Amanda, Harrison, James and Kai – as good a reason as any for coming home.

On the road, special thanks to Brendan 'Rexy' Green, Rebecca Jackson, Jonathon Dowson, Monique and Richard Sivret, and Pat and Barb McGowan, for good company and good laughs.

Thanks to Mike and Glenys Davey for timely financial assistance.

Thanks to Jude McGee for a great edit, and to all my good friends at Transworld as well: in Sydney, Heather Curdie, Natasha Ramia and Sophie Gemmell; in London, Alison Tulett, Simon Taylor and Sally Wray. My appreciation also goes to my agents, Fiona Inglis in Sydney, Jonny Geller in London.

Cheers to Tim Cox, Steve Cannane, Sarah McDonald and Francis Leach at ABC Radio and Triple J, respectively, for letting me onto their radio programs to talk travel.

Finally, I'd like to say thanks to Judy Green – the most famous Alby chick and original adventure travel girl next door. (If, God forbid, you don't know who Alby is, check out my website at www.petermoore.com.au). She showed that it is possible for a spunky blonde to wander world trouble spots in nothing more than a chamois bikini. She also gave me the twisted notion that travelling through third world shitholes was somehow glamorous.

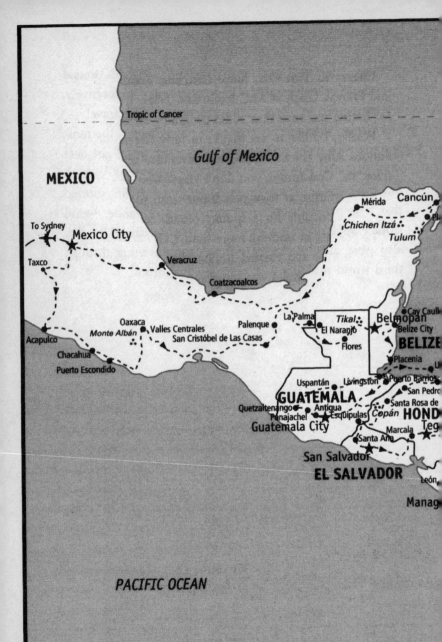

To Shana

CHAPTER ONE

Preparations

Annoying habit >>> Overpacking
Culprit >>> GND

I'm prepared to wager that there isn't a man on this planet who hasn't done foolish things during the first flushes of love. Some buy their new girlfriends expensive gifts. Others are talked into a new wardrobe of collarless jackets and string T-shirts. Some rash souls promptly propose marriage and then spend the next two years going through a messy divorce. Me? Well, I invited my new love – the girl next door – on a six-month journey through Central America.

We'd only been on a few dates – four, I think. I had spotted her one morning a few months before, having a cigarette out the front of her house before heading off to work in her business suit, her blonde hair in a shoulder-length bob. It had taken me all the time that had passed since that time to work up the courage to go next door and ask her out. But when we did go out it was so comfortable, so natural, I couldn't help but ask her to come away with me.

I know now it was because of a chemical imbalance in my brain. I was in love – mad with it – and my serotonin levels were shot. I was still in what scientists have recently labelled the period of pathological romance, a time when the inner chemistry of a smitten brain resembles that of someone suffering from obsessive compulsive disorder (OCD).

Donatella Marazziti, a psychiatrist at the University of Pisa, first noticed the phenomenon of pathological romanticism when she began looking for a biochemical explanation for OCD. She found the culprit was serotonin, a neurotransmitter chemical that has a soothing effect on the brain. OCD sufferers appeared to have low levels of serotonin, and, from her studies, so did people in the first stage of love. So when my friends told me I was crazy for taking a girl I'd only just met to a region prone to natural disasters and armed conflict, in a way they were right.

It certainly wasn't a plan that would have stood up to close scrutiny. Can you imagine what a trained psychologist, maybe even the esteemed Miss Marazziti herself, would have made of the whole thing? Me, reclining on the couch, explaining the reason why I thought a cute blonde was my ideal travelling companion through the likes of Nicaragua and El Salvador.

'Now Peter, how long have you known the Girl Next Door?'

'Well, I've only known *known* her for six weeks,' I'd sigh. 'But it feels as though we've known each other for ever!'

'And tell me, have you ever travelled with someone before?'

'Well, no. Not *really*,' I'd admit grudgingly. 'But it won't be a problem. The GND is so easygoing and laid back. We've been together for six weeks and we haven't even had a single fight!'

'Yes. I see,' she'd say, making a few notes in her notepad. 'Now, tell me again, where is it that you are planning to go?'

'Basically, a loop through Central America,' I'd say enthusiastically. 'We'll start in Mexico City and head south through Guatemala, Belize, Honduras, El Salvador, Nicaragua and Panama. Then we'll pop across to Jamaica for the cricket. Then Cuba. Then back to Cancun in Mexico before finishing again in Mexico City.'

'Hmmm,' she'd say, sucking on her pencil. 'Sounds pretty intense. Are you sure the GND knows what she is letting herself in for?'

It would be a valid point. In my mind I hadn't been thinking of the long arduous bus journeys, the active volcanoes, the shifting tectonic plates or the fact that we would be starting our journey at the tail end of the hurricane season. In my mind's eye we were frolicking on Caribbean beaches – albeit some of the less expensive ones – watching sunsets and gambolling dolphins – basically the sort of stuff you read in tawdry romance novels.

That was certainly how I sold the idea to the GND. I had already been planning to go to Central America before I had met her. To be honest, it was more the Mayan ruins and volcanoes and the fact that the Australian dollar could still buy you something there that had initially drawn me to the region. But when the GND started to seriously consider coming along, I shifted my focus onto things more coastal. She was contemplating throwing in her job as an office administrator, after all, and it would help convince her mother and father that their only daughter wasn't going to get kidnapped by mountain-based Marxist guerillas. In those serotonin-sapped days I may have even become convinced that it was because of the beaches that I'd thought of going to Central America and the Caribbean in the first place.

Thinking about it now, I doubt that I even had a scrap of serotonin in my system. How else do you explain the purchase of the companion fares? It was a special deal Japan Airlines were offering two people travelling together. In return for agreeing to fly every single part of the way with another person, both parties were offered a saving of $50 each on their airfares.

When the travel agent told me about it I should have said, 'Well, that's very nice, but as I have only been in this relationship for a matter of minutes, I think it would be wise just to take the normal fare, don't you?' She would have laughed knowingly and nothing more would have been said. But no, I had to talk to the GND about it.

'Do you think we should get the companion fare,' I asked cautiously.

'Do you think we should?' answered the GND.

'Do *you* think we should?' I repeated.

'Do *you* think we should?' answered the GND again.

From that moment, there was no way out of the companion fares. Although it only saved us $50 each, not to take the companion option would have suggested that we had doubts about the longevity of our relationship. Sure, it would have been sensible not to buy the companion fare. But as I was quickly finding out, love is rarely ever sensible.

It was the same when the GND showed me her packing list. I had asked her to make a list so I could go over it. I wanted to check for anomalies and – I don't deny it – prune it a little. I guess I had been left scarred by the only other time I had travelled with a member of the opposite sex. It was on a Marco Polo cruise around the Pacific. I was eleven and the woman in question was my mother.

There are no weight restrictions on cruise ships so my mother felt compelled to fill enough luggage to cover every contingency. My father struggled up the gangplank at the Sydney Overseas Terminal with half a dozen suitcases, stuffed solid and bursting at the seams with matching outfits for my sisters and me. Being the mid-seventies, each outfit was 100 per cent polyester, striped and in unnatural hues of orange, pink and brown. It never occurred to my mother that a) we didn't like the outfits or b) we didn't want to match our siblings.

As an only child my Mum didn't comprehend the acute embarrassment of wearing the exact same outfit – right down to the anchor-shaped buttons – as your kid sister.

She'd just buy this horrible material by the bolt and run up identical outfits in four different sizes.

Worse still, my mother had noticed in the brochure for the cruise that there were going to be activities nights – fancy dress, cocktail parties, theme nights – and she'd brought enough beads, baubles and buttons to knock up appropriate outfits for each of us. (I'm sure that somewhere in one of the larger vinyl suitcases there was a sewing machine.) It all paid off, though. Dad won the Tarzan look-alike competition - no one else's wife had thought of bringing along a loin cloth on a cruise to Fiji – and my sisters, dressed as fairies, princesses and ballerinas, won their appropriate sections in the fancy dress competition.

I was the only one who let the team down. Mum had brought a leotard along for me, figuring that I wanted to be a ballet dancer too, but I refused on the grounds that I wanted to be an individual. (The fact that I had a crush on the girl in the cabin opposite and was concerned about how she would react to me in a tutu may have had some-thing to do with it.) I was hoping to get out of the stupid fancy dress competition altogether. But my mother, being the resourceful woman she is, simply shrugged her shoulders and ran me up an outfit made from the shopping bags they got when they bought souvenirs in Suva. I didn't win my section, but the judges took pity on me and gave me a consolation, Best Use of a Brown Paper Bag, award.

So you can understand why I was a little nervous when the GND handed me her packing list. Especially when I noticed how long it was. It unfurled before me like one of those scrolls the old town criers used to read from.

'I've been good, haven't I?' said the GND.

I bit my tongue and smiled weakly. Then I noticed the hairdryer ... then the haircurler ... and then the hairspray, and felt compelled to speak. 'What do you need *those* for?' I spluttered.

'My hair is really thin and limp,' the GND replied matter-of-factly.

'Well, if it's thin it will dry quickly.'

'But because it's thin, I need to style it,' reasoned the GND.

'Style it? Just pull it back into a ponytail.'

'I *guess* it's getting long enough to pull back,' answered the GND, unconvinced.

'There you go,' I said proudly. 'I just saved you a kilo. No hairdryer, curler, hairspray – pump action or otherwise.'

The subhead *Cosmetics* caught my eye. The GND had foolishly listed each item individually: foundation ... powder ... blush ... eyeliner ... mascara ... lipstick ... cleanser (rinse off) ... moisturiser ... suntan lotion ... it was as if she was going on a Revlon shoot.

'The list *looks* long,' she explains. 'But remember. They're all *little* things.'

Then there were the personal grooming items: clippers ... tweezers ... scissors ... razors ... soap ... washer ... deodorant ... two-in-one shampoo—conditioner (I smiled at this concession to saving space!) – the GND was going to be the neatest, cleanest, clipped person this side of Managua. When I pointed this out she just made a face and pleaded, 'It's better for you!'

About a metre down the list I came upon the clothes:

two pairs of shorts – denim *and* canvas . . . four T-shirts . . . three dresses . . . two pairs of jeans – black and light canvas . . . one jacket . . . two long-sleeve tops . . . one spray jacket . . . one swimming costume . . . seven pairs of underwear and matching bras . . . four pairs of socks . . . one pair of walking boots . . . one pair of flat casual, light canvas shoes . . . one pair of sandals . . . and a cap.

'It's not a fashion parade, you know!' I spluttered. 'We're going to Central America. We'll be roughing it!'

I sat down, trying to catch my breath. The list was quite staggering. How would the GND carry it all? How would she lug it up onto the tops of buses and into the backs of utes? Would I end up having to carry some of it? I had a flashback of my father – sweating, staggering, cursing – and the gangplank bending under the weight.

'Oh, and by the way,' the GND smiled sweetly. 'I've decided to give up smoking two days before we go away.'

I think my serotonin levels must have been on the rise again. Because at that moment I had a spasm of what felt an awful lot like doubt.

Not much, mind you, but enough.

CHAPTER TWO

MEXICO CITY

Annoying habit >>> Lack of sympathy
Culprit >>> Peter

The GND and I arrived in Mexico City expecting to hear the lip, sip, sucking sounds of salsa but all we got were organ grinders. They were on every street corner in Mexico City, in natty grey uniforms, grinding out the most God-awful noises that sounded not unlike a cat having la vida loca sucked right out of it.

Now, I'm not exactly sure of the heritage of the organ grinding profession, but I'd put money on the fact that organ grinders weren't a common part of everyday Aztec life. I've always associated the trade with swarthy Mediterranean types wearing striped T-shirts and with a monkey sitting on their shoulder waving a battered tin cup collecting money. The Mexican organ grinder, however, wears a train conductor uniform complete with a snazzy peak cap, and instead of a monkey they send a similarly dressed human offsider to go and collect the coins.

There was no escaping them. We had a favourite place for breakfast, a huge, bustling cafeteria called Café La Blanca, where wizened old waiters in fading uniforms doled out breakfasts of refried beans and coffee to bored customers. An organ grinder and his mate stood either side of the door playing a mournful tune, causing customers passing between them to get into the cafeteria to cover their ears. Occasionally waiters would shoo them away and they would take up a spot across the street, their music only a little less intrusive. But when the waiter's back was turned they would scamper back to the cafeteria entrance. This would happen at least half a dozen times. By the time our refried beans arrived, the waiter would have simply given up.

There was one common factor between the Mexican organ grinders and others I have encountered elsewhere – the music they churned out was excruciatingly bad. It wailed and moaned, fluctuating in speed according to how tired the organ grinder's grinding arm was. Most hadn't learned the art of the smooth grind, so their tunes floated along on a path that was neither in time nor in tune. The music would speed up on the downward grind and slow down on the back upward pull, as if the organ grinder was releasing pressure on a cat's throat and then reapplying it again. Let's just say it wasn't the kind of noise that would move the GND to grab my arm, pull me close and say,

'Gee, I love you! I'm so glad I came along on a jaunt through this part of the developing world with you!'

Nor would have our first foray on Mexican public transport. On a short ride to Zona Rosa on the Metro to check our e-mail, the GND was goosed by some oversexed Mexican commuters. I guess I should have seen it coming. The carriage was crowded and as people got on and off we were separated, then gradually pushed further and further apart. We looked across the sea of black hair at each other and smiled, unaware that a group of teenagers in baggy pants were circling the GND and getting ready to strike. Then, somewhere between Pino Suárez and Isabel la Católica, the GND gave out a scream.

'Hey!' she yelped. 'Some guy just pinched my bum!'

It should have been an opportunity for me to step forward and take charge. I should have collared the offenders and made it clear that the GND's bum was not some piece of fruit to be tested with a squeeze for ripeness and freshness. Make them apologise to the GND for taking liberty with her butt. It would have been an ideal opportunity to put the GND's mind at rest, to show her I was a take-charge kind of guy, the sort of fellow an attractive blonde could feel comfortable and safe with travelling through dodgier areas of Central America.

It didn't work out that way. I was trapped, impotent, on the wrong side of the carriage. The boys used the crowd to avoid my grasps and got off the train at the next station, giggling at what they'd done. The best I could do was yell after them, calling them all manner of names – infuriatingly, only in English. To her credit, the GND laughed it off, joking that she had been given The Full Montezuma. All I could think of was the last words of the GND's father – 'You take good care of my daughter!' Just over 24 hours into the trip and I had already failed.

I must admit I was already a little sensitive about how the GND was finding Mexico. On the taxi ride from the airport on our first night she had been alarmed by the dark streets, the shuttered shops covered in graffiti, the piles of garbage and the lumpy prostitute on every corner. After reading in our guidebook that taxi drivers were often in league with criminal elements, she became convinced that the driver was taking us to a dark lane where young Latinos in tight white singlets and black jeans with wispy moustaches were waiting with switchblades to take all our belongings and carve their initials into our chests just for good measure.

Our hotel had also left her a little underwhelmed. We were staying in the rather modest Hotel Zamora, atop five flights of stairs, the climbing of which left the GND breathless. The room was tiny and dark and the attached bathroom kept making noises like a stricken U-boat in an old b&w war movie.

The GND had taken to naming the cockroaches and spent the moments before retiring each night reading the most alarmist comments from our guidebook. 'It says here foreigners are often kidnapped and held for ransom,' she said. 'You didn't tell me that.'

It's true. I hadn't. When I had been trying to convince her to join me on this journey I had focused on stuff like margaritas, salsa music, Caribbean beaches and the off-chance of running into Ricky Martin. I was hoping that the other, less savoury aspects of the region – the crime, the wars, the corruption – wouldn't need to be addressed until we were actually confronted by them. To be honest, I was kind of hoping that with a little luck I wouldn't have to bring it up at all. Instead I tried to brush her off with a rather weak, 'Oh, really?'

Another night it was Mexico City's notorious pollution problem that caught her eye. '"The pollution in Mexico City may cause a sore throat, headache, runny nose or insomnia,"' she read. '"People with serious lung, heart, asthmatic or respiratory problems are advised to consult a doctor before coming." Lucky I gave up smoking, heh?'

Aaah, yes, the smoking. As someone who has never smoked, I hadn't realised just how much of an issue giving up smoking would be. When we passed street vendors selling single cigarettes she would get that look on her face that Homer Simpson gets when he thinks of donuts and would say, 'Hmmmmm, cigarettes.' One afternoon she woke up from a mid-afternoon siesta in a bad mood and snapped, 'I want a cigarette.' After every meal or after every drink – and she claimed she was doing far more eating and drinking since she had given up the evil weed – she would sigh, 'A smoke would go down well.' She even admitted she was beginning to dream about smoking.

If ever I commented that perhaps she was getting a little obsessed I was hounded down. 'You don't understand.' she would cry. 'It's an addiction! They have university studies to prove it!'

I had a theory about that, and one afternoon I made the

mistake of voicing it. 'Have you ever thought that those studies might be funded by the cigarette companies?'

'Why would they fund something that says their product is addictive?' she replied. 'That would be bad publicity.'

'Not necessarily,' I argued. 'You think about it. If you're a smoker trying to give up and you backslide, you can soothe your conscience by telling yourself that you're addicted.'

The GND was unconvinced. It was easy to blame her cravings, the extra food she was putting away, the few extra pounds she was carrying, on a nicotine habit she had no control over. 'You can't just give up a habit of fifteen years without any side effects,' she huffed, tucking into a slice of flan from Casa del Pavo.

Her resolve was given a greater test the day we ventured out to Teotihuacán, the archaeological zone on the outskirts of Mexico City. Once Mexico's largest ancient city – up to 200,000 people are believed to have lived there at its peak – it is also the site of two of the tallest pyramids in Central America, the Pyramid of the Sun and the Pyramid of the Moon. In fact, at 70 metres high, the Pyramid of the Sun is the third-largest pyramid in the world.

The GND was aghast when I said we should climb them both. 'Why don't we just look at them?' she asked. 'Just take a picture of me with them in the background.'

I am of the opinion that if there is something you can climb you should climb it, be that a building, a mountain or an ancient stone staircase. (Strangely, it's an opinion I seem to hold only when I'm away. I'm more than happy to catch an elevator back home in Sydney). So I set off up the staircase of the Pyramid of the Sun, and beckoned the GND to follow, which she did, reluctantly.

From a distance the stairs had looked like they went up at a reasonable angle, but once we got up a bit it was more like climbing a ladder. I've never had a cigarette in my life, but when I reached the top I was wheezing like someone with emphysema. The GND took longer, stopping on every second step to take a five-minute rest. Even so, she reached the top in bad shape.

'This ... is ... when ... I ... wish ... I'd given up smoking years ago,' she gasped, collapsing onto the stone wall at the top, then rooting around in her daypack for her Nicorettes.

We sat in silence for a few minutes, gazing out across the site at the Pyramid of the Moon, which sat, equally as lofty, at the other end of Avenida de los Muertos, the Avenue of the Dead.

'I feel good,' said the GND unconvincingly, sitting on a stone and chewing on her Nicorette. 'I really feel as though I've achieved something. I wouldn't have been able to do this before I stopped smoking.'

The GND was under the mistaken belief that now that she had decided to give up smoking her lungs would somehow mysteriously repair themselves of the damage caused by 15 years of heavy smoking. Of course, not smoking for a week wouldn't have had any effect on the capacity of the GND's lungs, but in a rare moment of tact I bit my tongue.

Secretly, I was very impressed by the GNDs efforts to give up smoking. She was doing much better than I thought she would, and certainly better than I was. I had agreed to give up drinking Coca-Cola in sympathy. (I remember telling my agent that I was giving up Coke, and by the startled look on her face it wasn't the dark liquid refreshment she thought I was talking about.) I had barely lasted two days before I was sneaking off for a bottle of the black stuff from a street vendor on the corner opposite our hotel. The GND complained a lot, but at least she hadn't weakened.

Besides, it was a little ungracious of me to complain about the GND's smoking habit. After all, it was through smoking that we had met. Her fastidious housemate insisted that she smoke outside. The GND would stand out the front, leaning against the window sill, hidden by a giant fern in the front yard, watching people go by – watching me go by. One day she peeked out from behind the fern and said, 'Hi.' I said 'hi' back and it kind of went from there. If she hadn't been a smoker we may have never got together.

But the GND's struggles against the evil weed, no matter how heroic, were a trifling consideration. There was a bigger problem at hand – Hurricane Mitch. It had arrived the same day we did and had cut a swathe through Central America.

Mitch was the worst hurricane to hit the region in 200 years. Every country we planned to pass through over the next six months, every island we had intended to drop in on, had battened down the hatches and prayed for salvation. In Belize, locals had abandoned their homes and were huddled in makeshift shelters. In Guatemala and Costa Rica bridges had been washed out and crops ruined. In Nicaragua, a swollen lake atop a volcano had burst through the cone and unleashed an avalanche of mud that buried five villages. Even Mexico, while not directly hit, had endured severe flooding from the associated rains.

Honduras was the worst hit. Early reports were putting the casualties at 5000 dead, 11,000 missing and 550,000 homeless. The capital, Tegucigalpa, was buried in mud, while the rest of the country resembled an archipelago, with people stranded in trees, on rooftops and on small islands. The Honduran president, Carlos Flores Facussé, had declared it 'a disaster of historic magnitude'. Judging from the stories in the English language newspapers and from the horrific images on the televisions in bars and restaurants, it looked like our journey could well be over before it even began.

In the end, we made the decision to spend an extra month in Mexico before crossing into the countries more directly affected. The extra time would give us the chance to check out more of Mexico and allow us to assess more fully the extent of the damage in the rest of Central America. If it was possible, I still wanted us to go through all the countries in the region. We had come all this way, it would be a shame to miss any of it.

In any case, despite the alarmist comments in the guidebook and the little incident on the Metro, Mexico City was turning out to be something of a pleasant surprise, so a few more days there would be no real burden. Our choice to stay in the Centro Histórico turned out to be an inspired one. The heart of Mexico City, it was a stately collection of old European buildings and home to its best museums and most important monuments. It was bordered at one end by the Alameda Central – a thin sliver of green parkland where families strolled and young couples can-oodled – and the baroque Palacio de Bellas Artes. At the other end sat El Zócalo, the largest square in Central America and formerly the centre of the Aztec capital, Tenochtitlán, and bordered by the parliament buildings, the cathedral and the museum.

The Zócalo was my favourite part of Mexico City. At one end was the National Palace and the Supreme Court of Justice, where protestors from every corner of the country would camp out under hand-painted banners listing their grievances. They hoped to catch the eye of an MP as they arrived with their heavy police escort and bullet-proofed limousines. Groups of policemen in blue uniforms and the latest riot gear, helmets and shields milled around in packs, waiting to rush in should there be the slightest hint of trouble, but just generally passing the time. The police presence could not quell the communal, carnival atmosphere.

The National Palace is built on the sight of Montezuma's palace. Montezuma was perhaps the most famous of the Aztec rulers, and in reality, was the last (two rulers followed, Cuitláhuac and Cuauhtémoc, but they were both Spanish puppets). Regarded as much a god as a king, Montezuma had forseen the arrival of the Spanish – a little birdie told him, truly! – and believed that Cortés was the god-king Quetzalcóatl, returning from the east. This mistake gave the Spanish captain and his troops uncommon access to the city and to Montezuma himself, for they eventually took him hostage and killed him. The rest, as they say, is history. Cortés and his small band of men took over the greatest city in the New World, a city bigger and more sumptuous than any in Spain, and set about looting and subjugating the population. Now that I think about it, there may well have even been a salutary lesson for me in the story of Montezuma – be careful who you treat as a god or goddess – but if there was, I chose to ignore it.

At the other end of the huge square was the Metropolitan Cathedral, blackened by the ravages of time and pollution and with a distinctive lean as it sank into the sandy basin that Mexico City is built on. The cathedral, the largest and most spectacular in the New World, is built on part of the site of the Teocalli, or ceremonial precincts, of Aztec Tenochtitlán. Inside, the vaulted ceilings were obscured by a forest of green scaffolding. In the centre of the church a huge plumb bob hung from the ceiling, just in front of the main pulpit and a statue of Jesus being lifted off the cross. It marked just how off centre the church was. While I was there it was a good 15 degrees. Parishioners have to take their place on pews among a giant construction site.

More alarmingly, there were no doors on the confession boxes. Even though I am not a Catholic, I would think that such an arrangement would not be conducive to open and frank confession. You're hardly likely to confess to impure thoughts about the local butcher's daughter if Father just saw you clamber in. And what with all the racket in the cathedral, as workers erected new scaffolding, you'd have to yell to be heard.

'Imagine if you were telling the best bits when the

workmen stopped,' said the GND. 'It would echo around the cathedral.'

Imagine, indeed.

To the right of the cathedral, just off the Zócalo is the Museo del Templo Mayor. Built beside the excavated ruins of Teocalli's main temple, it houses the great archaeological finds from the city and from around the country. It's also where you'll find people dressed up as Aztecs and dancing for tourists, and the stalls selling the crap souvenirs. History, religion, politics. The Zócalo has it all.

Before we knew it we had been in Mexico City for a week and we had developed a routine. We would breakfast at Café La Blanca before heading to an Internet cafe to pick up our e-mail, invariably from friends and family back home haranguing us with the latest horror stories about Hurricane Mitch and begging us to come home or at least change our itinerary. Then we would seek out a Comida Corrida – the extraordinarily cheap set-menu lunches that form the basis of eating well and living cheaply in Mexico.

After lunch, we'd go to some tourist sight – another Diego Rivera mural perhaps. Diego is one of Mexico's best-known artists, and his murals are like precursors to the cover for the Beatles' Sergeant Pepper's Lonely Hearts Club Band. They are elaborate paintings, many metres long, featuring guest appearances from the big names of Mexican history, from Hernán Cortés right through to Don Benito Juárez. But instead of hinting that Paul was dead, Diego's pictures suggest it was the concept of democracy whose days were numbered.

After enjoying our dose of culture for the day, the GND

and I would then retire to some little cantina where we would teach the locals to stick a wedge of lemon into their bottles of Corona or Sol beer. Then a quick meal of rotisserie chicken from Gili Polo – rancho or normal, depending on our mood – before retiring satisfied, our fingers greasy, to our room. Life, it must be said, was good.

The GND must have been feeling more optimistic about our trip, because at the end of the week she felt comfortable enough to pull out her hair dryer. 'It's better for you,' she explained. 'If I feel nice, I am nice. My demeanour is better.'

Actually, I was grudgingly impressed by the GND's packing. Her pack was half the size of mine and a good eight kilos lighter. When we had slung our packs on the conveyor belt at check-in I had been preparing to gloat. Instead, her bag was well under the weight restriction of 20 kilos whereas my bag was a good four kilos over. (Okay, I have a guidebook fetish – at least half that weight was the small library of books on Central America at the bottom of my pack.) Luckily we were travelling on the companion fare and we were able to check our luggage together.

More impressively, every day she would magically pull some useful item from her bag. Each of the personal grooming items I had crossed off the list mysteriously appeared out of hidden corners of her bag at the appropriate time. When I got a splinter from running my hand along the banister of the staircase in the Hotel Zamora, she pulled out a small zipped bag and produced not only a pair of tweezers but cotton wool and surgical alcohol to swab the wound. Everything came in neat little packages that nestled together like an interlocking puzzle in similarly practically designed bags. Not only was I struggling to put my hand on something I wanted from my pack, it was a battle for me to even re-zip it after trying.

Nevertheless, I used the hairdryer to get my way on an issue we'd been divided over. I wanted to go to a corrida de toros, a Mexican bullfight. And the GND didn't.

Quite rightly, the GND felt that a bullfight was barbaric and bloodthirsty. I argued that it was sport. The back pages of Mexican newspapers were full of fight analysis, matador profiles – there was even a tipping competition. The English-language newspaper, *The News*, even ran a weekly column about the sport called 'Blood on the Sand'.

'How can you say stabbing a bull is sport?' she said. 'That'd mean any guy working in an abattoir is, by definition, a sportsman.'

There was no arguing the point. In the end I pointed to the hairdryer – the appearance of which had given me plenty of 'hand' as George from Seinfeld would say – and raised my eyes. The GND relented.

In Mexico, bullfights are an important part of life. They're held in Mexico City on every Sunday from October to March at the Monumental Plaza México, a massive concrete bowl that holds 48,000 people and is one of the largest bullrings in the world. It's the biggest bullfighting stadium in Central America.

The moment we emerged from the San Antonio metro station we knew we were heading for an event. Thousands of people streamed along the streets to the stadium, just like a crowd heading to a football match. Police stood on every crossroad, directing traffic and telling people looking for somewhere to park to move along. As we got closer to the stadium hawkers were selling cold drinks, tacos and thin cushions to soften the impact of the hard concrete seats. Outside the stadium a huge tent housed a makeshift restaurant where patrons were able to fill up on tacos and burritos. Elsewhere stalls sold souvenirs and paraphernalia like flags, T-shirts and soft toys of cute bulls.

I could have gone wild, but limited myself to cushions – red with a rather attractive 'Ole!' logo – and a poster advertising the bullfight. The poster was the kind of thing you see in houses that have a bar done up Hacienda style. The mounted bull's head was particularly fetching but the GND suggested I buy some tickets instead.

I joined a scrum of people attacking a series of holes in the stadium wall behind which sat ticket sellers. Each hole was marked with the type of ticket they sold. 'Sol', in the sun, or 'Sombra' in the shade, 'Barreras' (the area closest to the ring) or the rest, divided into 'Primer' or 'Segundo'. In the end, I bought two tickets in the shade about halfway up, a bunch of nuns pushing in before me and getting better seats.

Inside the huge bowl, or amphitheatre, seats in rows climbed steeply from the ring. After much consternation we found our row, and then edged along it, lugging our souvenirs and stepping on feet until we found our seats. After placing our cushions on the concrete steps that served as seats, careful to leave the 'Ole!' logo facing up, we settled in for the afternoon's entertainment.

It was quite a spectacle. The stadium was full and there

was a buzz of anticipation. Below was the brown dirt ring. Hawkers walked up and down between the aisles selling pizzas, ice cream and beer. A trumpet blasted over the speakers and a bull ran out into the ring, snorting, dashing wildly, wondering where the hell it was and what it was doing there.

After a few minutes four guys in matador outfits came out to muted applause and waved capes at the bull. Each was trying to distract the bull, hiding behind wooden walls when it tried to charge them. Nothing much was happening so I figured this would be as good a time as any to get a beer. The guy selling Coronas was only three metres or so from me, sitting on the stairs watching the fight. I called out. I waved. But he ignored me. When I did catch his eye he gave me a filthy look. People were starting to hiss at me, but I was determined.

'Hey Señor!' I called out in my best Speedy Gonzales accent. 'Una cerveza, pronto!'

Finally the girl next to me tugged me on my sleeve. 'He is not allowed to sell you a beer while the fight is on,' she explained in an accent not unlike Salma Hayek's. 'Please wait until it is over.'

Her name was Mercedes, and while the GND disagrees with me on this point, she looked a little like Salma Hayek as well. She had dark eyes and long, black, wavy hair. She was at the bullfight with her boyfriend – 'How you say, on a date?' – but offered to explain the finer points of the corrida de toros to us. This fight was only a preliminary fight – there were four on the program – and was basically a chance for a younger matador to practise.

Two guys on heavily padded horses came out with huge lances. 'These are the picadores,' explained Mercedes. 'It is their job to jab the picas [lances] into the shoulders of the bull, to weaken him.'

The four guys in matador outfits came back. This time they were each brandishing three long elongated darts, which they took turns jabbing into the bull's shoulder, once again with the intention of weakening him. When the matador finally emerged in his traje de luces (suit of light) the bull was well and truly shagged.

'This is called the "suerte de muleta", the exciting bit,' she said. 'The matador only has 16 minutes to kill the bull.'

Sixteen minutes to wave a cape around, tire the bull out and then plunge a sword into the poor animal's neck. Finally, the dead bull is dragged off, its head placed on a little trolley and the carcass tied to two horses, leaving a trail of blood in the sand that is quickly swept away.

As this bull was dragged off, I asked Mercedes the significance of the circles marked on the ring with lime.

'The ring is divided into three parts,' said Mercedes. 'A place to run, a place to fight and a place to die.'

'Sounds like most of my relationships,' I joked.

The GND looked alarmed.

With the corrida de toros finished, Mercedes waved the beer seller over. Throughout the fight, Luis had sat scowling and muttering in Spanish. He had brought his girlfriend to the bullfight, shelled out for some pretty good seats and she'd spent most of the time talking to a couple of gringos. Fearing that we were getting the lovely Mercedes into trouble, the GND suggested I buy Luis a beer. He seemed cheered by this and spent the rest of the afternoon reading the Mexico City colloquialisms listed in the back of our Lonely Planet guidebook, chuckling to himself and muttering the English equivalents like 'Cool, baby!' and 'Let's go cruising!'

The most exciting fight of the afternoon was between a matador called Fernando Ochoa and a bull called Esplendido. Fernando was a flashy matador, a crowd favourite who liked putting as little space between his cape and the bull as possible. When the bull knocked him off his feet, inevitably, it seemed to me, the crowd gasped and Mercedes clutched hold of Luis's arm tight. His three toreros, or mini-matadors, as I liked to call them, rushed into the ring to distract Esplendido, just in case the bull got it in his head to turn around and finish the job with a stomp. But Fernando, ever the showman, was back on his feet in a flash, dusting his gold pants and waving dramatically for the mini-matadors to go away.

'He is uninjured!' cried Mercedes. 'Thanks be to God!'

Fernando seemed unfazed by the fall, and if anything grew more and more reckless. He drew the bull through with a series of ten or twelve flourishes of his cape, each time tempting the bull's head lower towards the ground, and each time eliciting a louder 'Ole!' from the crowd.

'The lower the bull puts its head the greater the skill of the matador,' enthused Mercedes, before jumping to her feet and letting out a particularly loud and lustful 'Ole!'

Finally, just as his allotted time ticked down to the final second, Fernando withdrew the sabre from his cape and plunged it dramatically into Esplendido's thick neck. In the same continuous fluid movement he turned on his heel, his back to the enraged bull and bowed deeply to the crowd. It was the ultimate in arrogance and showmanship.

Forty-eight thousand people jumped out of their seats as if they had all just received a jolt of electricity up their butt. Coats, hats, roses, seat cushions, even small children, were tossed into the air and into the ring for Fernando to pick up, touch and then throw back to their original owners.

'He is so marvellous,' swooned Mercedes, clutching her hands in front of herself. 'And *sooo* handsome!'

Luis looked alarmed. I think it had finally dawned on him that it wasn't the gringos he had to worry about ruining his date. We'd be gone the next day, on a bus heading south to Taxco. Matador Fernando Oacha, slayer of the fearsome Esplendido, would be back in the same place, at the same time next week, doing daring deeds and winning the hearts of damsels all over again.

'Mierda!' he muttered, rubbing his eyes with the bottom of his palms. 'Un desmarde!'

It wasn't until I got my guidebook back that I could translate what he had said. Shit. What a mess.

CHAPTER THREE

Acapulco

(Mexico)

Annoying habit >>> Map hogging
Culprit >>> Peter

In many ways, arriving in Taxco was like a homecoming for the GND. Not that she'd ever been there before – this was her first visit to Mexico. Nor had she been there in a previous_life, either as an Aztec princess when the town was the ancient Tlachco, or as a miner when the Spanish discovered the rich veins of silver in Cerro de Huixteco, the hill behind the town. No, the GND knew Taxco courtesy of a travel and tourism course at Kogarah TAFE.

Since we'd been away I'd learnt that the GND had done quite a few courses after leaving school. There was a course on art history she did at a community college, a philosophy and English literature program at Newcastle University, as well as the odd computer course here and there. I've got to say, I was impressed. When I finished university I didn't want to study ever again.

Part of the travel and tourism course was a case study on a particular destination, the idea being to broaden the students' knowledge of destinations, so that when they became travel agents they could offer useful advice to clients. The students were given a list of places and the GND chose Taxco. If someone came into the travel agency to book a ticket to Mexico City, the GND could also suggest a visit to Taxco – an old silver mining town 170 kilometres south-west of Mexico City.

Taxco is a quaint little colonial town that clings to the side of a mountain. The streets are cobbled and narrow, barely wide enough for a single car to pass. The only vehicles seem to be taxis – either VW beetles or Kombi vans – that go only in one direction and only along a single route, like cars in an oversized slot car set.

We arrived late in the afternoon, and as we wound our way up the hill from the bus station in one of the Kombis, our destination etched in chalk on the front windscreen, the GND gave me a primer on the place. 'The first mine was built in 1531,' she explained. 'It was the first Spanish mine in North America. They found a bit of silver, but after 20 years or so it ran out. Then 200 years later a French guy called Borda turned up and uncovered a huge vein of silver. That's where all this came from.'

'All this' was the whitewashed colonial buildings, the cobbled streets, terracotta roofs, the tumble of bougainvillea and the quaint town squares. I guessed it was also the reason for the alarming number of silver jewellery shops.

'Oh no,' said the GND. 'The silver ran out again and the place became a ghost town. Until another guy, an American called Spratling, set up a silver workshop to try and revitalise the town. It was a huge success and soon the workers started setting up their own shops. Now there's more than 300 silver shops here.'

We got off the Kombi at Plaza Borda.

'That must be Santa Prisca,' the GND said, pointing to the magnificent rose-coloured cathedral at the far end of the square. 'I can tell by the twin spires. It's considered a treasure of baroque architecture. It was built by that Borda guy I was telling you about.'

That Borda guy was José de la Borda, a French adventurer who came to Mexico in 1716 and made and lost his fortune several times. His famous motto was 'God gives to Borda, Borda gives to God.' The church, built in the elaborate Churrigueresque style, was his way of saying thanks to God for letting him discover the vein of San Ignacio, a mother lode of silver unlike anything the world had ever seen.

The GND set off across the square and up Avenida Cuauhtémoc.

'If I remember rightly there should be a couple of nice old hotels overlooking San Juan Plaza,' she said. 'Cheap too.'

She was right. We found a great room in an old building overlooking the square and with views across the town towards the cathedral. As we watched the sun set over the hill, I commented to the GND that she seemed to know a lot about Taxco.

'It was my favourite part of the course,' she said. 'I came top of the class.'

As the town lights twinkled in the dust, I wasn't surprised. Who says self-improvement doesn't pay?

We ended up spending three days in Taxco. If I'd been on my own, I probably would have stayed only one night, frightened off by the abundance of silver souvenir shops where, to quote the GND, 'the discerning buyer was bound to find something to their taste'. But with the GND, the town worked its charms on me. We strolled hand-in-hand through narrow lanes, browsed in silver shops, and ate in restaurants where the waiters wore matching uniforms. We found a bar with a balcony overlooking Plaza Borda and went there every night to eat peanuts with spicy lemon seasoning, drink ice cold Sol and watch the cathedral turn different hues of rose as the sun set.

It was wonderful, too wonderful perhaps. I couldn't help wondering if this was what travel was all about or whether I was still the same guy who had hobbled through war zones and posed for photos with the mujaheddin. Then 'Acapulco H.E.A.T.' came on the television and I was snapped out of my reverie.

Acapulco H.E.A.T. was a modern Mexican version of 'Charlie's Angels', featuring sultry Latin equivalents of Farrah, Jacqueline and Kate fighting crime among the glitzy high-rise condominiums of Acapulco. The plot of each show revolved around the girls chasing criminals through exotic beach-side locations before retiring to some obscenely opulent mansion to frolic in a pool with very little on. As Acapulco was the next stop on our itinerary I had made a point of watching the show each of the evenings we were in Taxco, ostensibly as research, but mainly because I wanted to see what happened next.

While I had no problem with the overall concept of the program – who would? – I was disturbed by two aspects of the show. First, the guy who played the character of Bosley, a fat middle-aged 'gopher' for the Angels in the original series, was a good twenty years younger, 20 kilos lighter and sported long hair, a tan and the sort of six-pack you normally see on the cover of *Men's Health*. The second thing that alarmed me was how expensive Acapulco looked. It was all glittering neon, luxury cars and nightclubs spelt 'niteclub'. I was worried that we'd have to turn to a life of crime – hopefully running afoul of the girls at H.E.A.T. in the process – just to get by.

My plan to avoid languishing in a Mexican gaol was a lightning visit to Acapulco – that is, check out the cliff divers and then catch the next bus out of town. But as I was about to discuss it with the GND, 'Melrose Place' came on and I lost her for the rest of the evening.

I've never really understood the appeal of 'Melrose Place'. I guess any guy who doesn't have a penchant for Barbra Streisand and gourmet cooking can never hope to. But the GND, like every other urban female of her generation, loved it. In fact, one of the major stumbling blocks to getting her to come along to Central America was that Melrose wouldn't have finished for the year before we left. Worse still, the last episode she watched before we left saw Amanda being kidnapped. 'I wonder what's going to happen to Amanda?' was as frequent in our conversations so far as 'Gee, I really feel like a cigarette!'

Myself, I'm more of a 'Neighbours' fan. I guess I can just relate more to a guy called Toadie who lives in the suburbs of Australia than to Jake, Michael or, God forbid, Billy. And besides, that Anne Wilkinson is such a spunk.

As luck would have it, the episode of 'Melrose' showing on Mexican TV that night was the next one after the kidnapping episode that the GND had seen in Australia. And as luck would also have it, Amanda was able to escape her captors by hitting them over the head with a cast-iron frying pan that they had just used to cook her eggs. (Ungrateful or what?) So we were able to leave for Acapulco without the nagging question of what would happen to Amanda.

Despite my reservations about the welfare of my Visa card, I was quite excited about going to Acapulco. I've always associated the name with beachside cool – cocktails, lounge music, cat's-eye glasses and very loud shirts. To me it was girls wearing bikinis that looked like your grand-mother's underwear and a young, taut, handsome Elvis diving off the cliffs at La Quebrada. Basically, go and borrow *Fun in Acapulco* from your local video store and you'll get an idea of what I had in mind.

Our arrival was suitably dramatic. After four and a half hours along Highway 95 the bus entered the two-kilometre tunnel that would take us under the brown barren mountain from dusty shanties, car dealers and taco stalls to the glitz and glamour of one of the most famous beach towns in the world. In a divine act of synchronicity, 'Rockafeller

Skank' came onto my Walkman as we entered the tunnel, thumping in time with the neon lights as they flashed by, and reaching a crescendo as we burst through to the daylight on the other side. There, in front of us was Acapulco, the granddaddy of all Mexican resorts. And behind that, glittering and blue behind the skyline of condominiums, was the Pacific Ocean.

After the indulgences of Taxco I was determined to bring the journey onto a more frugal level. Much to the dismay of the GND I insisted a) that we stay in the older, cheaper part of town and b) we use the crowded city bus rather than a taxi to get there. The bus was not one of my better ideas. It took us half an hour to figure out which side of the road the bus to Old Acapulco left from. And when we finally got on one, we found it was more crowded than the subway in Mexico City.

Now it's never easy getting your bearings in a new city, especially on a crowded bus where your view of any landmarks or streets signs are obscured by the armpits of your fellow commuters. I discovered, however, that if I ducked down quickly at each stop I could catch a glimpse of what was outside the window. On one quick duck I spotted water and surmised from that we were somewhere along La Costera, the road that ran along the edge of the bay. On another duck, I spotted what looked like the Post Office and studied the map on the guidebook to see how far it was from the zócalo, the major landmark in the area where all the cheap hotels were.

'Why don't you just ask someone?' said the GND, a little annoyed. 'You're starting to frighten these people.'

Instead I kept ducking, knowing that any attempt from me to speak Spanish would only frighten them more. In the end, the GND asked a guy where the zócalo was and he pointed back over his shoulder, in the direction we had just come. And from the look on his face, we hadn't just missed it either. We scrambled off the bus and were left stranded on the wrong side of a very busy road.

The sensible thing would have been to cross the road, hail down a bus heading back towards the zócalo and ask the bus driver to tell us when we reached it. In fact that was the very plan the GND suggested. But from my reading of the map we weren't that far from where we wanted to go. If we headed up Inalambrica, turned right towards Avenida López Mateos and La Quebrada we'd only be a couple of hundred metres from the hotel we had decided to try.

'But if we catch a bus back to the zócalo we're only a block or two away from the hotels too,' she said. 'And we won't have to walk so far.'

I showed the GND the intended route on the map, and when she still hesitated, accused her of being lazy. I was so certain of my plan I set off up Inalambrica, forcing her to follow.

Any guy who has put his faith so totally in a map knows how this sorry tale ends. A few minutes in, Inalambrica took an unexpected – and in my defence, an unmarked – turn away from where we wanted to go, and streets and lanes that weren't even on the map started appearing with alarming regularity.

Of course, I didn't tell the GND this. I powered on with

a surety in my stride that suggested I knew exactly where I was going and everything was going to plan. Finally, when a small bay appeared where our hotel should have been, I swallowed my pride and asked directions from a guy sitting on a wall drinking beer. He pointed to a road just up ahead that wound its way dramatically up a cliff beside the bay. At that moment the GND caught up and asked if I knew where the hell I was going. I'm not sure if it was the look on my face or the realisation that I had involved someone else in this mad scheme but the guy started laughing.

The only thing I had going for me was that the GND did not yet know that the near vertical road ahead was the one we had to take. I decided to take the most sensible approach and make a pre-emptive apology.

The necessity of the pre-emptive apology was obvious. I knew I was in strife – I had insisted that we walk and had got us horribly lost. But if the GND was angry now (and she was) she'd be furious after climbing a hill in the hot midday sun, a pack on her back and nowhere in sight to buy water. By saying I was sorry, that I should have listened to her, and that it would never happen again, I could possibly limit the collateral damage. If I waved down a taxi, I could probably still get a peck on the cheek when we retired to bed that night.

If you need any proof that God is a woman, or at the very least a divine being with a very twisted sense of humour, I present that afternoon as Exhibit A. Every taxi driver in Acapulco, it seemed, was taking a siesta, and we were forced to walk the entire way. It was hot, it was difficult and by the time we got up to La Quebrada the

GND was fuming. I rushed into one of the tacky tourist shops that lined the road and paid way over the odds for a bottle of water, hoping in some small way it may help to appease her. It didn't, but luckily it was all downhill from there.

◙   ◙   ◙

I fell immediately in love with Old Acapulco and so did the GND. A collection of hotels, restaurants and ice cream stalls, it had the feel of a faded fifties beach resort – imagine the set of *Fun in Acapulco* if it had been left out in the elements for thirty years. There were shops selling souvenirs made from shells and our hotel was made from concrete breezeblock in the finest tradition of 1950s Florida chic.

At night, however, the zócalo had a distinctively Mexican feel about it. It was a pretty square, with trees and benches and surrounded by outdoor cafes and restaurants. Couples walked by holding hands, parents too, with kids holding helium-filled balloons in the shape of Bart Simpson. Mariachi bands wandered from table to table singing songs in such a haunting, plaintive way that you just knew the song was about a beautiful girl, unrequited love and perhaps an untimely early death.

The mariachi bands would normally play in the ornate wrought-iron bandstand, but it had been taken over by protesting students. They had draped the bandstand with banners listing their grievances, but to my untrained eye it looked like an excuse to drink beer, flirt with passing girls and sing loud drunken ditties that may or may not have questioned the size of their professor's willy.

The main reason we had come to Acapulco, however, was to see the world-famous cliff divers. On our first foray up to their rocky eyrie in front of the Plaza Las Glorias hotel we got to see them up close and personal. Looking more like Elvis circa 1976 than 1956, they waddled through the crowds in their skimpy sky-blue Speedos on their way to the cliff. The GND mistook them for under-dressed tourists.

'Look at those wallys,' she said. 'You'd think they'd put something on before coming to see the cliff-divers.'

Those wallys, however, risked life and limb four times a day and five times on Sunday to dive into a narrow stretch of water that fluctuated in depth from shallow to extremely fucking shallow depending on the swell. And despite their portly frames and bad seventies moustaches, they were regarded as love gods by the local señoritas.

I was given this alarming piece of information by Pancho, an ex-diver who was now selling the 10-peso ($1.50) tickets at the box office. 'The divers can have any woman they want,' said Pancho, before adding ruefully, 'Well, at least while they are diving.'

If you've seen *Fun in Acapulco* you know the drill for the cliff divers. Climb to the top of the cliff, bless yourself at the shrine of the Virgen de Guadalupe and jump. Then, if you've correctly picked the swell in the narrow channel 42 metres below, emerge from the water to rapturous applause. And that's pretty much how it went every time we went, except when the divers would dive in tandem, or at night, holding a flaming torch.

We ended up watching the cliff divers three times – twice

in the afternoon and once at night. I liked the way these pudgy guys were heroes in their community. We'd spot them on the streets of La Quebrada, being greeted warmly by the old men or being given discounts by blushing checkout girls. Before each dive they would parade through the crowd, receiving slaps on the back and admiring glances from the ladies. After the diving was over people would clamour around them to kiss them or have them touch their babies.

'You just wish you were a cliff diver,' said the GND. And I guess she was right.

On the last time we visited, Pancho's son, Carlos, was making his first dive in front of an audience. I asked Pancho how he felt Carlos would go.

'He is ready,' he said. 'I just hope he remembers all that he has learned.'

Carlos started well. He clambered up the cliff to the 20-metre mark as dextrously as the more seasoned divers and sat and watched patiently as they performed their dives. When his time came, he stood on the rock ledge, his small chest heaving as he sucked in the air nervously, watching the swell and waiting for the right moment. The right moment came – and so did another, and another. Just when it looked like young Carlos had lost his nerve he dived – arcing perfectly – and hit the water below as straight as a pin.

Carlos emerged smiling to the most enthusiastic applause of the day. As he climbed up from the water his dad gave him a hearty slap on the back and watched with pride as a group of young girls clamoured to congratulate his son and kiss him on the cheek.

Another all-Mexican, Acapulco cliff-diving love god had been born. Damn him!

Before we left Acapulco the GND wanted to go to a beach. She'd brought along her little blue swing dress on the promise of sand, sea and sun, and two weeks in she still hadn't had the chance to use it. The area in front of Old Acapulco was a working harbour, home to a constant stream of cruise ships filled with people shaped like beetles from the USA and cargo ships taking loads of new cars shaped like beetles to the USA.

A tentative foray up to New Acapulco, among the condo canyons of malls, McDonald's and neon signs, had proved disastrous. We were chased off the beach by security guards protecting their turf, the roped-off sand in front of every hotel. We slunk off while the more privileged ones – and, to be fair, the people who had spent a good deal more for their lodgings than us – paraglided, rode banana boats and did whatever else it is people do on overpriced holiday resorts.

After consulting our guidebook, we decided that our best bet was to catch a boat across the bay to Isla de la Roqueta. A small island at the southern end of Acapulco Bay, it had a couple of beaches and was reached by glass-bottom boats that went via a submerged bronze statue of the Virgen de Guadalupe as part of the price. We arrived to find the beach crowded with Mexican families, banana boats and guys with canoes full of souvenirs. It was raucous and crowded, with the rather uninspired backdrop of the port and condos of the cluttered Acapulco water front. We spotted a spare metre of sand, but if we'd sat down we would have ended up part of some impromptu game of beach soccer, a family feast or squashed by the belly of one of the huge Mexican guys with tiny, wispy moustaches and wearing equally tiny, wispy Speedos.

Instead, we followed a sign pointing along a bushy path leading to the zoo. The zoo was a rather sad affair, but we noticed another path, untended and neglected, that led off into the undergrowth, and we decided to follow that too. Just as we were about to turn back it descended down a staircase cut into stone leading to a little hidden cove.

The cove was beautiful, a small strip of golden sand arcing delightfully, surrounded by hills on either side. The water was clear and cool, and because it looked out towards the Pacific rather than Acapulco, there wasn't a condo, pleasure craft or overweight Mexican in sight.

The GND yelped in delight, stripping down to her bikini and dived in. 'This is perfect,' she beamed, splashing in the cool, clean water. And I had to agree.

A tree beside the staircase provided a nice patch of shade, so we ended up staying on that beach for a couple of hours, taking a dip every 30 minutes or so. The map incident? It was like it never happened. Hurricane Mitch? Perhaps if we ignored it, it would go away. It was romantic – perfect – and the entire time we were there the GND didn't once bring up smoking or chew on a Nicorette.

I've got to admit. It was nice to have someone to share it with. If I'd been on my own I probably would have taken a few photos, had a swim, and then wandered back to the other side of the island to catch the next boat back, *wishing* I'd had someone to share it with. But instead I got to live out the kind of holiday fantasy stressed-out couples are convinced will save their ailing marriages.

Our chances of getting the little cove all to ourselves again were slim, so we decided to make that perfect day on Isla de la Roqueta our last day in Acapulco.

'There'll be plenty more beaches like this anyway,' argued the GND. 'I mean, we haven't even got to the Caribbean yet.'

I remember wondering what would happen if there weren't.

CHAPTER FOUR

The Mexican Pipeline

Annoying habit >>> Excessive thriftiness
Culprit >>> Peter

As a rule, I don't like buying bus tickets in advance. I like to just turn up at a bus terminal and let fate dish out whatever it is she has in store for me. Sometimes it can be a couple of hours sitting in a ramshackle terminal counting geckos. At other times, a journey in a totally unexpected direction because that was the only bus with a spare seat. Time limits, I'd found, were a dangerous thing. They robbed you of the spontaneity of staying a little longer in somewhere you liked and punished you for the foolishness of having one too many before a big trip the next day.

Now that I was travelling with someone else, however,

I felt I had to be more responsible. So when the GND had suggested we should purchase our tickets to Puerto Escondido in advance, I readily agreed. We called into a travel agent the second day we were in Acapulco and, despite the girl telling us that we didn't need to buy our tickets, we did.

I guess after the map incident I'd lost my nerve. I'd been paying for it every day in Acapulco, deferring to the GND on issues I would normally take a stand on (the souvenir Virgen de Gaudalupe she wouldn't let me buy being perhaps the most illuminating example) and buying her more margaritas than our budget would allow. Buying the tickets, she said, was the sensible thing to do. And so would taking a taxi to the terminal.

Of course, it would have been a sensible thing to do if we hadn't slept in or if the GND could have decided which way she wanted to wear her hair that day or I could have re-zipped my bag more quickly. It would have been even more sensible if we had factored in enough time for the horrific traffic on the road that morning. As it was we had to abandon our taxi in the middle of the markets – a gridlock of buses, trucks, cars and wooden carts filled with roughly butchered meat pushed by boys without shirts on – and catch another one at the other end. We arrived at the terminal just as the bus was leaving, our taxi driver dramatically cutting it off as it left the terminal, not allowing it to proceed until we were on board.

The bus was an old Greyhound bus from the states, retired from service there after a hard and long life. The bus driver was in a bad mood, not helped, I would suggest, by our taxi driver's dramatic attempt to get us on board. He spent the first part of the trip telling an English backpacker with smelly feet to put his shoes back on and threatening at intervals to pull the bus over to the side of the road until he did. During the most heated altercation, the old Hollies song 'The Air That I Breathe' played on the radio. Obviously seeing this as some kind of divine message, the guy agreed to put his shoes back on.

The bus drove south along Highway 200, through dry hills and along a stretch of bitumen that was straight but dipped up and down like a roller coaster ride. Just before sunset the bus stopped at San José del Progreso, a shabby little town still 80 kilometres from Puerto Escondido. I saw a sign pointing down a dirt road to Chacahua, and in a moment of madness tugged on the GND's arm and told her we were getting off. The bus pulled off, covering us in dust and choking us with fumes, to leave us standing alone beside the road.

I'd read about Chacahua in our guidebook. It was described as an isolated village on a wonderful expanse of ocean, the perfect place, our guidebook said, to 'bliss out – for the day, a few days, weeks'. It could only be reached by boat from Zapotelito or along a rough, little-used road, impassable in the wet season, from San José del Progreso. I was guessing that this was the road I had spotted from the bus.

When we dragged our packs back to the turnoff and set them under a tree, the enormity of what I had done suddenly struck me. It was a Sunday, the sun was setting and we were waiting beside a tiny dirt road for a ride in a town where the only signs of life were the cars that went hurtling by on the highway, going somewhere else.

Now you're probably shaking your head reading this and asking: Why? Hadn't I learned anything from the map incident? Well, I had wanted to inject a little adventure into the trip. But by the way the GND was silent, it seemed I had injected a little danger as well.

'I'll just ask someone when the next bus is, shall I?' I said, anxious to get away from the silence.

I ventured over to a small shop, nothing more than a wooden shack, and disturbed the bored female shopkeeper, who was resting her head on her arm, sleeping.

'Chacahua?' I asked.

She lazily motioned towards the tree we were sitting under. I was encouraged. She hadn't look alarmed.

About ten minutes later, an old Dodge pick-up truck pulled up beside the shop. From the wooden slats at the back, it was used to cart cattle. But tonight it was carrying a football team, still in their uniforms, who jumped from the back of the truck to buy soft drinks and cigarettes. As luck would have it, it was the Chacahua football team, and being in a good mood (they had just beaten their arch rivals, San José del Progreso, 4–nil), they agreed to give us a lift back to their village. We spent the next two hours bouncing along a bumpy road in the back of a truck with a bunch of footballers singing songs and handing around a victory joint.

'This is wonderful,' whispered the GND, as darkness fell and the fireflies came out to play. 'It's like we're on a grand adventure!'

It made me happy to hear her say that. My gamble, it seemed, had paid off.

◼   ◼   ◼

When we finally arrived at Chacahua it was dark, except for a few hurricane lamps, and silent, except for the warble of music coming from a radio, somewhere. The radio was playing a song that sounded like the Gipsy Kings but featured, disconcertingly, a maniacal laugh. The places to stay were on the other side of a lagoon, on the spit between the lagoon and the ocean. One of the footballers indicated that we should wait beside the boats that were dragged up on the beach.

Lights flickered in the distance. The only other sound was the disembodied voices of men on the water, fishing, and the clunk of their oars. We sat on a low concrete wall where a few other people were waiting, not altogether sure if we were in the right place or even where we were going exactly. A guy finally wandered down to a boat, fired up the engine and motioned for us to get in.

I couldn't see the GND's face on that trip across the lagoon, but I know I had a big dopey grin on mine. The wind in my hair, the splash of the water, the darkness, it was all so exhilarating. My stomach was flipping with excitement. For the first time on the trip I felt as though we were doing something adventurous. When we were led to a rustic hut, down near the beach, by a small boy with a hurricane lamp, I knew we were.

The next morning I was even more delighted. Our hut was only a hundred metres or so from the beach, one of a collection built in anticipation of a rush of tourists that never came, and all fading and falling apart. Not that the owner was losing too much money. Each hut had a sandy floor with two beds and a couple of mattresses. There was no electricity, so there were no pesky light bulbs to change or power bills to pay. The shower was a well, surrounded by a wooden fence, where you had to pull up ten or so buckets full of water that you poured into a concrete holding tub and then scooped over yourself with a battered plastic bowl.

It was perfect. We got to hang out on a deserted beach in a tiny hut, where the only sound was that of the waves crashing on the sand. The friendly local restaurant would serve us huge meals of roasted fish caught that very day for next to nothing. And the weather during our stay was warm and fine. The fact that Hurricane Mitch had stirred up the sea to monster levels that made it dangerous to swim was the only blight on an otherwise idyllic set-up.

The only other person staying on the beach was Faro the Rasta, a Jamaican who had recently moved to Canada. He was built like a Kenyan long distance runner – tall, thin and complete with tiny shorts – but the rest was pure Rasta – long dreadlocks swept under a red, green and yellow crocheted hat, various trinkets and a pointy little goatee beard. He'd been in Chacahua for a week and wasn't as enamoured with it as we were.

'The people here are holding something in, man,' he said. 'I've been playing down the restaurant and they won't even give me a soda.'

Faro had been playing his guitar for tourists who came

to Chacahua on day trips from Puerto Escondido.

'These tourists come in, have a long lunch, pay lots of money,' he whined, 'and I don't even get a god-damn soda.'

Faro had been playing at the restaurant on the promise of free lunch. The GND asked why he didn't say something to the owner.

'I did!' exclaimed Faro. 'Man, you won't believe this story!' He crouched down, grabbed a handful of sand and began. 'After a few days,' he said, 'I decide to complain to the boss guy. He says, 'Do you like oysters and prawns?' I rub my hands together. Of course I do. I been livin' on beans and rice for close to a year. He says, 'Okay, come back tonight.' I go back that night and we go out on his boat. I think, 'That's okay, we're on his boat, I can dig that.' Anyway, we get out there and he gets me throwin' out nets. If I wanna eat oysters and prawns, I gotta catch them. He just sits back and drinks beer, watchin' me. I'm throwin' out nets and pullin' 'em in. Throwin' out nets and pullin' 'em in. And there are twigs and spikes from the mangroves tangled in the nets, cuttin' my hands. I say, 'Man, this is bullshit. My hands are my livelihood!' He gets pissed off and just drops me in the middle of nowhere. Never did get my oysters and prawns. But I learned my lesson. They feed me first, then I play!'

※　　　※　　　※

We waited for the boat to Zapotelito at the restaurant, an open area of tables and chairs protected from the hot sun by a roof. The restaurant also acted as the town wharf, meeting place and focal point for the entire village. School kids played in the water, waiting to be taken by boat to the school on the other side. A candidate for the upcoming elections for governor, wearing neat jeans, a polo shirt and expensive looking shoes, dropped in to share a beer and chew the fat with the owner. After an hour, the boat still hadn't come, so a woman, dressed in her finest clothes for the big trip south, waded into the lagoon to cool down.

'Is she mad?' said the GND, horrified. 'Her mascara will run!' The GND was flabbergasted and was still going on about it when the boat finally arrived and the woman sat beside us, a pool of water forming instantly around her.

The boat trip took us through the heart of Lagunas de Chacahua National Park. In the distance, blue grey mountains folded into one another. Before us, guys in dugout canoes threw fishing nets into the placid water. Occasionally, the captain would take a short cut, turning the boat into a channel through the mangroves, which pressed in on each side, or stop at a small wharf where farmers waited with sacks of produce to be taken to the market.

It took us two hours to reach Zapotelito, and after that our journey to Puerto Escondido was fairly uneventful. The taxi we caught from Zapotelito to the highway was pulled over by the police for overcrowding, but judging by the civilised way money changed hands, it was an accepted and normal part of the journey. Once we got to the highway we waved down a bus to Puerto Escondido, which dropped us off at the dusty lot that serves as the town's bus station. There we caught a colectivo, a van with a few seats in the back, to Zicatela, the surfer ghetto a kilometre or so away.

The surf at Zicatela is known as the Mexican Pipeline and after three days in Chicahua, where we only had Faro for company, the number of foreigners was astounding. They were mostly there for the surf and were all brown, thin and good-looking. They wandered along the beach in bikinis and sarongs and boardshorts, checking out the waves and looking for all the world like they'd just come from shooting a Calvin Klein commercial.

The road beside the beach was lined with restaurants selling fresh juice, wholegrain breads and vegan lasagna, where those who weren't surfing picked at their meals and boasted about the waves they had caught. I immediately felt conspicuous. I can't surf. And unlike the GND, I do not tan instantly. I began to wish we were back in Acapulco, where the tourists at least had the decency to have puffy physiques, pale skin and loud shirts. I could blend in there. Here I felt like the new kid at school. Like everyone was looking at me and judging me for not being cool enough.

A few discreet inquiries at the hotels near the beach confirmed my worst fears. The rooms were expensive. The GND wanted to take one, but encouraged by our Chacahua experience I was determined to find the cheapest room at Zicatela. I found it at the Hotel Azucena.

The Hotel Azucena was set in a damp hollow facing the beach, just up from the Grizzly Bar, where Vietnam veterans in wheelchairs spent each day drinking themselves into oblivion. Its wooden cabañas were set around the open-air restaurant, and the entrance was guarded by a guy in a wheelchair who seemed to spend most of his time sleeping.

The GND took one look at the shared bathroom and declared that she would be washing in the ocean.

Our cabaña was damp and humid, with a tattered mosquito net and a fan that struggled to work. On the first night we discovered that the mosquito net had more holes than a cola drinker's teeth, including a very large hole at the top through which the mosquitoes would pour in squadrons, circling down to us like 747s at Heathrow. I made the mistake of sleeping naked and after a restless few hours of swatting, turned on my torch to discover that three mosquitoes had settled down for a feast on the tip of my penis. I waved them off but the damage had been done.

My yelp of horror woke the GND. She pointed at the blisters that had formed instantly and laughed. 'Ha, ha, ha!' she guffawed, 'You look like Mr Blobby!'

Just who Mr Blobby was and how the GND knew what his penis looked like would have to be a topic tackled at some other time. As soon as the grey light of dawn filtered through the cracks in the woodwork, we packed our bags and found a better room – at three times the price, mind you – further up the beach. I resisted the urge to itch in fear of being arrested.

Our new room was wonderful. After our cabaña at the Azucena, it seemed almost luxurious. A hammock hung at the front of the room, completely surrounded by windows with views over a palm tree to the ocean. The bathroom was clean and spacious, in dazzling white tiles that were scrubbed clean every day. The bed was huge, with crisp clean sheets. On the floor were large terracotta tiles; the walls were whitewashed and bright. A large fan swished lazily overhead. And there, in the middle, was a mosquito net in perfect condition.

'You won't have any problems with mosquitoes,' assured Maria, the girl showing us the room. 'We spray the rooms each night.'

We said we'd take the room and thanked Maria enthusiastically.

'You are not Americans, are you?' she stated blankly.

We shook our heads and asked if it was our accents that gave us away.

'It's your behaviour,' she said. 'Americans act like emperors.'

Our new hotel had a pool and the GND insisted that we go down and have a swim straight away. She had been adamant that we got a room in a hotel with a pool, which to me seemed a little superfluous considering we were staying near a beach. If we were going to lash out on a luxury, I had argued, why not get a room with a TV, preferably cable, and preferably with all the sports channels. Then, if the weather turned bad, or an evening slow, we could retire to our room and get the latest football scores.

The GND was not convinced by this argument, and with my credibility in tatters after the mosquito incident, I followed her obediently down to the pool in my new Mexpipe boardshorts, careful not to scratch. And it was good: cool, still, relaxing, especially during sunset or night. The beach, in contrast was crowded, dirty and hot. In the end, we spent most of our days in the pool.

We spent most of our evenings in the Everyone Bar on

the rooftop at the front of the hotel, which sold half-price margaritas at sunset. The bar was owned by a guy called Felipe and most evenings we would sit and chat. One night I asked him where the name, 'Everyone Bar' came from.

'Because everyone has an idea on how I could run it better!' he chuckled.

I thought it was fine. It was an open veranda with a clear view over the beach and to the sunset. The wooden tables, suspended from the ceiling, were cut in the shape of surfboards. And every evening as the sun set, all the drinks were two for the price of one.

'One Norwegian guy said I needed to change the music I played,' explained Felipe. 'The next night he brought one of his own tapes and insisted I put it on. He said that it would fill the bar. It was death metal stuff. People were too scared to come in.'

Another guy, an American college student, claimed he could fill the place in five seconds. 'He stood at the front window and yelled "Free beer",' laughed Felipe. 'It took me a hell of a time to convince them they had to pay.'

The GND and I ordered some margaritas. Felipe was training a new barmaid and he carefully showed her how to put all the ingredients in the blender. When she brought them to our table they were cold, refreshing and very, very strong. As the sun sank over the horizon, a fiery red ball, we decided we liked the Everyone Bar just as it was.

After a few days we ventured beyond our pool to visit Puerto Escondido, a twenty-minute walk away, down along the beach and around the rocky headland. The rocks were supposedly the hideout of thieves who would rob tourists as they returned home, but all we saw was a sad-looking donkey tied up, waiting for someone to ride it, and the regulars of the little shack that was a bar, passed out in the sand.

Puerto Escondido was where the Mexicans holidayed. Full of tacky hotels that clung to the hill behind the town, it was here, too, you could find cantinas, restaurants, ice-cream stalls and tacky souvenir shops, as well as entire Mexican families strolling around with their shirts off in the hot midday sun. Down on the beach, Mexican fathers with generous bellies, dressed in Speedos barely bigger than a handkerchief, played with their children in the surf. The kids would call out to their mother to join them, who, after a decent number of refusals, would reluctantly come in, usually still wearing her clothes in a display of modesty. Then they'd all get out, flop on the sand, eat burritos and guzzle from family-sized bottles of Mexican soft drink.

The contrast with the scene back at Zicatela was astounding. There the western tourists would set up on the beach metres apart, careful not to invade the personal space of their fellow sunbakers. At Escondido family groups spilled onto one another, invading, and then sharing, not only space, but food and drink as well. The effect was that the beach became one big communal gathering. I liked it. A lot.

◙   ◙   ◙

After a week Maria asked if we were staying longer. At first I though she was trying to get rid of us for hogging the pool, and I promised we would cut down the hours we spent in it.

'No, it's not that,' she laughed. 'It's just that the international surf contest starts next week. We need to know how many rooms we'll have available.'

Hmmmm. Even more tanned, thin folk? I had advanced my tan a little, but it was still in that disturbing bright-pink mode.

'There's also a Miss Puerto Escondido Bikini Competition,' Maria added, although I don't know why.

Now while the prospect of seeing the world's leading surfers held little appeal, I was intrigued by what a bikini competition would be like in Mexico. (To be honest, not having ever been to one, I wondered what a bikini competition would be like full stop.) If the contestants were anything like the girls on 'Acapulco H.E.A.T.' it could be quite a hard-fought competition.

Unfortunately, my plea to stay for research purposes fell on deaf ears. The GND claimed that all the silicone on show would give me the wrong idea altogether on how breasts are meant to behave. She said it was time to head on, to Oaxaca, up in the mountains, where it was a good ten degrees cooler and where everyone wore thick coloured shawls and ankle-length skirts.

Damn.

CHAPTER FIVE

Oaxaca

(Mexico)

Annoying habit >>> Chronic leg shaking
Culprit >>> Peter

We caught a bus to Oaxaca with the fattest family in
Mexico. The mother, father, daughter and son had a
combined weight greater than the entire World Wrestling
Federation, and, judging by their pinkish tones, had just
spent a couple of days by the beach at Puerto Escondido.
They occupied two rows of seats on both sides of the bus
and blocked the aisle with the hangover of their considerable
bulk.

What I found most fascinating about the family wasn't
their size – although, in most parts of the world, except
perhaps the southern states of America, that would be

enough to excite considerable comment – but the sheer cubic volume of food they put away. Before the bus had left the bus terminal the mother put away three tortas and a two-litre bottle of cordial. Over the first two hours of the trip the family ate burritos, tacos, chicken and big greasy chunks of ham, smacking their lips and wiping their hands on the back of the seat. At one point, something must have gone down the wrong way because the mother spluttered and coughed, shaking the bus like an earthquake. Then she sat picking the crumbs and little pieces of food from her cleavage.

'Must have just given up smoking,' I said to the GND. She was not amused.

The family waddled off at Cerro el Vedri, a tiny village in the foothills of the mountains that didn't look big enough to support their eating habit. The bus, free of their impressive weight, continued on, winding its way up the mountain with considerably more vigour and purpose.

It is 310 kilometres from Puerto Escondido to Oaxaca, climbing from sea level to over 2500 metres, and passing from deciduous tropical forest to spectacular stands of pine and oak forest. At its highest point the road seemed to be winding its way through the clouds, the valleys on either side hidden by mist. The air was thinner, it was cooler and there was moss hanging from the trees. Just before Oaxaca the road dropped into Valles Centrales, a region altogether drier and rockier.

Oaxaca is widely regarded as one of the most beautiful cities in Mexico, a place of low Spanish buildings and narrow cobbled streets with a lively plaza. But we didn't see that at first. We arrived at the second class bus station, classed that way because of the type of bus we caught, but equally indicative of the bus station itself. It was a huge dirty place where poisonous exhaust fumes lingered in the thin mountain air and snotty-nosed kids roamed in packs looking for someone to pickpocket.

My impression of Oaxaca wasn't improved by the fight I had with the bus station toilet attendant. After seven hours on a bus I was dying to have a pee. I frantically searched the bus station to find a toilet. There it was, just behind a taco stall. As I walked through the door I heard a bloodcurdling yell, a banshee, from behind me. It was a toilet attendant demanding that I pay him one peso (ten cents) to use the toilet. He was angry, it seemed, because he thought I was trying to sneak in.

Normally, he would have been right. As an Australian I get morally outraged at having to pay to go to the toilet. If we ever get rid of the Queen and get ourselves a Bill of Rights, the right to use the porcelain for free would be as passionately defended by Australians as Americans defend the right to bear arms. And don't go claiming that the money is used to keep the toilets clean. It never is. Besides, we'd prefer our toilets filthy than have to pay for them.

But this time it was an honest mistake. The guy was sitting 20 metres from the door, trying to cover the ladies toilet 20 metres away on the other side as well. He started swearing at me in Spanish, so I swore back at him in English. Finally, I flicked the one peso at him with a sneer. I try not to do that sort of thing, karma and all that, but I was distracted – seven hours is a long time to spend on a bus without spending a penny – and he bugged me. If I was lucky, he'd just think I was American.

Luckily the bus station was not indicative of Oaxaca, nor was the toilet Nazi representative of the people of Oaxaca, just as my behaviour with the toilet Nazi was not representative of my behaviour during my stay there. Over the next week the GND and I found Oaxaca and its people to be gracious, charming and delightful.

We took a room in the heart of the city, just across from the market and only a couple of hundred metres from the vibrant zócalo. We'd wandered the cobbled streets, admiring the old houses and enjoying the cafes, restaurants and bars. On the streets and in the markets, villagers from all over Valles Centrales sold rugs, brightly painted wooden animals and leather belts and shoes. Elsewhere, hawkers sold delicious flans and Oaxaca's famous stringy cheese by the kilo. Young boys wandered the streets selling the local delicacy, deep-fried grasshoppers, by the plastic bag full.

On market days, the streets around the zócalo were transformed into a huge flea market. Among the stalls selling crafts, clothes and cheap tools and kitchen appliances made in China, villagers set up huge makeshift kitchens, doling out meals that were filling and delicious. The GND made an attempt on a giant chicken taco, smothered in cheese, sour cream and avocado, but even in her current mindset she couldn't finish it. In the end, a tubby boy, well dressed by Mexican standards, asked it he could have it. By the way he tucked into it I figured that he must have just given up smoking as well.

At night we'd wander down to the zócalo, where there always seemed to be some sort of parade. Sometimes it might feature giant figures that spun around, known as 'Baile de los Gigantes' (Dance of the Giants); at other times, brightly dressed folk with fruit on their heads twirled their way through town. I could never quite figure out what the festival was for. At first I thought it may have been the Guelaguetza, an ancient Indian maize festival that had been fused with Christian celebrations for the feast of the Virgen del Carmen, but that was held in July, not December. I think the good folk of Oaxaca just liked putting on their best frocks and prancing about.

The city so captured our hearts that the GND and I started seriously discussing the idea of coming back and buying an old colonial house to live in. I could write a book about our experiences – like Peter Mayle had done in Provence or Frances Mayes in Tuscany – describing the trials and tribulations of buying and renovating in Oaxaca. The GND could learn to speak Spanish and cook Oaxacan food, and then invite our neighbours over for dinner so I could chronicle their idiosyncratic personalities.

Just as we were polishing this idea – doing the sums, deciding on what shade of terracotta for the walls, picking out iridescent throw rugs for the couch, that sort of thing – we met an older American couple in a restaurant just off Avenida Bustamante. They sat in the corner staring into their coffees, but perked up when they heard us speaking English. After we finished eating, they came over and introduced themselves.

'Do you mind if we talk to you?' the woman asked. 'We

don't get much chance to speak English these days.'

They were the Rubensteins, Val and Sol, originally from Queens, New York, but now of Oaxaca, Oaxaca. They had planned to retire to Florida, but when Sol got sick – they didn't go into details, something about his gall bladder – they didn't have insurance, so the money they'd put aside for the condo in Florida was spent on hospital fees. With what little they had left, all they could afford to do was rent an old apartment in Oaxaca.

'It seems romantic at first,' Val said. 'But you soon get sick of the faulty water pipes and blackouts.'

'We thought the kids would visit too,' Sol said. 'But they have to fly to Mexico City and change planes to get to Oaxaca. It's too much of a hassle, too much money.'

They were trying to learn Spanish. They were trying to fit in. 'But we're too old to be making friends here,' they sighed. 'Now we just strike up conversations with other tourists.'

It was a sobering encounter. The GND and I never spoke of our dream of owning a colonial house in Oaxaca again.

That afternoon, as we wandered down Hidalgo browsing through the craft stalls for a knitted hat for the GND, a man handed us a flier for La Cucaracha Restaurant and Mezcal Shop. Mezcal is the local firewater, a variant on the perennial Mexican favourite, tequila. The flier featured a picture of a cockroach (for that is what cucaracha means in Spanish) holding a bottle, lying sozzled under a cactus. The flyer boasted that it had 'the best Mezcaleria in the world' – over 50 varieties of mezcal and 100 varieties of tequila. More importantly, it promised free snacks with drinks.

Brilliant! A real live La Cucaracha bar! I was so excited I started singing the song as we walked down the street. How could we come to Mexico and not go to a bar named after the tune favoured by more hoons in hotted-up cars for their air horns than any other. Unfortunately, the GND had less fond memories. For her, hearing La Cucaracha was invariably followed by a wolf whistle and a 'Show us your tits!' To her credit though, she agreed to go along.

The bar was set in a lovely old building with wrought iron window bars and a flagstone floor. It had also only just opened for the night.

'I am Jorge,' said the barman, the only other person there. 'And I am your waiter for the evening. How may I help you?'

I told him I wanted the best mezcal he had. He brought me a lemon-flavoured mezcal in a glass set in a wooden handle, which looked a lot like an egg timer. I downed it in one and asked for another.

Mistaking me for some kind of mezcal aficionado, the waiter took me to another room to show me a mural explaining the process of making mezcal. The rows of algave growing in fields; the harvesters in their white pantsuits and hats felling the plants and removing the spikes; the algave 'piñas' being loaded into carts pulled by donkeys; the distilling process; and, finally, a crude representation of people enjoying the end product.

'We have a saying,' he said. 'Para todo mal mezcal, y para todo bien tambien – as a remedy for everything bad, mezcal. And to celebrate everything good as well.'

While there is no evidence to suggest that the natives of

Mexico had distilled any hard liquors before the arrival of the heavy-drinking Spanish, they were more than a little partial to a fermented drink called pulque. Jorge said they even had a group of gods called the 400 Rabbits, each one representing a different way to get drunk. He took me to another part of the room and showed me a mural that was, in effect, an early community service announcement on the dangers of drinking. It was a cautionary tale about Cuextecatl, an Aztec chief who had one too many to drink.

'Even though Cuextecatl had drunk four,' Jorge explained, 'he asked for yet another. He became very intoxicated, very drunk. He was not conscious of his actions, and there, in front of the people, he removed and cast aside his loincloth.'

The picture was tastefully done, concealing Cuextecatl's private parts with a ceramic mug.

Jorge continued. 'He was completely naked,' he said. 'The people counselled together because he had done something indecent in throwing aside his loincloth, in becoming very intoxicated. And in shame Cuextecatl went away.'

I told Jorge I could relate to poor old Cuextecatl. Personally, I was impressed that he got to five. I would have been casting aside my loincloth after two.

To finish the evening, Jorge brought me a mezcal with pickled scorpions floating in the bottom. He claimed it was an aphrodisiac. The GND begs to differ. She said that when I got back to our room that night I simply passed out.

Now, I don't want you getting the idea that the GND and I spent our entire time in Oaxaca stumbling from one mezcal bar to another, or even one restaurant, street-side hawker or market kitchen to another. We spent at least a couple of hours at Santo Domingo and the Oaxaca Regional Museum.

Santo Domingo was one of the most beautiful churches I had ever seen. Built between 1575 and 1608, it is squat yet stately, like many of the grand buildings built in areas prone to earthquakes. A journalist at the *Oaxaca Times*, Oaxaca's original English newspaper, said that the church touched his soul 'softer than a lover'. While I wouldn't go that far, it was an extraordinary building, framed by date palms, mini-algave plants and the mountains behind. Inside, the lavishly gilded interior, especially the family tree of Santo Domingo de Guzmán, is breathtaking. This elaborate ceiling was designed to ensure that worshippers' eyes were turned to heaven, and it does the job. It's hard to believe that at the height of the anticlerical movement in 1862 the church was used as a stable by government troops.

The museum is housed in the old priory attached to Santo Domingo. It had just been remodelled, and the history of the region was presented in a flashy multi-media, interactive way, but unfortunately only in Spanish. Luckily there were lots of buttons to push and touchscreens to touch, so I was easily kept amused.

My favourite part was the display of treasure discovered in Tumba Siete (Tomb Seven) at Monte Albán, the Zapotec–Mixtec ruins on the edge of town. The highlight was the video, a low-budget Indiana Jones recreation of the discovery of Tomb Seven. It opened on a dark room, with the deep baritone voice-over booming out 'Tumba Siete!' very much in the manner one would announce *The Mummy* or *Dracula*.

The light faded up to reveal an old professor digging at Monte Albán with a dashing young archaeologist, Alfonso Caso.

They spend hours piecing together what they have found. They know there is another tomb somewhere, Tomb Seven, but where? The professor goes to town in his old Model T Ford for supplies. As he putters back up the hill, the Model T struggling under the weight of boxes of moustache wax, the old professor spots young Alfonso running down the road, mad with delight and holding aloft a glittering pendant. 'Tumbe Siete!' he cries. 'Tumbe Siete!' Finally, they'd discovered Tomb Seven.

And what a find. The Mixtecs had buried one of their kings in an old Zapotec tomb and had loaded it up with gold, exquisitely crafted silver, amber, turquoise, coral, jade and pearls. They'd even tossed in some intricately carved jaguar and eagle bones for good measure. To my untrained eye, most of it looked like the kind of stuff you'd buy off a middle-aged hippy woman in Byron Bay, but apparently it was worth millions.

Inspired by the video, we decided to visit the ruins of Monte Albán that afternoon. The ruins were perched high in the hills above Oaxaca and were reached after a treacherous minibus ride along a narrow, winding road that threatened to crumble and fall into the valley below and was nothing like the well-graded road the professor had negotiated in his Model T.

The only other tourists on the minibus were a retired couple from the Gold Coast in Queensland, Gwen and Jack. They wore matching khaki safari vests with a badge featuring the Australian flag sewn on the left breast and flinched every time the minibus flung around a corner. They were in the middle of a three-month journey around Mexico and were even more startled by our travel plans.

'Haven't you heard about Hurricane Mitch?' they gasped. 'There's nothing left of Central America!'

To prove her point Gwen reached into her backpack and pulled out a copy of *Time* magazine. The cover featured a corpse, bloated and stiff, in a muddy field that may have once grown maize. The headline said 'Land of the Dead', while the subhead told how Central America was struggling to recover from Mitch, which was described as a disaster of enormous magnitude. Inside there were more horrific pictures – helicopters ferrying survivors from flooded villages, families pulling what they could from homes covered in mud. Nicaragua's Minister of Defence was calling the area around Casitas Volcano 'a national cemetery'. Crops had been destroyed, people were starving and children were suffering from deadly septic infections set free in the flooding waters. Worse, the governments in these countries, underfunded from years of war and crippling international debt, were woefully ill-equipped to handle the catastrophe. The GND read the magazine over my shoulder, horrified.

The devastation caused by Mitch was much worse than we had first feared. We'd allotted six months to get through Central America, swing by Jamaica for the cricket, and pop into Cuba, before heading back to Mexico City from Cancun. And we'd already been in Mexico for close to four weeks – by my original plans we should have been in Guatemala by now. And, by the look of things, the extra month we'd agreed to spend in Mexico before venturing into Mitch-affected territory might not be enough. I got off the bus and entered the ruins at Monte Albán wondering if we'd ever get out of Mexico.

The ruins of Monte Albán sit atop brown hills surrounded by dramatic mountains. From the top of the Southern Platform, a stone edifice with a wide staircase, we had a panorama of the site, across the Grand Plaza to the Northern Platform and the tombs. With a little effort, I could imagine a bustling metropolis of skilled artisans, priests and farmers. Once, this collection of stones was one of the most advanced cities in the world, with a highly sophisticated system of government at a time when Europeans were still wallowing in shit. Now the descendants of this great civilization sat in the shade cast by the stone monuments, smoking cheap cigarettes and waiting for unsuspecting tourists to pass, silly enough to buy tacky souvenirs from them.

The GND and I sat there in silence, our thoughts still on the article in the *Time* magazine. The GND turned to me and grabbed my arm. 'You wouldn't take me anywhere dangerous, would you?'

I promised I wouldn't.

◼   ◼   ◼

Inspired by Monte Albán, we agreed that we'd visit the other major sights of Valles Centrales. We set off bright and early the next day, hoping to avoid the tourists and at least have a little time at each of the ruins to ourselves. It soon became apparent, however, that we were being followed by a coachload of French tourists.

At first I thought it was a coincidence. Like us, they had sensibly decided to start at Mitla, the Zapotec ruins furthest from Oaxaca. From there we planned to call into Yagul to see the remains of a ball court, the second largest in existence, high on a cactus-covered hill. Then, just as the sun was setting, we'd pay a visit to El Tule to see a huge 2000-year-old cyprus tree, picturesquely dwarfing the church next to it and with the widest girth of any tree in the Americas. I soon became convinced the French tourists had been sent on a special international mission to annoy the crap out of me.

Consider the evidence. While we were struggling to get from one ruin to another on crowded local buses, even walking the 1.5 kilometres from the highway to the hilltop ruins of Yagul, the French tourists had the services of a large air-conditioned coach. Despite this, or maybe because of it, they arrived at each of the places only moments after we did.

Secondly, consider their blatant disregard of tourist photo etiquette. This etiquette – a French word, funnily enough – is all that stops major tourist sites around the world from becoming places where much blood is shed. You see someone taking a photo, you walk around the back of them. You wait for a few seconds for them to take the photo (the photo taker gets a little flustered and rushes the shot – one of the few pleasures afforded by this etiquette) thank yous are exchanged and every one is happy.

But that wasn't how it worked with that coach load of French tourists. They swarmed over every ruined building, across every ancient mosaic, through every ball court, walking into photos, more often than not *between* the subject and taker. If someone asked them to move there was no apology, just a gallic shrug if you were lucky, an obstinate refusal to move if you were not.

They were worse with the set shots. Every tourist spot has the set shot, an object, sight or animal in front of which everyone wants to have their photo taken. At Mitla it was the Columna de la Vida (Column of Life), a stone pillar that you wrap your arms around to see how long you have to live. (Inexplicably, the closer your hands get to touching the closer you are to death.) Most tourists scampered up, flung their arms around the pillar, flashed a goofy smile to their friend or partner taking the photo and moved on.

Not the French. Not only did they ignore the queue the rest of us had quietly formed, they took forever to strike the pose they were most happy with. They would drape an arm and try a sultry look over the shoulder until the guy taking the photo would say 'Oui! Oui!' and whatever it is in French for 'Beautiful beautiful, work the camera baby'. Then, just before taking the photo, the photographer would notice a hair out of place. Half an hour later, the photo (or, more often than not, photos), would be taken. Then the rest of the coach would take their turn.

Finally, I present as evidence the way they were dressed. In the manner befitting the world of international intrigue, they were stylish. Not in a tailored tux, James Bond kind of way, but in a way that said well travelled but careful not to get grubby while doing it. On the face of the evidence, I'm sure you'll agree that they were sent to annoy the shit out of me. It was obvious, really.

What wasn't so obvious, well to me, anyway, was why I was beginning to do the same to the GND. On our last night in Oaxaca, as we ate in our favourite restaurant, a small, smoky place with wooden floors and a barman who knew how to mix a margarita just the way the GND liked them, there was a palpable sense of tension in the air.

'That's really annoying you know,' said the GND.

'What?' I asked defensively.

I thought she was talking about the way I ranked everything on my plate and then ate it in order, saving my favourite thing until last. A previous girlfriend used to make a big deal about my eating habits. She said it was delayed gratification, and indicated I was borderline psychotic. She had said it was a symptom that many serial killers display.

'No, the way you shake your leg all the time.'

'Oh, that!' I said relieved, smiling.

'It's really annoying,' she said. 'Can you stop it?'

The short answer to that was no. It was something I'd been doing all my life. Like a dog that automatically moves its leg when you scratch its belly. It gets worse when I think. (I'm doing it now even as I write – I'm beyond help.) During my final university exams, it was going up and down like a piston, and to this day, the girl who was sitting next to me claims she didn't get enough marks because I distracted her.

In well-built places, preferably with concrete floors, it is not generally a problem. But on rickety wooden floors, like there in the restaurant, you could measure the effect of my shaking leg on a Richter scale. The GND was clearly peeved so I made a serious attempt to stop. The trouble was, it took all my concentration to do it.

'Why have you stopped talking?' said the GND. 'Are you upset that I asked you to stop shaking your leg?'

'No, it's just that I need to concentrate.'

The GND looked at me, disbelieving. But almost to prove the point, my leg started shaking again the moment I answered her questions.

'This is ridiculous,' she snapped. 'Just finish your meal. We're going.'

Usually, I could put the GND's irritability down to a nicotine craving. But tonight was different. It seemed that I was causing it.

CHAPTER SIX

Chiapas

(Mexico)

Annoying habit >>> Tactlessness
Culprit >>> Peter

We caught an overnight bus to San Cristóbal de Las Casas, a colonial town in the heart of Mexico's troubled state of Chiapas. It was a 12-hour, 630-kilometre journey that took us from the heights of the Sierra Madre de Oaxaca to the low-lying Isthmus of Tehuantepec and then back up into the mountains again. The guidebook warned of bandits stopping buses on the long stretches of lonely highway, but it wasn't the bandits I was worried about. It was motion sickness.

I've always been a little prone to motion sickness. When I was a child I'd spend the long drive up the north coast for Christmas holidays staring blankly out of the window while my sister amused herself for hours reading the latest *Dolly* magazine. Even if I tried to read the wrappers off Fantales, lollies featuring film star biographies that Mum gave us periodically if we behaved ourselves, I would be bringing those chocolate-covered caramels back up all over the vinyl interior of our sky-blue Valiant stationwagon. On long journeys I had to keep myself happy by counting petrol stations. Thirty years later, it was only the prices on the bowsers that had changed.

I knew I was in trouble when I noticed the TV monitors hanging from the roof of our coach. Now, don't get me wrong. I can occasionally watch a video on the bus, but only when it is travelling along a super smooth piece of black top, on a stretch as straight as an arrow. Unfortunately, the road out of Oaxaca was a tightly twisting mountain road that plunged dramatically back to sea level via a series of switchbacks and hairpin bends. And in the grand tradition of Mexican highways it was peppered with topes (speed humps) built at a height and an inclination determined to do the most damage to the undercarriage of even the sturdiest of vehicles.

The sensible thing to do would have been to sleep and ignore the movie. And it should have been easy. It wasn't a terribly good movie – some New York mob movie dubbed into Spanish – but it had subtitles in English and I couldn't stop myself from reading them.

It was a bit like the cocktail phenomenon: when at a crowded and noisy party, you can instinctively hear your name above the Chemical Brothers being played at 240

decibels. If ever I turned my head, or
woken by the thud of the bus coming back
a particularly high tope, my eye was immedi
to a particular word in the subtitles. Then the n
then the next, until I was reading the whole damn
When the words started swirling I put my hand to my
forehead and noticed with alarm that it was wet and
clammy. I pointed both the overhead airconditioning vents
towards myself, gripped the handles and tried to fight back
the nausea. Every time I nearly had it beat, another word –
usually a damn verb – jumped out and sucked me back in
again.

The GND was beside me, being thrown side-to-side by
the curves of the road, happily reading *Memoirs of a Geisha*.
I began hallucinating that the chin of the geisha on the
cover had melded with the GND's, which was especially
freaky when she turned and smiled occasionally. When I
dry-retched, very nearly bringing up the greasy enchilada I
had foolishly tucked into at a stall across from Oaxaca bus
station, she put down her book and felt my forehead.

'Oh my God, you're sweating like a pig,' she cried, before
turning back to her book.

When dawn broke I had only been able to snatch a few
moments sleep. We were at sea level now, the roads were
straighter, but the topes no less stratospheric. We passed
through the Chiapas state capital, Tuxtla Gutiérrez, a bowl
of orange street lamps. The bus crawled through the deserted
streets, making a brief stop at the bus station before heading
towards the mountains and San Christóbal de las Casas.

Those two hours were the most enjoyable of the trip.

The road was winding again, but now, in the grey light of dawn, I could look out the window and watch the world go by. It was a magic world, too, with pine-clad mountains broken occasionally by maize fields and small huts with smoke seeping through the wooden slats. Indians wearing impossibly bright, embroidered shirts appeared suddenly in the mist, carry baskets or hoes and making their way to till the maize fields that clung precariously to the folds in the steep mountains. We had entered a different world now, an isolated world where the people had the kind of closed, exotic faces that suggested that their mother and father didn't get off the mountain much.

At what seemed to be the highest point of the mountains the bus turned off the main highway and plunged into the Jovel Valley. San Christóbal sat smoking and stirring to life at the bottom, a postcard-perfect colonial gem, looking sweet and mystical in the early morning fog. But when the bus finally pulled into the bus station on the edge of town I was tired, cranky and more than a little seedy.

As soon as the bus stopped I grabbed my pack and set off up Crescencio Rosas towards the centre of town like a mad man. I wanted the chill of the crisp morning air on my face. I needed a brisk walk to get the blood pumping through my veins. I was desperate to shake the fog that had settled on my brain, a hangover of my nausea.

I'd like to think that is why I told the GND she was lazy when she finally caught up and quite sensibly suggested we get a cab. Why, when she asked to see the map, I told her that she couldn't read maps so why bother. And why, when she complained of blisters, I told her she should have brought more sensible shoes. It was like I'd fallen into the Jim Carrey movie, *Liar Liar*. Where I had been careful to check my words during heated moments earlier on the trip, now I was saying whatever came into my head.

If I'd had any sort of sense I would have slapped both hands over my mouth and not said another word. If I'd been in a better mood I would have apologised. Instead I powered on up Madero towards the Hospedaje Bed and Breakfast, which our guidebook described as the 'best deal in town', all the while berating the GND to get a move on. We finally got there and when she said that she wasn't sure about the room, I said, 'We could get another one ... but we're not!' and promptly collapsed on the bed. The GND sat on the edge of it sulking. If my leg shaking had annoyed her, I had really pissed her off now.

As I lay there on the lumpy mattress looking at the stained ceiling, I contemplated how different it was travelling with someone. On my own, I would still grumble, but to myself, internalised, kicking a few stones or pushing that little bit harder to get up a hill to take out my frustrations. I knew I should apologise, but I also knew that would be admitting that some line had been crossed, maybe a line that we couldn't get back over. Instead, I took a nap, hoping that the GND would blame my churlish behaviour on the bus trip and that when I woke up it would be all forgotten. I think John Gray, the guy who wrote *Men are from Mars, Women are from Venus* would have said I was retreating into my cave.

After a nap, the GND and I went for a wander around San Cristóbal. I had woken in a much better frame of mind – it *had* been the seediness that had effected my demeanour – and the GND, perhaps in a spirit of reconciliation, chose not to remind me of the horrible things I had said. The clouds that had hung low over the town giving it an enchanting air on our arrival had not cleared and were now low and oppressive. Indians from surrounding villages, loaded with stuff for the markets, scurried about scowling, shooting dark glances at the riot police who stood on every corner.

San Cristóbal had obviously been a major tourist spot – that was evident by the number of cafes, the brightly restored colonial houses and the number of shops selling knitted ponchos. Then there was the lovely plaza lined with trees, the centrepiece being a fine colonial kiosk. But there was also a real sense of menace, not helped at all by the riot policemen in their sinister black uniforms, bulging from the latest in US-supplied body armour.

Of course, it could have just been the weather. Grey skies can often put people in grey moods. I remember that from when I was living in London. Most days it was grey and drizzly and everyone shuffled about with their heads down. On those days the local newsagent would toss me my change with a 'Harrumph'. On the few days that the sun was out, however, the city and its people were transformed. People walked around smiling, the buildings appeared bright and cheerful and the newsagent actually asked me how I was doing. Maybe it was the same in San Cristóbal.

My bet, however, was that things still hadn't settled down since the Zapatista uprising in 1994. On January 1 of that year the town shot to world-wide prominence when an armed peasant group calling itself the Ejército Zapatista de Liberación Nacional (The EZLN, or Zapatistas, as they are more commonly known) attacked and sacked government offices and took over the town. Their stated aim was to redress the wrongs committed against the ancestors of the Tzotzils and Tzeltals who had moved to these highlands after the collapse of lowland Mayan civilisation. When the Spanish arrived in 1524 and made it their regional headquarters, the Indians lost their land and suffered new hardships in disease, taxes and forced labour.

The Zapatista rebels were driven out of San Cristóbal by federal Mexican troops after a few days, and they retreated to a remote corner of the Lacandón jungle near the Guatemalan border. But not before the world's attention had been drawn to the plight of the Chiapas Indians, and their leader, a masked figure known only as Subcomandante Marcos became a cult figure for those wanting change in Mexico and around the world.

It has been said that the Zapatista uprising was the first indigenous uprising to effectively manipulate the media. Subcommandante Marcos, it is argued, stage-managed the whole affair rather well. The balaclava, for example, was an inspired move. Not only was it eminently practical for hiding one's identity, it also acted like the trademark, or an icon, of the peasant rebellion. Where posters of Che Guevara had once adorned the walls of college kids around the world it was now the balaclavad Subcomandante Marcos.

The Zapatista movement had also created a whole new cottage industry in Zapatista-related souvenirs. All the

European tourists were bypassing the weavers' collectives and heading straight for the Zapatista merchandising. Not that I can talk. On that first morning in San Cristóbal I bought a Zapatista doll key ring and the GND bought a small woven horse with two rebels riding on its back from a stall in the markets around the Templo de Santo Domingo.

I was surprised, actually, at how openly the stuff was being sold. There was even a stall flagrantly selling badges, pamphlets and booklets, newsletters and other political tracts calling for the overthrow of the oppressive Mexican government. Having said that, the guy behind the stall did have that look about him that he was ready to run at any moment. His eyes scampering from side to side, and when I bought an EZLN badge from him he mumbled something to me from behind his hand. My Spanish wasn't good enough to know whether he was offering a private audience with the subcomandante or warning me to get out of town. The atmosphere in the town and the heavy police and army presence, made me think that he was trying to give me a warning – we still had time to get out. The GND said I was just being paranoid. Besides, she had found an embroidered jacket and wanted to know if I thought it suited her.

Later that afternoon, just east of the plaza, we were approached by young Indian girls wielding exercise books. They said they were doing a school project. Their teacher had told them to get the names and countries of foreigners visiting their town. Could we fill out the book for them. Of course. It was a simple task. I filled in my name . . . my country ... my thoughts on San Cristóbal. Like dozens of other tourists. Then I noticed the last column. 'Donation.'

'Cheeky buggers!' I thought. The audacity of it made me chuckle, especially when I noticed that all the donations were in dollars, not pesos. I filled in $0 and gave the book back with a smile.

'Don't be mean!' said the GND.

The girl read it, quickly checked out my donation and let out a dismayed 'Hey!' before punching me in the stomach and storming off.

'That certainly took the grin off your face,' said the GND, allowing herself a small smile. 'It serves you right.'

The girl stood at the end of the passageway, showing my entry to her friends and pointing me out to them. I knew that if the revolution came I'd be top of the 'People Who Must Mysteriously Disappear' list.

❖   ❖   ❖

That night it was misty and drizzling, and we were the coldest we'd been on the journey so far. We ate at a small restaurant with an open fire. A traveller sat warming her hands and on noticing our guidebook – the new Lonely Planet guide to Mexico – asked if she could read it while we ate. I suspect it was simply a pretext to talk to us when she gave it back. Her name was Amanda. She was American and she had come to Mexico to work through some issues and find herself.

'When I found myself,' she told us unashamedly, 'I was shocked at what I was.'

She was equally shocked by our plan to head down

through Central America. 'God, it's a mess down there,' she said. 'I just saw it on CNN.'

I tried to look nonchalant, but my leg started shaking – for the first time since Oaxaca – giving away my real concern.

'I've heard that Costa Rica won't let you in after you've travelled through Honduras or Nicaragua,' she said. 'They're worried about cholera.'

The news alarmed the GND, enough, it seems, to stop her from noticing my shaking leg. I changed the subject by asking Amanda if she'd noticed a weird vibe in San Cristóbal.

'*Yes!*' she exclaimed, slapping the table. 'It's like something heavy is about to happen! I was up in the mountains today and I heard 30 minutes of gunfire. Something's goin' down!'

Later than night something was coming up. A dodgy taco the GND had bought from a street vendor for lunch. Our room at the Hospedaje Bed and Breakfast was one of the cheaper rooftop ones, so for the GND that meant a mad dash to the concrete shower and toilet block at the end of the roof when nature made its frequent calls.

It was a quiet night, so the GND's affliction was graphically audible. It soon became obvious that as well as a dose of Montezuma's Revenge, the GND was also throwing up. I lay in bed, trying to block out the sounds with my Walkman, not altogether sure if our relationship was ready for this kind of, um, intimacy yet. Most couples don't have to deal with these kinds of noises, even after twenty years of marriages. Yet here, just over a month into our trip, I was listening to the GND doing her best cappuccino machine impersonation. Having said that, though, her dexterity was astounding. She had problems at both ends, yet from the noises coming from the bathroom, she had a 100 per cent accuracy rate. I was impressed. And judging by the appreciative murmurs coming from the other rooms, so were the other guests.

Eventually, the GND returned to our room exhausted and spent and collapsed into a fitful sleep. I couldn't sleep, though. Not because of my stomach – I was untouched by whatever it was that had upset the GND – but because of the explosions I was hearing periodically throughout the night. At first they were muffled, the dull thuds somewhere up in the mountains, but soon they were closer, louder, echoing in the empty streets.

I was convinced it was the start of something. The English language newspapers had been full of stories about the stalled talks between the EZLN and the government. A group of foreigners called Pastors for Peace had been arrested ferrying food and supplies to pro-Zapatista villagers. The mood of the town, the high military presence, Amanda's experiences, the guy from the Zapatista stall: it was obvious – what I was hearing was the start of a revolution.

I lay in bed waiting, but when I didn't hear the rattle of gunfire – the logical next step in any armed conflict, I would have thought – I decided to go out on the roof and see what was happening. The GND woke and asked me what I was doing.

'I'm going to see what the explosions are.'

'Explosions?' she asked, looking down at the sheets. 'Are you sure it wasn't me?'

'No, listen,' I said. Another thud.

'It sounds like fireworks to me.'

'Maybe,' I said. 'But why are they letting fireworks off at four in the morning? It's the start of something, I'm telling you.'

Up on the roof, the grey light of dawn was peaking from behind the mountains. I watched for about ten minutes, just long enough for the cold to seep into my bones and to determine that the explosions were indeed just fireworks. They fizzed up into the sky on a slight arc before exploding with a flash, making the local dogs bark. The GND, even in her unfit state, was right.

'Was it fireworks?' she asked when I returned to the room.

'Well, I think so,' I answered grudgingly. 'But that doesn't mean it's not the Zapatistas. Maybe they're letting off fireworks at these odd hours to lull the army into a false sense of security and . . .'

'But the battle hasn't started, right?' interrupted the GND.

'Well, no,' I replied.

'Good, because I've got a battle of my own,' she said leaving the room. A few seconds later, the valley echoed with the sounds of a very different kind of fireworks.

■   ■   ■

By lunchtime the next day the GND was feeling well enough for us to venture out. Gifts of corn snacks from the shop down the road and my thoughtful gesture of opening the door for her whenever nature called had made her better disposed towards me than of late, and, I'd like to think, helped speed her recovery. As long as we kept an eye on where the nearest toilet was, or the nearest bush, we could still have a look around. We decided to visit Na Bolom.

Na Bolom was the home of Danish archaeologist Frans Blom and his wife, the Swiss anthropologist and photographer Trudy Duby-Blom. Frans discovered a number of old Mayan sites; Trudy took photos of remote Lacandón tribes people. Now that both had died, Trudy in 1993, their home had been turned into a museum and volunteer centre for folk with left-leaning views.

While we were there, admiring Trudi's stunning portraits of the proud Lacandón Indians, as well as the pathway lined with half-buried bottles, bottles collected from Fran's long drinking sprees with his good mate Diego Rivera, the artist, I got to talking to one of the guys working there. Pepe was a striking man, with long dark hair and strong features. He dressed in jeans and a vest, with suitably exotic trinkets around his neck. He was obviously a favourite with the female volunteers at the house. I told him I wanted to visit Chamula, one of the outlying villages around San Cristóbal and renowned for its intense religious practices and equally intense hostility towards outsiders. Pepe had been born there and agreed to take us.

We caught a minivan from the markets up into the hills. It dropped us off at a crossroad marked by a huge sign welcoming us to Chamula but also warning us that photography at the church or during rituals was strictly forbidden. A single concrete road led down to the town, which was further down in a valley. To our right were the ruined remains of an old church and graveyard, scattered with fading streamers, pine needles and branches and rubbish from celebrations for the Day of the Dead.

As we made our way down the road towards the town, a gaggle of children, their clothes dirty and ragged, appeared begging us to take their photographs. 'I thought villagers from Chamula didn't like their photos taken,' I said to Pepe.

'They don't. These kids just want you to take their photo for money.'

Realising that we weren't about to take their photo, they abandoned us and went to hang around the entrance gate to a large modern house bristling with satellite dishes and with a BMW parked out the front. I asked Pepe if it belonged to one of the rich landowners the Zapatista were fighting against.

'No!' laughed Pepe. 'The guy who owns that place is more powerful than that. He is the local Pepsi distributor.'

'The Pepsi distributor?' echoed the GND and I in unison.

'Yes. The only richer man in the valley lives over there,' he said pointing to an even grander place with even more satellite dishes and a Mercedes parked in the driveway. 'He sells Coca-Cola.'

Sensing that he needed to give an explanation, Pepe continued. 'Because the people here believe that cola has healing powers,' said Pepe, matter-of-factly. 'In Chamula, it is magic!'

'Black magic!' laughed the GND, getting in the line before I could, damn her.

Readers may be surprised to learn that this was not the first time I had heard of the healing powers of Coca-Cola.

My mother had always forbidden me to drink Coke because she said it would rot my teeth and make them fall out. But when I was at university, one of the other students, a mature-aged student who practised law during the day and always appeared in class dressed immaculately in a three-piece morning suit, used to make quite a show of drinking a 1.25-litre bottle during the lesson. When our tutor questioned him about it, he simply replied that his doctor had prescribed it to ward off colon cancer. I don't know if it's true, but to this day I've always quoted him to people who claim that my Coke consumption is excessive.

In Chamula, however, Coke's restorative powers went beyond preventing colon cancer. Shamans had started using it in healing rituals, shaking it until it went flat and then giving it to their patients to drink. (They had previously used coffee, but obviously liked the more show-stopping volcanic effect of a shaken Coke.) When the sick people perked up – the caffeine and sugar hit, no doubt – it became a vital part of all healing rituals. The sales of Coca-Cola went through the roof. It wasn't long before Pepsi caught wind of this and brought the Cola Wars to Chamula.

'To prove that Pepsi was just as good,' said Pepe, 'Pepsi started giving a commission to shamans if they recommended their clients bought Pepsi. Then so did Coca-Cola. Now shamans are sponsored by particular brands.'

It all sounded a bit far-fetched to me, but when we arrived in the town square it became obvious Pepe had been telling the truth. The entire square was covered with Coca-Cola and Pepsi billboards. Each restaurant, shop, mechanic, or bicycle repair person had shown their allegiance to one cola or the other by tacking a sign over their doorway. Pepe said that friendships, marriages, and families in Chamula were all divided along these cola lines. Here, in a tiny Mayan village in the southern highlands of Mexico, the Cola Wars were being fought at their most fundamental level. And nowhere was it fought as viciously as in the town's church.

The church stood on the far side of the plaza, freshly whitewashed and with streamers and pine branches hung across its gaily coloured door. The church had been built between 1522 and 1524 and within its walls a unique blend of Catholicism and Mayan beliefs was practised. The Chamulans, for example, believe that when Christ rose from the grave he became the sun, and they had simply replaced their various gods with saints. St John, for example, replaced the corn god and took on all the duties previously undertaken by that deity – guaranteeing bumper crops, warding off pests and that sort of thing.

In the early days the church fathers turned a blind eye, happy to have recruited such eager new souls to their religion. But when more and more Mayan practices were incorporated – the sacrifice of live animals, for example – a line was drawn and the church was excommunicated. It still is, and the result is that the Chamulans practise a very bizarre form of Catholicism to this day.

Inside the church it was dark and the smell of incense was overwhelming. When my eyes adjusted to the light I let out a gasp. All the pews had been removed and the floor covered in pine needles (a symbol of happiness, apparently). Pale light streamed in through the thick smoke and fell upon shamans who had set up on the floor in regular intervals to ply their trade. Locals sat before them, lit candles in rows, the sick and infirm lying or sitting up the front. The shamans were waving eggs or chickens over the ill as they drank glasses of flat cola.

'The chicken or the egg soaks up the illness,' explained Pepe. 'After ten minutes or so, the shaman will break the egg or kill the chicken and study it to find out what is the problem. Then he will recommend a cure.'

Elsewhere villagers kneeled before the various statues of saints that sat in niches around the church, lighting coloured candles or leaving glasses of Pepsi or Coke as an offering. Other women dressed the saints in clothes made especially for them.

'This is creepy,' said the GND, shuddering.

I've got to admit that the chanting, the smoke, the animal sacrifices all made me feel uneasy too. For a boy brought up in the traditional three hymns and a sermon style of religion it felt very pagan. I had an uneasy feeling that either us or the church was going to get struck by lightning. We beat a hasty retreat. On the way out, I noticed half a dozen saint statues leaning against the wall, ignored and gathering dust. I asked Pepe why they were so neglected.

'They are the shamed saints,' he answered.

They were from the destroyed church we had seen on the way into town. They hadn't saved the church from the earthquake, so now they were condemned to sit at the back of the newer church and see the other saints being lavished with offerings. It was their version of purgatory.

Back in the square, it seemed my version of purgatory

was coming to end – the GND consented readily to having her photo taken. She'd been loath to do it of late because my constant requests for her to pose in front of any object of interest 'aggravated' her. My efforts in checking my tactlessness and curbing my leg shaking were obviously paying dividends. She was still feeling a little off-colour, however, and joked that she could do with a cola.

'Pepsi or Coke?' smiled Pepe.

Just so it didn't look like we were taking sides, we decided to have one of each.

CHAPTER SEVEN

Palenque

(Mexico)

Annoying habit >>> Sexual adventurism
Culprit >>> GND

It wasn't until I got onto the bus taking us to Palenque and was startled by the music playing on the radio that I realised what had been so disconcerting about San Cristóbal. It had been quiet, unnaturally so. There had been no mariachi bands, no Mexican pop songs featuring maniacal laughter – just a heavy, oppressive silence, punctuated by the odd firework exploding. Sadly it took Cher asking in a warbling voice if I believed in life after love to realise it.

The bus climbed out of the valley, through green fields and pine forests, and after an hour damp thick walls of vines and jungle closed in. The GND was quietly concentrating on her bowel movements so I struck up a conversation with another gringo sitting opposite who was wearing a 'Pastors for Peace' T-shirt.

His name was Dave and he had the pale, thin look of a born-again Christian, and sported the limp mousy hair and scraggly goatee beard they tend to favour. The Pastors for Peace had been in the Mexican newspapers lately – five had been arrested and deported for visiting Zapatista-friendly villages without permission – so I asked him if he had been among them. And, if so, why he hadn't been deported.

'It was all beat up by the Mexican press,' he said. 'Five of us who were leaving the country anyway were "expelled". Those of us who weren't were allowed to stay.'

They had made the mistake of visiting a village that hadn't been nominated on their visas, a village, as it turned out, that was pro-Zapatista. Dave claimed they didn't know about the village's leftist leanings – in this region a pro-Zapatista village can be right next to a pro-government one. They had simply asked in San Cristóbal which village needed aid the most and that was the name they were given.

'The government knew we were coming,' said Dave. 'When we arrived with our trucks the road into the village was blocked by the army. Trouble was, the road was too narrow for our truck to turn around, so they had to let us go through to the village. We took our time turning around and unloaded the stuff anyway. I think that's what pissed them off.'

After the army searched their vehicles they were allowed

to go back to San Cristóbal. It was only after they got back and noticed that things had been 'souvenired' by the army – sunglasses, torches, passports, that sort of thing – and they complained that the trouble started.

'Our leader called a press conference and said we were only helping people who were very poor and in need,' said Dave.

That's when the Mexican government made up the story about the expulsions. 'Don't let the façade of normalness fool you,' Dave added. 'It's very tense down here. Seventy-five per cent of the Mexican army is stationed in Chiapas.'

Almost as if to prove his point three army Hummers full of soldiers passed, heading back towards San Cristóbal.

'The US gives the Mexican government $215 million a year in military aid to help fight drugs,' he snorted. 'Most of it ends up here, like those Hummers, in a region that is not a big drug region. You figure out what the Mexicans are using the money on!'

About 80 kilometres before Palenque the bus started winding its way down the jungle-covered mountain to a vast plain that stretched forth towards the Yucatán Peninsula and the Gulf of Mexico. We were in a different Mexico now. Where the jungle had been cleared in the mountains for maize, here it was cleared to graze cattle. Instead of struggling along with sacks on their backs, the locals on the plains drove pick-up trucks. The brightly coloured outfits of the highland Indians were replaced by jeans and white cowboy boots. The air too was different. In San Cristóbal it had been clear and crisp. Now it was thick with humidity.

On the outskirts of Palenque the bus was stopped by a military roadblock. When a soldier got on board, I got a little excited. Perhaps they were looking for Dave. Maybe he had been expelled after all, but had escaped from the two inept guards taking him to the airport and he was now a fugitive. (Obviously they still had his bag – surely he would have changed his T-shirt otherwise!) Unfortunately, the soldier merely stood at the front and addressed the passengers in Spanish. I couldn't make out what he was saying, but his tone and demeanour suggested that it went along the following lines:

'If there are known terrorists on board, would they please make their way to the front of the bus.'

An uneasy silence.

'No? There are *no* terrorists on board?'

Again, silence.

'*No* Zapatisas among you lot?'

Uneasy shifting in seats.

'Are *you* sure? I'm only going to ask once.'

Silence.

'Okay. Well, have a nice day!'

The soldier got off the bus and we were allowed on our way.

I've never understood the purpose of these kinds of roadblocks. I'd come across them before in other troubled areas of the world – Colombia, Rwanda, Denmark – and exactly the same thing happened at all of them. A soldier got on board, stood up the front of the bus and made an announcement, and when nobody stepped forward, got off again.

Why don't the soldiers ask for identity papers or at least walk down the aisle eye-balling passengers in the hope that one will crack and make a run for it? But they don't. They rely on the honesty of the terrorist to own up and make their way in a quiet and orderly fashion to the front of the bus.

Of course, I couldn't understand a word the soldier said so I'm merely speculating. The guy could have simply been asking if anyone had a spare cigarette.

There are two Palenques – the archaeological ruins that are home to one of the most important Mayan cities ever discovered and the scruffy town nearly seven kilometres away. The turn-off to the archaeological zone is marked by an oversized statue of a Mayan ruler's head stuck in the middle of a roundabout.

Palenque, the town, is merely a collection of squalid, ramshackle buildings deteriorating prematurely in the thick humid atmosphere. It starts at the chaotic bus station, surrounded by collapsing cantinas, mechanics shops and a Pemex fuel station, where coaches sit revving, belching out fumes, while minivans scuttle among them, splashing through puddles and drenching unsuspecting people trying to get anywhere else but there. The rest of the town stretches for two kilometres in this fashion, an ugly but lively scar.

We got a room in a hotel near the park, the nearest thing Palenque had to a town centre. Our room was clean and bright with an overhead fan. It also had an attached bathroom, an added luxury the GND insisted on after her public humiliation in San Cristóbal. An American guy, unshaved and unwashed, a displaced Vietnam veteran by the look of him, sat in the doorway of the hotel fashioning Mayan pyramids out of Styrofoam.

'What do you think of my pyramids?' he asked with a manic look that suggested that the truth – that they were crap – was not the most sensible answer.

'They're good,' I lied.

'Wanna buy one?' he asked. 'Only 100 pesos!'

That was $20. I wouldn't have taken one even if he gave it to me. 'We've just started our travels,' I squirmed. 'We couldn't carry it.' That part was true. The things were ridiculously big.

'Sure you could carry it,' he argued. 'They're only light!' Sensing my scepticism, he handed me one. 'You could post it home. The post office is just around the corner.'

I begged off, saying I would think about it. I didn't want to upset him in case it triggered a Vietnam flashback and he mistook me for Charlie.

'Great for Christmas,' he yelled after us as we scurried away to our room.

Even though it was Saturday night, a quick wander around Palenque revealed that there was not much going on. The central park was nice enough, a pleasant place to sit and watch the freshly washed locals parade, the young boys flirting with giggling girls, or shoe-shine boys plying their trade. We ate a filling dinner of beans and rice in an agreeable restaurant, chosen by the GND purely on the basis of its two-for-the-price-of-one margarita deal. We strolled along the main drag, Avenida Juárez, bought an ice cream and looked through shops that all seemed to sell penlight batteries and Maglite torches. Although it was miles from any border, Palenque had a real frontier feel, a town full of smuggled goods and crap made in China.

When we finally retired to our room for the night we realised that our hotel was right next to a Pentecostal church. I'd noticed a large number of Pentecostal churches once we had hit the plains from the mountains, but I hadn't noticed this one. Now the Saturday evening service was in full swing. And instead of murmuring and quietly chanting over a bottle of Coke, like the highland Indians of Chamula, these guys had a fully amplified band and took an all-singing, all-dancing, 'hallelujah' approach to their religious observances.

I've got to say that hotel rooms affected by noise don't bother me that much. In my time on the road I've stayed in a number of places that would have been shut down by municipal noise codes and have still managed to sleep, the worst two being the Busha Beni Lodge in Zaire with the attached disco, and the Friendship Lodge in the Philippines with the complimentary rutting Swedes next door. In comparison, especially when pitted against the decibels the Swedes had produced, the noise from the church next door was minimal.

Having been brought up a Seventh Day Adventist, however, I knew all the tunes they were playing from my childhood at church. And although they were in Spanish, I found myself involuntarily singing along. Just as I was about to nod off, I'd hear the opening bars from another childhood Christian classic and I'd be off again. The GND couldn't sleep either, but was amused by my involuntary warbling. 'I didn't realise you were such a religious man,' she teased. 'It's a shame you can't sing, you might have found your calling.'

In the end she cuddled up to me, to block out the music I suspect, and quickly fell asleep. When I finally drifted off an hour or so later, I was mumbling the words of 'Jesus Loves the Little Children'.

The next morning we got up early to get out to the Palenque archaeological zone before the Pentecostals started their Sunday morning service. It was an inspired move. We arrived at the gates of the park just as it opened at 8 am, the morning air still cool and the mist still hanging low over the jungle. There are close to 40 square kilometres of ruins at Palenque and only a dozen or so of the 500 buildings believed to be on the sight have been excavated. The city fell into decline sometime around 1500 AD, and with the region around Palenque boasting the highest average rainfall in Mexico, it wasn't long before the jungle reclaimed its own.

The jungle's voraciousness was such that the ruins sat undiscovered for over 200 years. Cortés came within 40 kilometres of the city, yet neither he nor the Tzotzil Indians he met had any idea about it. In 1773 some local Indians stumbled upon what they called 'stone houses' and told their priest. A few Spaniards visited the site, but it wasn't until Count de Waldeck turned up in 1831 that the world took notice.

The count produced a series of drawings and descriptions that compared the ruins to those in ancient Greece and

Egypt and even suggested that Palenque might be the lost city of Atlantis. His claims were entirely fanciful, of course, but they inspired American explorer, John L Stephens, to undertake a more serious investigation of the site. Along with Frederick Catherwood, they cleared some of the jungle and wrote an exhaustive study of the site.

On my insistence, our first stop was the Temple of the Count, a stone pyramid in the north of the site where Count de Waldeck had lived for two years. The count had become something of a hero to me and I had taken to reading out passages about him to the GND from a booklet about the ruins I'd bought in town. Called *The Easy Guide to Palenque* it described the count as an adventurer who'd come into the middle of the jungle and set up camp atop one of these temples with what it quaintly described as a 'local lady friend'.

From the Temple of the Count we made our way across a stream to the Temple of the Foliated Cross, an intriguing temple that had partially collapsed to expose the unique construction techniques. A team of workers were slashing the thick lush grass with machetes. I decided to take a photo and the GND sat on a slab of stone beside me, a sheet of black plastic where the workman had laid some of their tools behind her.

Noticing I was taking a photograph, one of the workman put on a particularly energetic show and unwittingly lopped off the head of a snake that had been hiding in the grass. Its decapitated head whistled past the GND's nose and landed on the sheet of plastic. She shrieked and then fell into a catatonic silence. I picked it up and showed it to the guy who had killed it. He ran away, alarmed, crying, 'Mucho peligroso!' – very dangerous!

I was upset that he didn't appreciate that I had picked up the remains of the snake from the back of the head. Growing up on the outskirts of Sydney, I had quickly learned which end of a snake was dangerous and how to avoid it. Red belly black snakes were always slithering onto our place, and if my dad wasn't home from work it was my duty to kill them. Our dog Sally would bail them up and I'd cut off their heads with a shovel.

'Mierda?' I asked the guy, saying Spanish for shit, but meaning to say 'muerte', the Spanish word for deadly.

'Si, Mierda!,' he replied, cautiously coming forward to get a closer look at the snake. 'Y muerte!'

Shit and dangerous.

Killing the snake was obviously the highlight of this guy's day, maybe even week. He called other workers over and animatedly re-enacted the story: 'I was just slashing away, and whoosh – I cut off the head and nearly hit that gringa over there!' The other workers nodded gravely and then shook their heads in disbelief. When another group of workers wandered by, he called them over and told the story all over again. Half an hour later, when we were clambering over the Temple of the Jaguar, he was still pointing us out to workers who hadn't heard the story yet.

To escape the attention – believe me, it gets a little wearisome waving and smiling inanely all the time – we made our way to the Queen's Bath, a natural sink below a waterfall on the Otulum River. It was a pretty spot and a dip in the chilly water helped soothe the GND's jangled nerves.

'This is perfect,' she said, swimming towards the waterfall. And it was.

Finally, we made our way to the Temple of Inscriptions. If you've ever seen any pictures of Palenque, chances are they featured this place. It is a stepped pyramid, topped by a small temple, the tallest and most prominent of Palenque's buildings. I'd like to say that after a month free of cigarettes the GND was able to scale the 69 steps to the top with ease. The truth is, she was reaching for the Nicorettes by step 32.

'Imagine how hard it would have been if I hadn't given up smoking,' she huffed. I think it was beginning to sink in, however, that her lungs wouldn't miraculously heal overnight.

The top of the Temple of Inscriptions affords a fantastic view back over the Temple of the Jaguar and the jungle, and on the rear wall of the temple there are three panels with long inscriptions in Mayan hieroglyphics. In the heart of the temple, at the bottom of a flight of steep, slippery steps, lies the tomb of Pakal.

Pakal was Palenque's most famous ruler, the guy who built the most significant temples and whose jewel-encrusted skull and jade death mask was the pride of the Mexico City Museum until the mask was stolen in 1985. His intricately carved stone sarcophagus lid remains in the tomb, too heavy and awkward for a thief to lift.

Descending the staircase, the air grew thicker and staler the lower we went. We passed other visitors returning from the bottom, bathed in sweat, stopping to catch their breath. Near the bottom, the staircase turned back on itself, leading to a stone entrance where inside, illuminated, lay the sarcophagus lid.

The carved stone lid showed an image of Pakal encircled by serpents and was quite impressive, but the room was small and cramped and the air thick, so after a cursory glance I turned to leave.

The GND grabbed my arm and stopped me. 'Listen,' she said. 'There's no one else coming.'

She was right. It was quiet. The only sound was the distant chattering of the people we had passed on the way down.

'Let's get up to some hanky-Palenquey!' she said with a smirk.

'What, here?' I asked incredulously.

Personally, I've never really understood the appeal of sexual congress in public places. To me it was just the quickest way to get arrested or embarrassed nationally when the photos came out. But the GND was insistent. Obviously my renditions of Christian classics the night before had stirred something deep inside her.

'I bet your good friend the count wouldn't have been so hesitant,' she teased. 'I'm sure his "lady friend" wasn't just there for company!'

I hesitated, but in my heart I knew she had me there. I crossed my heart, asked the ghost of Pakal for forgiveness and did what I had to do.

◙　◙　◙

I woke up in a foetal position with the GND checking my pulse.

'You passed out,' she said defensively as I flickered back to consciousness. 'I was just checking your pulse.'

I pulled my wrist away sharply. 'You thought I was dead!' I said. I was lying on the bathroom floor at our hotel.

'What did you expect!' she exclaimed. 'All that stuff you said about upsetting the spirit of Pakal yesterday – I was freaked out.'

I clambered back into bed. I'd been sick all night and I knew I had a dose of giardiasis – I'd had it once before in Kenya and the symptoms of watery rice stools and burps that smell like farts were pretty hard to miss. I sent the GND up to the town centre to get me a course of Flagyl and a bottle of Coke, just in case.

We had planned to head off to Guatemala that day. But when the GND returned with the Flagyl tablets and mopped my brow with a wet towel I figured it was best to put it off for another day. It was nice to be fussed over, and besides, if we jumped on a bus to the border, who was to say I wouldn't pass out again?

'Why are men such sooks?' asked the GND, passing me a magazine and a chocolate bar that she'd bought for me as well. 'You didn't do all this for me when I was sick in San Cristóbal!'

I clutched my stomach and groaned, skilfully avoiding having to answer that question and getting another glass of Coke poured for me to boot. As long as I didn't push it too hard this illness was proving to be a godsend. Nursing me back to health, the GND seemed to forget she was ever annoyed with me. When she organised for a TV to be brought to our room it struck me that maybe I hadn't upset the ghost of old Pakal with our dalliance at all.

CHAPTER EIGHT

Tikal

(Guatemala)

```
Annoying habit >>> Laziness
Culprit >>> GND
```

When we set out for Guatemala early next morning the Christians were quiet and the Vietnam veteran pyramid maker was nowhere to be seen. The morning air was still crisp and cool, and teams of workers lined up at the council depot at the bottom of the park to receive brooms and buckets to clean the streets.

We had noticed this ritual every morning we had been in Palenque – townsfolk, women and children mainly, queuing up for a couple of hours, cleaning the streets. After getting a broom, they would mill around on their designated block in groups, laughing and chatting, until one caught sight of a supervisor. Then they would sweep furiously for a few minutes, waiting until the supervisor passed (invariably pointing out a few spots that they missed) before getting back to their gossiping. At 8 am, just as the humidity and the heat hit again, they filed back to the depot, returned their buckets and brooms and returned to whatever else it was they did for the rest of the day.

Our plan was to cut across the top of Guatemala via Flores, pop into the Mayan ruins at Tikal, and then continue on to Belize. There were two ways of getting to Flores – the straightforward route via Frontera Corozal, the one favoured by every tour operator in town, and the more adventurous route via Tenosique, La Palma and El Naranjo, currently out of favour with everybody. This was the route I favoured, simply because it involved a four-hour speedboat ride up the Río San Pedro and passed through a town named after an orange.

The bus trip to Tenosique passed without incident. Although it looks close to Palenque on a map, there is no direct road between the towns, so instead the bus took a circuitous loop through Catazajá and Emiliano Zapata. This was cattle country, a land of pick-up trucks, cleared swamps and towns set up specifically to service rural needs. The towns were nondescript and mostly named after figures in Mexican history. Emiliano Zapata, despite being named after the rebel leader, was not an exciting town. Apart from the statue of Zapata marking the start of the town and a new John Deere tractor showroom, it was no different to the other new towns that had sprung up to service the cattle farms, on land only recently reclaimed from the jungle that surrounded it.

Our plans to get to La Palma in time to catch the boat to El Naranjo hit a snag in Tenosique. Tenosique was an older town, set up by the Spanish as an administrative centre, and altogether scruffier. Our guidebook said that orange colectivos (vans) left from outside the markets for La Palma starting at 6 am. What it failed to say was that the market was a small abandoned market on the outskirts of town, not the main market in the centre of town. The GND and I spent a good two hours wandering around the town's main markets asking vegetable sellers for directions in bad Spanish and being evicted by the owners of orange-coloured vehicles that we had taken to be the colectivo to La Palma. Eventually, a guy selling carrots took pity on us and bundled us into a taxi, giving the driver explicit instructions on where we wanted to go.

We were dumped in a poor part of town, next to a building that may or may not have once been a market, and beside a single orange van. The driver was asleep across the front bench and we woke him to confirm he was going to La Palma, before we let the taxi go.

'Si,' he nodded wearily. 'Hora tres' (three o'clock). And then he went back to sleep.

It would have been difficult to pass two and a half hours in Tenosique and keep one's sanity at the best of times, but in its suburbs it was well near impossible. The first hour passed okay – the GND and I simply used it as an opportunity to get to know each other a little better by listing our top ten movies, books and albums. The second hour, however, dragged and we had to resort to throwing stones at a can to amuse ourselves. When other passengers began appearing with sacks of stuff they had bought at the markets back in town I felt like hugging them. Right on three o'clock the driver started the van and we all clambered in. A Spanish language version of 'Achy Breaky Heart' was playing on the radio, which raised my spirits immeasurably.

The van bounced its way along a dirt road through scrappy farmland. It was clear that the pace of life was slower and gentler in these parts. When we stopped to pick up an old guy, he dipped his cowboy hat and gave a polite buenas tardes (good afternoon) to everyone on board. We passed a father leading his two daughters home from school, still in their school uniforms, on the back of horses. Everyone spoke in polite murmurs and thanked the driver with a heartfelt gracias when he dropped them off at gates that seemed to be in the middle of nowhere, far from any sign of civilisation. The first signs of civilisation, in fact, was La Palma itself, and even then it was little more than a collection of wooden huts and a concrete restaurant down by the river.

It was at this restaurant that the van finished its journey. The driver motioned towards a small concrete dock beside the river, indicating that this was where the boat into Guatemala would depart from. We asked him when and he shrugged his shoulders. The waitress in the restaurant didn't seem to have any better idea when the boat, or launcha, as they liked to call it in these parts, would be leaving. Nor did the cowpokes who were sitting around drinking beer. We ordered a couple of Cokes and a plate of beans and rice and decided to sit outside and wait. When the sun sank spectacularly over the river, we figured that the boat wasn't coming and we'd better find somewhere to stay for the night.

This seemed to be an even more difficult concept for the waitress to comprehend than when the boat would leave. From what I'd already seen of La Palma, I'd deduced that it was unlikely the place would have a hotel, so I used all the Spanish words I could think of to indicate a dry and comfortable place to bunk down – habitación (room) ... domitorio (dormitory) ... cama (bed). When these all drew blanks I did a complex routine of charades that indicated that the GND and I had had a very long day, were extremely tired and wanted to go to sleep.

'Ahhh! Domir!' she said and pointed to a ramshackle building up a hill that served as a general store.

The store was basically just a wooden shack with a counter, behind which was stacked cans of beans and packets of biscuits, chips and washing powder. It was staffed by a girl so bored that her upper body was sprawled across the counter, her head resting on her arms, her eyes staring blankly into the middle distance. When I asked her for a room she became confused, then apathetic and then went blank again. When I asked her again, she shook her head and shrugged her shoulders.

I went back down the hill to the restaurant to the waitress and questioned her again in pidgin Spanish. 'The shop, it has rooms?'

'Yes, yes,' she seemed to say, treating me as if I was an idiot. 'I already told you that.'

I went back up the hill, this time questioning a lady who had just come out of the shop. She looked like a Mexican version of Mrs Mangel in 'Neighbours', so I figured she'd know everyone's business and whether the shop was running a little domir action on the side. She looked at me as if I was crazy as well.

'Rooms?' she seemed to say. 'It's a shop. Can't you see that?'

'If we'd taken the more straightforward route, we'd have been there by now,' snapped the GND when I returned again and told her the news. She was tired and cranky and keen to have a wash and a sleep. 'Go and ask the waitress again!'

I nearly lost my temper and was about to blurt out 'You go and ask the bloody waitress!', but in a rare moment of tact and diplomacy I checked my tongue. My standing as a world traveller was diminishing so I did as she said.

The waitress rolled her eyes and yelled something to her boss out in the kitchen – no doubt a derogatory comment about my mental faculties. She grabbed me by the arm and dragged me back up to the shop. The girl was gone, and in her place was the kindly old man who owned the place. He took us down the side of the shop and showed us a selection of rustic rooms, all with mosquito nets and a stand fan. The waitress gave me a look that said 'Der!' and left before I could thank her.

Having secured a room for the night, I asked the shop owner in faltering Spanish what time the boat left for El Naranjo. Quickly and confidently he said, 'Manana, Quattro.' Tomorrow. At four.

In Spanish, manana has two meanings. Did he mean 'manana' as in morning, or did he mean it as in 'manana' – tomorrow? That's the trouble with trying to determine a departure time when you're struggling with a language – you never quite have the sophistication to note subtle differences. 'Manana, manana?' I asked, hoping it meant tomorrow morning.

'Si!' he said confidently. 'Manana, manana.'

I wished I'd had his confidence.

At 3.45 am, the GND and I were huddled by the river with our packs, rubbing ourselves against the cold. It was quiet except for the frogs croaking and the occasional rooster crowing, a pleasant change from a few minutes earlier when our departure from the shop–hotel had set off every dog in La Palma (by the sound of it, they outnumbered humans three to one).

My father, a plumber, had always said that dawn was the best part of the day, and would often drag my sisters and me out of bed to share breakfast with him, just so we could see it. I didn't really appreciate it back then, but this morning, as the first few orange streaks filled the sky, I had to say he had a point. It was a beautiful thing watching the river stir to life – birds shaking their feathers dry, smoke rising from a hut, the plop of a fish jumping. The only thing that spoiled it was that by 6.30 am the boat still hadn't arrived. Nine, 10, 11, 12 and it still hadn't come.

To be honest, I wasn't that fussed. It was a pretty enough spot, under flowering trees, beside a river in a town that to describe as somnolent would be adventurous. We set up camp at a table, our packs around our feet, and ordered drinks and meals periodically from the restaurant. It's amazing how patient you learn to be when you are travelling. Back home I'd be up at the customer service desk, berating some poor attendant and demanding my money back. Here I just went with the flow. Sometime, eventually, hopefully, a boat would come and we would be on our way. For the time being, I was happy enough reading *Memoirs of a Geisha*.

I was a lot more relaxed about how things were going with the GND as well. Sure, we were having our 'disagreements', but whereas earlier in the trip I saw that as an indication that our relationship was flawed, I now realised that it was a natural consequence of two people spending every waking hour with each other. Hopefully the damage from Mitch in Guatemala would not be so bad and we'd be able to enjoy the mountains, the ruins and the beaches as I had imagined we would only a few months before.

By four, children were wandering back home from school and fishermen were returning to town with fresh-water fish a metre long. I'd finished the book, and had long given up hope of the boat coming that day. The GND and I decided to go back to the shop–hotel and get a room for the night. Just as we got there a small boy came running after us yelling 'Launcha! Launcha!' pretty much in the same manner that Tattoo yelled 'Da plane! Da plane!' in 'Fantasy Island'. Sure enough, a flat-bottom boat was waiting at the concrete dock just below the restaurant. We were going to Guatemala after all.

The boat roared away from the dock, planing through a huge arc of spray and down the river towards the border.

It was just the GND and me, and two women who had appeared from nowhere once it was determined a boat was leaving for El Naranjo. Our captain was a boy about fifteen, but the way he manoeuvred across the broad river and then through the narrower passages lined with low-hanging trees, suggested that he had made the journey many times before.

The scenery was beautiful, with bright green plains and mountains in the distance. White egrets, startled by the roar of the outboard engine, rose from the river and flapped lazily into nearby trees. Above us the sky was flecked with pink from oncoming sunset but ahead there were angry purple clouds, heavy with rain. Twenty minutes later we were in the middle of a torrential rain storm.

Our fellow passengers had obviously done this trip before because as soon as the rain started they brought plastic sheets out to pull over themselves. The GND and I, however, were unprotected. At first I hunched my shoulders, convinced that somehow this would stop me from getting totally wet. But after ten minutes I realised this was useless and just relaxed, opening myself to the weather. Soon the rain was dribbling down the collar of my T-shirt and through the gap at the back of my jeans, tickling my arse. At the speed we were travelling, the rain stung against my face. It was invigorating and cathartic and I found myself laughing. I turned to the GND and she was laughing too.

Two hours into the journey the rain stopped. Somehow this was worse. The rain had been warm, but once it stopped the wind chilled our wet clothes and had us huddling together, shaking with cold. As night fell the boat stopped at a building that marked the border with Guatemala. Behind the building, beyond a small lake dotted with flowering lilies, stood a Mexican army camp. Our boat driver indicated that we should follow the stones that formed a path of sorts through the lake and present our passports.

As we hopped along the path I wondered what the immigration guy would make of us. We were drenched, our clothes – and our hair – clinging to us, our shoes squidging unbecomingly. If we were entering I'm sure we'd have had a hard time convincing immigration officials that we were of sound mind and able to support ourselves. But we were leaving the country, so the officer, resplendent in battle fatigues and brandishing a Maglite of impressive proportions, simply copied our details into a ledger and wished us a pleasant evening.

As we hopped back down the stone path, through the ponds and lily pads, the GND turned to me and smiled. 'I'm glad I'm going out with you!'

I was glad too. The boat ride, the rain – even sitting around all day – it had all been quite an adventure. This was the first border crossing of our trip and it had set a pretty high standard. I was happy to have found someone who enjoyed it too.

By the time the boat had set off again night had fallen. The rain had stopped, but the clouds hung heavy and low, blocking out the moon and stars. Despite the darkness, our boat continued to hurtle along the river, the boy driving it dodging submerged logs and powering through bends almost on instinct. I offered him the use of my torch but he didn't want it. His eyes were adjusted to the darkness.

About an hour after we had left the immigration post, just after the boat roared around a bend and through a mangrove swamp, the guy threw the boat into a wild spin. It was the kind of manoeuvre you'd see in a James Bond movie, executed by a trained stunt person, not a teenage boy just starting to sprout facial hair. At first I thought he'd lost control of the boat, but when the boat finally came to rest and he cut the engine, I saw that he had executed the manoeuvre to avoid hitting another boat that was floating aimlessly down the river.

There was a teenage boy on the other boat, and from what I could gather, he was returning to El Naranjo too, but had run out of fuel. Our driver threw him a rope and pulled the other boat alongside ours. The woman next to me started tutting and speaking under her breath to the other woman. 'It's that young Julio,' I imagined her saying. 'Never carries enough fuel. If his mother has told him once she's told him a thousand times. And look, now he's nearly got us all killed!'

My torch was called for – neither boat had one – and the delicate procedure of transferring fuel was undertaken. It was dark and the only sound was the splashing of water against the boat and the clunk of oars and boats clashing together. Once the fuel was transferred, the other boy tried to start his boat. It took a couple of attempts – there was probably a little bit of air in the fuel pipes – but soon the engine spluttered to life and he was on his way again. We followed in his wake towards a dull glow on the horizon.

El Naranjo made La Palma look like a bustling metropolis. It seemed to consist of three stilt buildings built over the river and a small collection of boats tethered against them, all sitting in complete darkness. Our driver indicated for us to wait beside the boat and soon the town's immigration officer came along and welcomed us to Guatemala. He spoke English, and after stamping us into the country and taking a $4 fee for 'extending' his office hours, he arranged a room for us in one of the buildings that sat over the river.

'There is no power and the bathroom is just a drum of water,' he apologised. 'But it is the only hotel in town.'

I asked him if there was anywhere to eat and again he apologised.

'Everything closes early in El Naranjo. Maybe tomorrow!' he said. Then anticipating my next question, he told us that the first bus to Flores left at 7.30 am.

'Buenas noches!' he called out as he hitched up his trousers and made his way back into the darkness and up the only road in town.

With my Maglite weakly illuminating our path, we made our way along the veranda of the 'hotel' and found our room. It was a bare room with a bare bed and no mosquito net. The floorboards had wide cracks and nothing underneath them but the river. Just as I was anticipating the problems with mosquitoes the heavens opened again, the rain making enough racket on the roof to drown out the sound of an approaching 747.

It soon became obvious that mosquitoes would be the least of our troubles. The tin roof had more holes than an outback road sign. We huddled on the bed in our wet clothes, trying to avoid the water dripping from the roof. It was like sleeping on a wet sponge, and finding the only dry spots entailed the sort of contortions you see in a half-an-hour game of Twister. When a mosquito started buzzing in my ear, I knew it was going to be a very long night.

The next morning we were up at daybreak, hanging our clothes along the veranda, hoping that in the hour or so before the bus arrived we might be able to dry them a little. The GND was in surprisingly good spirits. She had accepted the uncomfortably wet night as all part of the adventure of travelling. How her spirits would have fared if it was like that every night, was another question. But for that morning, at least, she was cheerful.

In the grey light of dawn I noticed that El Naranjo was bigger than I'd first thought. There was an army camp just across the way and a Mayan rock carving under a shelter. The army boys were up early, exercising, jogging up the road in formation, chanting one of those songs you see in American movies, but in Spanish. They spotted the GND and hollered and waved like juveniles – understandably, I suppose, with blondes being in short supply in these parts. The GND waved back, excited.

A beat-up bus drove into town around nine and the driver kindly waited for us to grab our damp clothes and shove them in our packs. His offsider, a young boy of around 13, opened the baggage compartment at the back of the bus and helped us with our bags.

'Welcome to the bus to the island of Flores,' he said beaming. Unfortunately that was the only English he knew.

Our guidebook described the road from El Naranjo to Flores as 'shocking' but in the time since it had been written the Guatemalan government, obviously stung by Lonely Planet's criticism, had made the road's improvement a priority. It had been freshly graded, and in many parts, workmen were sealing it with asphalt. Until nature, neglect and the weather took their toll again, it would be one of the best roads in Guatemala.

I decided I liked Guatemala, and judging by her smile, I guessed the GND did too. The passengers, despite intermittent rain, put their windows down to let fresh air into the bus, something that never happened in Mexico. The area we passed through was less developed than Mexico, marked by low limestone hills, a few farms cleared in the jungle and the odd village of wooden huts and produce stores. The road suggested that there were big plans for the area, and perhaps one day soon it would be prime cattle country, just like the Mexican ranches on the other side of the border. But for the time being it was pretty much untouched.

We reached Santa Elena, the town opposite Flores, just before lunch. It was a muddy, scruffy town without any redeeming features, apart from the fact that it was the largest town nearest to the ruins at Tikal. The area had apparently suffered from flooding during Mitch, but it was hard to tell what was damage from the rain or simple neglect. We spent a day there, not because we wanted to, but so we could do our washing and check our e-mails.

We received one e-mail from a friend warning us that the road to Tikal had been destroyed by Hurricane Mitch.

This was obviously news to the guy who quite happily sold us a ticket on the minivan heading to Tikal the next day. As it was, the road from Santa Elena to Tikal was the best road we'd travelled on so far, a 71-kilometre ribbon of asphalt as smooth as Julio Iglesias. We arrived just after lunch, with time enough to book into the Jungle Lodge and then pay a visit to the ruins.

The Jungle Lodge was originally built to house the archaeologists excavating and restoring Tikal. It had attractive gardens, a large dining room with overhead fans and a veranda from which you could look out across the jungle. It was all terribly nineteenth century and, to be honest, quite out of our price range. But its rival, the Jaguar Inn, wasn't renting out camping equipment anymore – despite our guidebook saying it did – and by the time we subtracted the cost of getting back to Flores from the price of the cheapest room at the Jungle Lodge, staying in Flores didn't work out any cheaper. I didn't tell the GND that was my reasoning, of course. I said that after the dank night at El Naranjo she deserved a special treat.

Having said that, I always feel like a bit of an impostor staying in places like the Jungle Lodge. Even freshly washed and shaved, I'm sure my scruffy demeanour gives me away, or, at the very least, the slight flinch in my hand will when I pay for the room with a US dollar bill of a denomination I could happily live on for a week. But whenever I do indulge, I've got to say I enjoy it immensely. And with the GND, I enjoyed it doubly so. With her involved, it was always easier to justify blowing the daily budget.

Tikal is like the Indiana Jones version of Mayan ruins,

a lost city of steep-sided pyramids hidden by vines and creepers, with a soundtrack of squawking birds and growling monkeys. It is set on a low hill and in an area rich in flint. It is believed that it was the abundance of flint that led the Mayans to settle here. While not exactly a precious commodity these days, flint was extremely valuable back in 700 BC. It was used by the Mayans to make clubs, knives, arrowheads, spear tips and other nasty, pointy things to help them subjugate the surrounding area. Before long Tikal was one of the most important cities in the Mayan world.

Scholars attribute the rise of Tikal to a brutal new method of warfare developed by its warriors. Instead of tackling their adversaries hand-to-hand on a plain, the soldiers from Tikal used auxiliary units to encircle their enemies and throw spears at them from a distance. This early use of 'air power', the brainiacs argue, caused fewer home-side casualties and allowed Tikal to become the dominant kingdom in the region.

For mine, the real reason for Tikal's success lies in the names of the rulers at the time. In the mid-fourth century AD, when the guys from Tikal were kicking Uaxactún butt, they were led by King Great Jaguar Paw and his general, Smoking Frog. In 562, when the wishy-washy Lord Water took over, the city fell into decline. Then, when the city rose to prominence again around AD 700, it was under tutelage of the Elvisesque King Moon Double Comb. If further proof of my theory is needed, note that King Comb only found success after ditching the less authoritative moniker of 'King Chocolate'.

The GND and I entered the archaeological park around

three o'clock, following a platoon of soldiers in full battle fatigues, each with an AK-47 slung over his shoulder. The man taking tickets at the gate said that they often did manoeuvres in the park, brushing up on their jungle warfare skills and discouraging robbers from attacking tourists at the same time. Today, however, they were going into the park as part of a special preparatory drill – the US First Lady was visiting the site in two days' time. 'And I don't mean Monica Lewinsky!' he said with a wink.

A path led through towering trees and vines, alive with the sounds of the jungle. Occasionally one sound cut through, a startling noise that was a cross between a roaring lion and a rampaging t-rex. It was the mating call of a randy howler monkey. 'It sounds like something from a horror movie,' said the GND with a shudder. 'If I didn't know it was a monkey, it would freak me out!'

Hurricane Mitch had kept a lot of tourists away from Tikal – the Guatemalan newspapers were reporting that numbers were down 70 per cent – so the GND and I had the place pretty much to ourselves. When we came upon the Great Plaza, home to the steep-sided temples you see in all the brochures and guidebooks, it was still and quiet, except for the sound of a woodpecker attacking a dead tree. We clambered half way up Temple II and sat down, soaking up the atmosphere and pretending that we had stumbled upon a lost civilisation. It was a conceit we quite happily revelled in until we were disturbed by a family of German tourists twenty minutes later.

From the Great Plaza we made our way along a path to El Mundo Perdido, the Lost World. The path wound its way around huge mounds, covered in jungle, with a few exposed stone blocks the only indication that underneath was yet another marvel of the ancient world just waiting to be restored. Not so long ago, all of Tikal had been like this.

On finding the Lost World, we clambered to the top of the South Acropolis to watch the sun set. It was a fantastic view, the nearest temples and pyramids – the Plaza of Seven Temples – right in front of us, and beyond that, as far as the eye could see, a canopy of jungle with just the tops of some of the other pyramids poking through. The sun sank over the jungle, a burning ball of orange, as a pair of toucans settled on a tree just across the way. It was enthralling and uplifting and we stayed as long as the light held out before scrambling down the back of the pyramid and towards the Great Plaza. Here we met a soldier who kindly led us back to the entrance.

'Tomorrow you must watch the sunrise from Temple IV,' he said. 'It will be the most beautiful thing you have ever seen.'

We ate in one of the cheaper restaurants near the park entrance and then returned to our hotel and sat on the veranda, the jungle pressing in on all sides. It was like one of those really bad Tarzan movies and I half expected to see yellow eyes peering out of the jungle at us. If I had, I would have insisted that the hotel manager light fires around the perimeter of the lodge to keep the wild beasts at bay.

'Imagine what sunrise will be like!' I enthused, genuinely excited about getting up at 4 am the next morning and tramping out to Temple IV.

The GND, however, said she didn't see any sense in getting up that early. As far as she was concerned, we had just seen the sunset and the sunrise wouldn't be any different. Nor could I sway her with my fanciful images of the morning mist and the sounds of the jungle coming to life. 'You go,' she said. 'I think I'll have a bit of a sleep in.'

A sleep in? That was the sort of thing you do on a wet Sunday back at home, not at one of the most amazing archaeological sites in the world. I couldn't understand how the GND could come all this way and not do it. It was a once in a lifetime event and the GND wanted to catch some extra zzzzes?

'Just video it and I'll watch it later,' she said, unaware, I think, of just how flabbergasted I was becoming. Things had been really good since Palenque. We'd been enjoying each other's company – even the wet night at El Naranjo had been fun – and a romantic jungle sunrise would have topped off things rather nicely. Her refusal to come along confused me, and to be honest, hurt a little too.

When I got up the next morning I made as much noise as I could but the GND didn't stir.

At the ruins, I made my way to Temple IV as the soldier who led us back to the entrance the night before had suggested. But when I clambered up a rickety ladder to the top of the mound it sat upon, I discovered that he had given everyone else staying at Tikal the same advice. The steps at the top of the temple resembled a football stand, packed with people rubbing themselves against the cold and passing Thermoses of hot tea. And when the sun rose, it couldn't get through the grey wall of mist that had swallowed the whole site. The highlight of the morning was when a racoon-like coati snatched the bag of a Japanese tourist and scooted down the embankment with it.

I returned to the Jungle Lodge cold, damp and tired.

'Did I miss much?' the GND asked sleepily when I 'accidentally' woke her coming back into the room.

'No,' I answered grudgingly. I wanted to lie and tell her that it was the best sunrise I had ever seen in my life, but my mood would have given me away.

'I thought so,' she said, turning back to sleep. 'Wake me in half an hour and we'll go. I want to be on a beach in Belize by this afternoon.'

CHAPTER NINE

Caye Caulker

(Belize)

Annoying habit >>> Scratching bites
Culprit >>> GND

Getting to a Caribbean beach before the end of the day was not totally out of the question. We were only a couple of hours away from the Guatemala–Belize border, and although we would have to travel the breadth of Belize to get to the coast, Belize was only 131 kilometres across at its widest point. As far as travel tasks go, it was very doable.

'My first Caribbean beach,' mused the GND as we packed to leave Tikal. In her mind's eye we were already on a palm-fringed, dazzling white beach. 'The girls back at the office will be so jealous!'

Our quest for sun and sand did not start well though.

Getting to the road leading to Belize was not a problem –
there were regular minibuses back to El Petén and Flores
from Tikal, and their drivers were more than happy to
drop us off at the corner of the crossroads. Our predicament
was that buses heading into Belize passed at less regular
intervals. We sat on a log, eating stale corn snacks and
drinking warm Coke bought from a small shack behind us,
and waited for two hours before a bus came along. And
when it did it was already nearly full. We took up our
positions under the smelly armpits of Guatemalan day
workers and Belizean smugglers and braced ourselves for
our second border crossing.

Our guidebook described the road to Melchor de Mencos,
the town closest to the border, as one of the worst in
Guatemala. But like the road from El Naranjo to El Petén,
it was being rebuilt in a flurry of IMF and World Bank-
funded capital works projects and passed through scrubby
farmland with barely a bump. We reached the border just
in time for the Guatemalan customs official to extract an
extra 60 quetzals out of us by feigning that he was about
to close to go to lunch.

The Belize side of the border at Benque Viejo del Carmen
was a more laid-back affair. The immigration official, a big
bear of a man, took our passports and on noticing we were
from Australia, smiled.

'Ahhh, the land under,' he beamed. 'Welcome to Belize!'
The Caribbean was now officially only 131 kilometres away.
The GND grinned with delight.

Like Australia, Belize is a constitutional monarchy, an
independent country but with the British monarch still the

nominated head of government. And also like Australia, Queen Elizabeth features on the back of some bank notes and on all the coins. All these similarities were comforting, but none more so than the fact that English was the official spoken language.

Now, I know that different languages and different cultures are all part of the rich fabric of planet Earth and are indeed a delightful part of the whole travelling experience. But as a linguistic moron with a highly developed inability to master any languages, it was with a great sigh of relief that I reached a country where I could speak English freely and enjoy the simple pleasure of understanding and being understood. Unfortunately, all that understanding got me in those first moments in Belize was that the next bus to Belize City would not be leaving for another hour.

The bus was already there. It sat beside the road, seemingly abandoned by its driver. It was owned by a company called Batty Brothers, and like the bus we had caught to the Belize border, it was an old American school bus. But unlike Guatemalan buses, which are invariably plastered with pictures of Jesus and have crosses hanging from the rear-vision mirror, this bus was largely unadorned. The only embellishment was a notice for the Batty Brothers Christmas Sweepstakes, made on a computer and complete with tacky clip-art pictures of holly and Christmas presents. Under the catchy heading of 'Win! Win! Win!' passengers were informed that they could win a turkey, champagne, T-shirts and the highly sought-after prize of round-trip, premier Batty Brothers bus tickets.

There wasn't a bus shelter or shady tree for us to sit

under, so we got on the bus and waited there. We were joined by Polly, a young English girl who had come to Belize to work after finishing school. She was blonde and buck-toothed and spoke with an incredibly posh accent. She had just visited Tikal and was heading to San Ignacio to catch up with friends before going back to England. Polly had lived with a family on Caye Caulker, one of the tiny coral islands off the coast of Belize City, in a household where there were only two rules – no rasta boyfriends and no drugs. More importantly, she had been in Belize when Hurricane Mitch struck.

'I was on Caye Caulker when it hit,' she said. 'Everyone on the island was evacuated inland to Belmopan or San Ignacio.'

Apparently an American marine biologist living on the island stayed longer so she could take photos. 'I've seen the photos,' said Polly. 'They're amazing! Huge waves – when you get there you'll understand how bizarre that is. In the end she had to decide between taking more photos or saving herself and her seven-year-old son. She got the last boat off the island.'

The GND sat with her mouth open, her Caribbean dreams taking a battering. I could almost hear what she was thinking – 'The palm trees, tell me it didn't get the palm trees!'

'It was scary,' continued Polly. 'Even in San Ignacio, 116 kilometres from the coast, people were stocking up on food and water. There were rumours that the shops would be closed for two weeks. I stayed in a hostel. There were two Israeli guys who really didn't comprehend what was going on. They'd just arrived from Guatemala and couldn't understand why no one would rent them a car. I told them to buy food and they came back with a can of beans and a bottle of water.'

I asked Polly how they kept up to date with what was happening.

'TV mainly,' she said. 'The hostel had a satellite so we were watching the Weather Channel from the US. The weather man kept reassuring Americans that Mitch wouldn't reach them. Apparently a cold front was turning it back towards Central America!'

After the worst of Mitch was over Polly returned to Caye Caulker and helped with the clean-up.

'For two weeks all anyone did was clean up the mess. There was stuff everywhere.'

In a tremulous voice the GND asked Polly if there was anything left.

'Oh yes! Only a few buildings were destroyed,' she said brightly. 'But all the wooden wharves are gone and there's not much of a beach left. The good news is that you'll have the place pretty much to yourselves. The hurricane has scared away most of the tourists.'

The GND was in shock. She had a sugar white sandy beach with palm trees in her mind, not a muddy stretch of land covered in twisted, broken palm-tree carcasses. I worried whether this state of affairs would affect her willingness to continue with the rest of the trip. After all, the promise of Caribbean beaches had been a major factor in getting her to come along. Luckily the bus driver got on board, started the bus and turned the radio on at full volume. The loud reggae music drowned any chance of discussion on the topic and, thankfully, any more horrific tales of destruction from Polly.

San Ignacio was only 15 kilometres away, nestled in the Macal River valley and surrounded on one side by mahogany forest and on the other by farmland. It was a pretty little town, bustling with life, and a snapshot of the unique racial make-up of Belize. Creoles sold drinks and tropical fruit to German-speaking Mennonite farmers in their straw hats, green shirts and britches, who were in town to sell their produce to Taiwanese or British traders or buy stuff for the farm from Lebanese shopkeepers. Polly got off here and wished us well.

'Don't worry about Caye Caulker,' she said. 'It's still lovely, and with less tourists the locals will be much friendlier.'

The worst effects of Hurricane Mitch had bypassed San Ignacio, but the heavy rains that came with the hurricane had caused the Macal River to burst its banks. Part of the town's landmark suspension bridge, the Hawkesworth Bridge, had been washed away, so our bus had to go further down the river where bulldozers had made a temporary causeway to get across to the other side. It would hold only until the wet season began again, but the locals hoped that would be enough time to repair the damaged bridge. Soon we were on a single strip of asphalt travelling through farmland.

'This reminds me of the outskirts of Sydney,' said the GND.

She was right. It could have been Rossmore, the five-acre, semi-rural environment on the edge of Sydney where

I grew up. There were neat weatherboard houses, most two-storey, with signs saying 'Lawn Mower Repairs Here' or 'Manure for Sale'. And there were the mandatory 'car in pieces' on the front lawns as well as the occasional market garden and chicken shed. The only thing missing was a board listing the meeting times of the local Lion's and Rotary Clubs and a sign proclaiming that this was a 'Tidy Town'. Instead, Belize had 'Tidy Highways', with signs proclaiming that the next two kilometres was kept litter-free by Chongs Chinese Restaurant.

The outskirts of Sydney are not Born Again like Belize though. The roadside was a forest of signs advertising 'The House of Prayer' and its promise of 'Prayer without ceasing'. Elsewhere there was a sign for the 'My Refuge' Christian group, listing the frequency of their radio station (the only place you could hear their band, 'The Chosen Generation Gospel Band'), the phone number for their counselling hotline and their e-mail address for a little on-line religious action. When we passed the Messiah Christian Bookshop and a Jesus Saves bus, I became concerned that we had taken a wrong turn somewhere and ended up in the deep south of the USA.

Between these towns were the huge orange orchards that are the mainstay of the Belizian economy. Financed largely by the Taiwanese, the orchards sported signs in Chinese characters, so I could fall once again into my usual state of ignorant bliss. The only time I was shaken from it was when a young guy got on the bus wearing a T-shirt that proclaimed 'Save Albert and save Belize'. I didn't even bother trying to think about that one.

Forty-five minutes later we were in Belmopan, the capital of Belize, purpose-built after Hurricane Hattie flattened Belize City in 1961. It was built in the geographical centre of the country, well away from the threat of killer hurricanes, and like all such enterprises it hadn't really worked. The various government departments, in prematurely decaying two-story concrete buildings, a few cars in the driveway, sat alone surrounded by cleared land. The planners had hoped that the spaces would be filled in with ancillary services, but they remained abandoned blocks, overtaken by weeds and rusting car bodies, with the occasional grazing horse being the only sign of life.

The bus station was lively, though, a chaotic muddy block surrounded by food stalls and a busy market. Every bus in the country passed through it and we stayed there long enough to buy a Big H orange juice and a handful of delicious meat pies. When it was time to go the bus driver got back on the bus and in a deep sonorous voice reminded people about the Christmas raffle.

'Customers, we are having a Christmas raffle,' he boomed. 'Write your name and address on the back of your ticket and drop it into our offices in Belize City. The raffle will be drawn every Saturday until Christmas.'

The 63 kilometres to Belize City passed without incident. The closer we got to Belize City, the more obvious it was that the road had been a recent imposition. Settlements were named after how far they were from Belize City. Belize Zoo, which had been started when some animals were rounded up for a wildlife documentary, was at Mile 29. JB's Watering Hole was at Mile 32. Every settlement, restaurant and roadside bar advertised itself using the same method.

At Mile 1½ we came upon Belize City cemetery. The road went through the middle of the cemetery and at one point was divided by a verge filled with headstones.

'Look,' I said. 'The dead centre of Belize.'

The GND, to her credit, laughed. Our relationship had already progressed through so many stages – from its romantic beginnings to the irritations of Oaxaca and back to a more romantic footing again – and she was still laughing at my bad jokes. I guess that was as sure a sign as any that things were still in good shape.

From all reports Belize City had escaped Hurricane Mitch relatively unscathed, but you wouldn't know that looking at it. It was a shambolic collection of clapboard houses in various stages of ruin. Though once bright and cheerful, they were now faded and neglected, with the mainly dark tenants sitting on the verandas looking off into the distance scowling. The narrow streets were full of cars in a similar state of disrepair and the sidewalks were cluttered with people selling assorted junk – mostly plastic and seemingly of no inherent value. If they caught you looking out at them, the townsfolk returned your gaze with a look that was at once dangerous and nasty.

'It's like we're in Harlem,' said the GND, alarmed at how reality had diverged from the image of Belize she had in her mind.

The bus pulled into a compound that may have once in the 1960s been a modern bus terminal but now served as the city urinal and squatter camp. The docks were still a good few city blocks away through some of the roughest neighbourhoods, so we decided to catch a taxi to save time and our personal safety. Normally I would have just put my head down and walked, but I could see by the concerned look on the GND's face that a taxi was in order this time.

The docks were no better. The buildings were just as shambolic, the locals just as scary. We bought our tickets from a guy who told us to go straight through the terminal to the dock. The boat, a long speedboat with a covered space for luggage up front and bench seats around the side, was beside the dock. People were starting to jump on so we handed our baggage to a guy on deck and got on board. We had barely settled in, between two rastas wearing crocheted beanies and mandatory Bob Marley T-shirts, when a tall, thin man in slacks, shirt and tie ran up yelling, 'Baggage only! Everyone out.'

Of course, no one listened to him and he became quite agitated. 'Get out of the boat!' he screamed. 'The boat will not leave until everyone gets off!'

It occurred to me that this kind of defeated the whole purpose of having a passenger boat service, but decided against pointing this out and instead told the man that the guy selling the tickets had said to go straight through.

'I'm the manager here!' he screamed, his eyes bulging. 'You listen to me, not him!'

The two rastas laughed.

'I can't believe it!' he continued, shaking his head in rage. 'I make an announcement and everyone ignores it!'

Once everyone had got off the boat, he ordered us back on again. If that had been the end of it the boat may have set off for Caye Caulker pretty much on time. But just as we had all settled into our places two tourist policemen came onto the dock and ordered a scruffy looking rasta off the boat, as well as the western woman he was travelling with. She was in her fifties, tanned and leathery, wearing ethnic clothing that needed a good wash. She and her boyfriend were both off their faces – not from dope, but something harder – and refused to budge. In the end the police dragged them off the boat physically, their ghetto-blaster, seemingly their only possession, nearly ending up in the canal in the process. I asked the guy next to me what it was all about.

'He is . . . troublesome,' he said, pausing while he searched for the right words. 'There are a lot of drugs on the island and the police are trying to stop it before it gets too out of hand.'

Finally, at dusk, and only an hour or so late, the boat pushed away from the dock, chugged up the canal and then roared onto the Caribbean Sea. The water had a platinum sheen to it and reflected the flecks of pink and mauve in the sky. Belize City soon faded into the distance, looking more and more like a collapsed house of cards, and we made our way through channels bordered each side by mangroves towards the Drowned Cayes.

The Cayes appeared like mirages, clumps of mangrove or shimmering white beaches topped by wooden huts. The wind was cool in our hair and there was a tang of salt spray on our lips. It was the first time we had seen the ocean since Puerto Escondido, and it was clean and invigorating. I turned to speak to the GND, but the roar of the outboard engine was too loud, so I just smiled. She smiled too. This is what she had come to Central America to see.

By the time we arrived at Caye Caulker, 33 kilometres north of Belize City, the sun was below the horizon. The sky turned dark blue and then deepened to rich black, dotted by the first of the evening stars. While we waited on the concrete pier for our bags to be unloaded, we were accosted by an ageing rasta, touting a hotel room for $15. It was the cheapest hotel on the island, he said, but I told him that we already knew where we were staying – Polly had given us the name of a cheaper place – and thanked him.

But this guy had attitude and wouldn't take no for an answer. 'What is the name of the place!' he demanded.

I knew the routine. If I told him the name of the place he would say that it had been destroyed by the hurricane or come up with some other kind of cock and bull story about the sad demise of the said establishment. 'Look,' I said, trying to keep my agitation under control. 'It was recommended by a friend. Okay?'

'How long did you know this person?' he shot back.

'Two weeks,' I lied.

'That's not very long to be friends,' he spat. 'Not a very long time to trust their judgment!'

'Well, it's longer than thirty seconds,' I retorted, my agitation now clearly apparent. 'Now if you don't mind, we've got a hotel to find.'

Furious, I grabbed my bag and set off down the sandy road towards the centre of the island, the GND running to keep up. It wasn't the touting that had made me angry.

That's an everyday part of life when you're travelling. It was the sanctimonious attitude of the guy, and the whole chip-on-the shoulder rasta routine.

'He was just trying to be helpful,' reasoned the GND, struggling to keep up.

But he wasn't. He wanted money from us. And he was trying to put a whole white guilt thing on us while he was doing it, insinuating that we weren't going with him because of his appearance.

We found the hotel Polly had recommended without much trouble. It was only $7, a bargain in Belize, but you got what you paid for. It had the feel of a seaside holiday home that had been left abandoned and locked up for too long – musty and mouldy – and with a bathroom covered in slime. As we left to find somewhere to eat, we ran into the rasta from the dock. Apparently, this had been the hotel he had been touting – albeit for double the price.

'It's funny how you end up with the things you are running away from!' he sneered.

'You know what I reckon is funny?' I thought. 'You just missed out on your $8 commission.'

The rasta had put me in a bad mood for the rest of the evening, and left me ill-disposed towards all the others on the island. As we wandered down the sandy streets, past the restaurants and shops, they seemed to be everywhere, shuffling around, more often than not with a chunky white girlfriend, saying 'Hey mon' and greeting each other with the kind of handshakes that need slow-motion replays to understand. The GND found it exotic and exciting, but in my current mood I found it annoying. She reckoned I was jealous because they were so cool so effortlessly. She may well have been right.

We ended up eating at a place called Wish Willy's, partly because their prices were the most reasonable, but mainly because I liked the name. It wasn't a restaurant as such, just a wooden platform with tables and hurricane lamps. The chefs, two knock-about rastas, cooked from a barbecue made from a forty-four-gallon drum. They were friendly and laid-back, without the bullshit of the tout, and spent most of the evening joking and laughing with the patrons. Better still, their food was absolutely delicious. We had a fish dish that melted in your mouth and then teased your tastebuds with all manner of delicate flavours. Looking at the guys you'd think they'd have trouble cooking an egg, yet here they were dishing up the best food of our trip.

'We're definitely coming here again,' said the GND, licking her lips in a manner I hadn't seen since Oaxaca.

The next morning we changed hotels, checking into Daisy's, a two-storey clapboard house down near the water that had mosquito screens and overhead fans. It cost a little more, but the bathroom was clean and the rooms airy. With that sorted we went for a walk. Having arrived after dark, we hadn't seen much of the island, and now in the light of the day we could assess the damage caused by Mitch. A lot of cleaning up had been done, the sandy lanes were all neat and swept clean, but everywhere locals were hammering and patching, sprucing up or rebuilding what had been knocked down and beaten by Mitch.

It was the businesses on the reef side of the island that had borne the full brunt of the waves stirred up by the hurricane, and many had been abandoned. The wooden hut that had been the office of Island Girl Grafix, home of the island's graphic designer and internet cafe, was on its side. The Rainbow Restaurant was in two parts, its owner cutting it in half to make the job of pushing it back on the side of the road it was originally on easier. Elsewhere, the trunks of palm trees flattened in the storm were being cut into small pieces and stacked neatly beside the road.

Seemingly unaffected by the hurricane were the electric golf carts – the only vehicles on the island – that whizzed up and down the sandy lanes. They were plastered with advertisements for establishments that in all likelihood hadn't survived the disaster – 'Jan's, for all your shopping needs' and 'Popeye's Pizza, we deliver' – and continued to go about their everyday duties of helping old folk do their shopping and driving home locals who had had too much to drink.

Now that we had reached the Caribbean, the GND wanted to hit the beach. Caye Caulker had only ever had a thin strip of beach, but after Mitch had come a-calling what little there was had been washed away. The only place to swim now was the Split, a canal that cut the island in two at its northern tip. There wasn't a beach as such, just a concrete retaining wall that you could sunbake on or dive from into the water. Locals warned about swimming in the Split – it was a popular short cut for powerboat owners, and there had been several accidents involving unsuspecting swimmers, some of them fatal. That day, however, there was a greater danger afoot. Sandflies.

Apart from my run-in with the mosquitoes of Zicatela,

I've never really had a problem with biting insects. As a generously hirsute person, I've found that most insects give up after a few seconds of trying to penetrate the matted hair on my body. Unfortunately, the GND presented them with a deliciously accessible meal. Within seconds of laying out her towel she was set upon by tiny black insects intent on sucking her dry. Unfortunately, diving into the water gave only temporary relief, and the instant the GND clambered back onto the wall they attacked again. One day in and the GND's dream of a blissful Caribbean holiday was in tatters.

'They don't tell you about the sandflies in the brochures!' she cried indignantly. I couldn't even pacify her with a meal at Wish Willy's. When we had gone back that evening the place was dark and unattended.

The next day the GND awoke to find her whole body covered in sandfly bites. She must have been allergic because the bites were marked by red, welty mounds, topped by blisters of pus. As she had only been wearing a bikini, there were few places left untouched. Worse, she couldn't stop scratching them.

'Don't scratch!' I said. 'You'll only make it worse!'

'I can't help it!' she moaned. 'They itch!'

I told her if she kept scratching she would scar.

'Get me some calamine lotion!'

I found a whole shelf of the stuff at the local supermarket and it seemed to do the trick for the GND. We daubed it in big pink splotches on each of the bites – on her thighs, back, arms, torso, even her face. She looked like a freak and was too embarrassed to leave our room, so I went to the general store to get her a cold drink. On the way I ran into Willy from Wish Willy's.

'What happened to you guys last night?' I asked.

Willy laughed a laugh not too dissimilar to Muttley's in 'The Wacky Races'. 'I cooked up some hash cookies, mon. We ate too many and passed out. I only just woke up.'

I asked him if he would be open that night. A meal at Wish Willy's was just what the GND needed to shake her from her funk.

'Oh sure, mon!' he cried. 'I make you special lobster dish.'

When I took the GND there that night, it was dark and deserted. Again.

The next day the GND's bites had subsided enough for us to go on a snorkel tour of the reef with Rico, a Hispanic guy whose boat had been used to ferry people to the mainland when Mitch hit.

As we masked up and put our flippers on, he gave us a word of advice. 'Do not touch the coral. You will kill it and it will cut you.'

Rico came into the water too, leading us through the reef, pointing out things of interest with a metal rod and surfacing periodically to tell us what we had just seen. 'That was an Eagle Ray,' he said on one surface. 'That was a Rainbow Flounder,' on another. But most of the time he shook his head gravely. There wasn't much coral left. The waves created by the hurricane had stripped the reef clean, like corn off a cob. The ocean floor was littered with broken coral. Colourful fish darted around, anxious from not having the camouflage of coral to hide in, and not altogether sure where it was they should be darting.

When we clambered back onto the boat, Rico lamented the effects of Mitch. 'Tourism is down 90 per cent,' he said. 'And this is the time we make most of our money for the year.'

Rico had abandoned the island for two days and came back to find his boatshed halfway across the island. He had spent the first two weeks after the hurricane cleaning up. 'You wouldn't believe all the rubbish,' he said shaking his head. 'And the piers, every one of them was damaged.'

Rico told us this as he skilfully manoeuvred through the narrow passages in the reef. We were heading to Shark Alley, where we would be swimming with sharks and sting rays. The locals feed them to make sure they are always there and they are quite used to swimming with humans. It was to be the highlight of the trip and Rico assured us it really wasn't that dangerous.

The GND still wasn't sure. 'I don't know about swimming with sharks,' she said. 'It seems a bit unnecessary to me.'

It was the same argument that she had used at Tikal. I argued that if she only wanted to do things that were necessary she should have stayed in Sydney. Why had she come all this way if she wasn't going to do anything out of the ordinary? To me that was what travelling was all about – stepping out of your comfort zone, doing something a little foolhardy even. Having said that, when Rico gave us last-minute instructions on arriving at Shark Alley, I began to wonder if it was necessary myself.

'The sharks are reef sharks,' he warned. 'They might

not have teeth, but they suck. And their suction is twenty times greater than a vacuum cleaner. Do not hold out your hand.'

But the stingrays, it seems, were the ones we had to worry about. 'If you step on a ray it will strike you with its tail. It will not kill you but it will be very painful. If you want to push one off you do not use your hand. This will only provoke them. Gently use your flipper.'

Just as I was about to ask Rico why a stingray would be 'on' us anyway, the boat stopped and we were immediately surrounded by sharks. They circled the boat, their brown fins cutting through the water. More alarming were the large grey shadows of the stingrays, waiting to get it 'on'.

'There's *no way* I'm getting in there,' said the GND emphatically.

For the moment I let the issue rest. My heart was beating a little faster and it was taking all my powers of persuasion to convince myself to go in. I hadn't come this far to chicken out, so after a quick prayer I jumped in, waiting for a bite or at the very least, to look down and find a shark Hoovering off a couple of layers of my skin. Disappointingly, the sharks continued to circle slowly, keeping their distance.

The stingrays, however, had other ideas. They swam straight at me, narrowly avoiding collision by suddenly sweeping below me. Sometimes they swam over the top of me, blocking out the light of the sun temporarily. It was scary and exhilarating and somehow compelling. I swam back to the boat to get the GND.

'You've got to come in! It's amazing!' I cried.

Unfortunately this seemed to freak the GND even more, especially when I dived back in so readily.

Now Rico was feeding the rays. They would come up to him, wrapping their bodies around his torso as they ate out of his hand. I had never seen anything like it. I turned to go back to the boat to insist that the GND come in, and found that she was in the water beside me. I could make out her eyes in the mask, wide open with awe and horror.

Later, back in the boat, she was shaking. I asked her what she thought.

'I'm not sure that I enjoyed it,' she said. 'But I would have regretted it if I hadn't done it!'

After a few weeks of getting annoyed with the GND's reluctance to do things – getting her to climb a Mayan pyramid had been like pulling teeth – that moment I felt something altogether different. I think that it might have been pride.

To celebrate we went to Karaoke night at the Oceanside Bar. Everyone on the island was there – the rastas, the guys from the general store, even Rico. Each had their favourite tunes, the songs they belted out each week. A gang of rastas did 'Exodus' by Bob Marley. The girl from the hair salon did the Whitney Houston classic 'I Will Always Love You'. Rico did a slow, mournful Spanish number that had every-one wiping tears from their eyes. It was a great night – cold Beliken beers for me, margaritas for the GND and our toes wiggling in the sand floor. (We'd stopped wearing shoes after our second day on the island, following the lead of the locals.)

After one too many Belikens, my third, I think, I got it

in my head that the GND and I should get up. We scanned the song menu, and after our first choice, 'Arthur's Theme', wasn't available, we decided upon the Gloria Gaynor classic, 'I Will Survive'. When we finally got on stage, the Belikens and the magaritas kicked in and the GND and I did a high energy – some would say 'shoutie' – version of the song. The people of Caye Caulker looked on in shock. The rastas sat with their mouths on the floor, our obvious energy out of keeping with the more laid-back vibes of their music. Others laughed nervously, not sure altogether if we were serious. When we had finished and sat down Rico came up and congratulated us on our bravery. 'You better be leaving tomorrow!' he laughed.

Energised, we walked back to Daisy's arm in arm along the sandy road, a breeze in the palm trees. It had been a fantastic day – the sting rays, the sharks, and maybe even the singing. Nevertheless, it would probably be best if we took Rico's advice and were on the first boat out the next day.

CHAPTER TEN

Placencia

(Belize)

Annoying habit >>> Always eating
Culprit >>> GND

The speedboat trip back to Belize City the next morning was rougher than our trip over, and the passengers huddled together to try and avoid the spray. It was a mixed crowd – a few locals and what seemed to be all of the tourists we had seen during our stay on Caye Caulker. One, an incredibly brown English girl, sat opposite us, her tanned breasts swinging freely under a loose tie-dyed shirt.

The waves were choppy from a morning southerly, so her breasts were putting on quite a show. Even more disconcertingly, whenever she leaned forward they were entirely visible. Every guy on the boat watched them –

some more discreetly than others, the level of discretion directly affected by the distance they were from a life partner. The captain was particularly blatant, and seemed constantly distracted from the task of manoeuvring through hidden reefs by the urge to ogle. I'll admit I took a peek or two – something in my DNA compelled me – but I thought I was being very discreet about it. A sharp dig in my ribs from the GND suggested that I hadn't been as discreet as I thought.

'What!' I protested, surprised at being caught out.

'I know what you're doing,' she hissed. 'You all are. You're so pathetic!'

I denied it, of course. Men are conditioned from an early age not to admit to anything – it's a basic survival instinct. You just take stock and make sure it doesn't happen again. But despite being caught that morning – or maybe because of it – I found my eyes being drawn irresistibly towards the breasts. It was like the 'Seinfeld' episode where George gets caught looking at the head of NBC's daughter's cleavage. Jerry tells him not to – warning him that it's like looking at the sun – but George is still compelled to look. After another jab in the ribs, I decided to pick a point on the horizon and not take my eyes off it until we reached Belize City. Luckily that point was Belize City.

The English girl went to the airport – I know this because like every guy on the boat and every male working at the terminal I watched her wave over a taxi and ask the driver to take her there. The GND and I, however, had decided to spend a day or two in Belize City so we set off up Front Street to find a room.

Just before Hydes Lane we were accosted by an old drunk called Winston who asked us where we were from. 'Ahh, Australia,' he slurred. 'You have the largest barrier reef in the world. You are the largest consumers of beer in the world. And your capital is Canberra.'

I was impressed. Most people think the capital of Australia is Sydney.

'I'm very good at capitals,' Winston said proudly. 'Ask me any and if I get it right you can buy me a beer.'

'Okay,' I said. 'What's the capital of Burundi?'

After a few minutes of thinking he looked at me with a pained look on his face and whined, 'I don't know!' The thought of the beer he'd just missed out on was almost too much for him to bear.

'Oh, don't be mean!' said the GND. 'How would he know that? Give him an easy one!'

'Okay,' I said, a little chastened. I'd thought the exercise had been to test his knowledge, but it seemed the GND saw it merely as a pretext to hand the guy money. 'What's the capital of India?'

'Bombay?' he said hopefully.

'New Dehli, I'm afraid.' I went to walk off but the GND hit me.

'Ask him another one. And make it easy!'

'Okay,' I said. 'What's the capital of the USA?'

'Oh, I know that one,' Winston said excitedly, jumping up and down. 'New York!'

'That's right,' I lied, handing him a dollar.

In gratitude he insisted on writing the name of a hotel in Belize City for us to stay in.

'Only $40 a night,' he said. 'Make sure you tell them that I sent you!'

We had another place in mind, the Marin's Travelodge, a place our guidebook described as a 'well-kept yellow wooden Caribbean house with a comfy swing on the veranda' for only $12 a night. When we got there, however, it was a pile of blackened rubble.

'It burned down a couple of weeks ago,' called out a dark girl standing on the opposite corner, correctly surmising what we were there for. She introduced herself as Grace Jones and said she'd take us to another guesthouse nearby. She was jittery and spoke like a person who had just swallowed a fistful of barbiturates. I asked her what had happened.

'Trouble with the police,' she said quickly. 'Supposed to pay money. Pay money too late. House is burned down. This place good though. Just took two people, they love it!'

The place was the Downtown Guesthouse. It was clean, small and neat and was protected by a high fence topped with razor wire and a heavy security gate. It was run by a bird-like Indian woman, who showed us our room before returning to a parrot she was teaching to sing 'Happy Birthday'.

The GND wasn't particularly keen about spending too much time in Belize City. While it had a real Caribbean feel to it that was quite a contrast to the Latin countries we had been passing through, our guidebook made it sound like a crime zone, the kind of place where foreigners couldn't walk ten metres without being mugged, raped or killed. Her fears certainly weren't eased when we stepped out of our guesthouse, supposedly in the 'good' part of town, and found a team of armed policemen had two boys up against a wall at gunpoint, frisking them.

Nor did it help that the old swing bridge across Haulover Creek was being repaired, forcing us to cross a temporary bridge further up river that deposited us in the heart of the city's bar district. From here the city centre was a tense 500-metre walk away, past honky-tonk bars and brothels and with a soundtrack of loud music, smashing bottles and shouting. Drug dealers, drunks and bouncers watched us pass, silently checking out the GND. The GND commented on the dangerous vibe, as you would if you were being sized up by a guy built like a house with a serious drug problem, but I wondered if it was really dangerous or whether we had been wound up by our guidebook.

Regardless, it didn't take us long to see everything we wanted to see in Belize City. Battlefield Park, St John's Cathedral and Government House were all clustered near the waterfront and each was charming in a rundown, faded clapboard kind of way. We found a musty old bookstore with week-old newspapers that we devoured until the angry owner chased us out of her shop, shouting that it wasn't a library. The real find was the roadside caravan that sold tiny meat pies, spicy and delicious, that the GND ate by the dozen.

Elsewhere, the city centre was dusty and rundown and humid so we returned, via Bar Alley, to the other side of the river and the Fort George district, home to the mysterious National September Celebration Office. After chancing upon the bakery that made the meat pies the GND was so taken by, we returned to our guesthouse tired and stomachs full. We had seen Belize City. Tomorrow we would head south to Placencia, and towards Guatemala.

We were woken at six the next morning by the parrot screaming 'Wake up! Wake up!' The GND was hungry, so I went back to the bakery and bought her some of the pies she liked fresh out of the oven. On the way back I called into the general store next to the hotel for an orange juice. It was run by a Chinese lady in her late fifties, and that morning she was chatting with a guy who was leaning against the counter, drinking a beer. He wore a basketball singlet and tracksuit pants and was clearly not impressed by my purchase of juice.

'Don't you like beer?' he asked in mock disgust.

I assured him I was quite partial to a Beliken or two, but usually in the evening, not at the crack of dawn. He seemed to take this okay and introduced himself as Charles. He asked where I had been and where I was going and was pleased to hear that I was heading south. He was a policeman in Dangriga, a town where we would be changing buses on our way south to Placencia.

'It is less dangerous down there,' he said. 'The worst thing that will happen to you is that they will steal your things. Here they want to injure you as well.'

The Chinese shopkeeper tutted in agreement.

'Things real bad now,' she said in a stilted Chinese accent. 'New government like human rights. Let killers out gaol!'

'Human rights is rubbish!' said Charles. 'We should be

like America. If you kill someone then you are killed!'

The Chinese woman nodded her head vigorously. 'You right!'

'You know,' he said, turning to her, 'I've shot four people.'

'Really!' said the Chinese woman. 'You kill them?'

'One,' said Charles. 'An escaped convict. He had a gun.' Not sure whether I was one of those damned human rights loonies, he checked his tone. 'I'm not proud of it,' he said. 'It's just something I had to do.'

'But imagine how many lives you saved!' said his Chinese fan. Charles shrugged and drained the last beer from his bottle. He'd save more, I thought, without the early morning drinking binges.

◉   ◉   ◉

By ten we were on the morning Z-Line bus to Dangriga, heading back out along the Western Highway to Belmopan and then south along the charmingly named Hummingbird Highway. The highway passed through huge citrus and banana plantations, the Maya Mountains looming to the south and west. The road was unpaved and heavily corrugated, making the 170 kilometres to Dangriga extremely slow going.

Dangriga is the second largest town in Belize, built on the spot where the North Stann Creek meets the Gulf of Honduras. When we entered, it looked like a small dusty town by the sea. Judging by the signs that lined the road leading into town, they also had a problem with their civic image. 'Dangriga is decaying,' said the first, just on the outskirts of town. 'Let us preserve this town, let us fight to save it. Keep drugs out of our community.'

Another, just opposite the bus station, had more specific ideas about what needed to be done. 'I must clean up my Dangriga,' it announced. 'My job: No drugs. No violence. No crime. No corruption. My reward: A healthy community.'

We were told in Belize City that we would have to change buses at Dangriga, but after we had taken our bags off the bus, abandoned our seats, discreet inquiries revealed that the bus we had just got off was in fact continuing on to Placencia. By the time we got back on, all the seats had been taken and we were forced to stand among the other passengers, all wearing brand new T-shirts. There were only two designs – blue shirts with a striking slashed white cross on the front advertising the PUP party or the plain white shirts with the red logo of the UDP. The recent elections may not have brought economic prosperity or civil reform, but it had updated everyone's wardrobe. I wondered why the local council in Dangriga didn't print off a run of T-shirts to get their message across.

The road south to Placencia was bumpy and dusty and in a worse state than the one to Dangriga. On dusk we left the Southern Highway and approached Hopkins, a tiny fishing village of wooden huts by the sea. Fishermen were dragging wooden canoes onto the beach and hanging nets out to dry, their wives sweeping leaves into piles and burning them. As we left the village and headed back to the highway, surrounded on either side by reeds higher than the bus, darkness fell.

Journeys in the dark always seem to take longer and it

wasn't long before the GND and I were shifting uncomfortably in our seats (we'd secured a couple at last when a young family got off at Hopkins), wondering when we would arrive in Placencia. Without any scenery to distract us, just darkness, it was difficult to guess how fast we were going or how much ground we had covered. Thankfully Christmas was only a couple of weeks away, so the few settlements we passed were gaily lit with Christmas lights and the radio station the bus driver was listening to was playing reggae versions of Christmas classics.

At a crossroads the bus stopped for a few minutes in front of a brightly lit compound, a banana packing plant, still operating well into the night. In a huge shed workers dipped huge hands of bananas into water tanks, washing them before putting them onto a conveyer belt that delivered the bananas to another part of the shed. Here other workers broke the hands into more manageable sizes and packed them into boxes. To the right of the shed were the workers' dormitories, where those who weren't on shift stood outside smoking cigarettes, the doors of the dorms open, revealing tightly packed bunks. Belize has a high population of itinerant workers from Guatemala, Nicaragua, Honduras, even Mexico, and while the conditions are harsh and primitive, the wages were high compared to the countries they come from. At the end of the compound the bus turned down a narrow road and towards the sea.

'I wonder what sort of Christmas they'll be having,' said the GND.

◼   ◼   ◼

The Belize Tourist Board calls Placencia 'the caye you can drive to', a laid-back village at the southern end of a long, narrow peninsula. As we approached the end of the peninsula the other passengers started getting off, disappearing down tiny sandy paths towards the pale glow of hurricane lamp lights. As each person got off I had the uneasy feeling that we should be getting off too, and squinted into the darkness hoping to spot some kind of landmark that would allow me to get my bearings on the map. Soon the bus reached the end of the road – the fuel depot – and we were the only ones left on the bus.

After my disasters with maps to this point I had hoped that in Placencia, at least, I would be able to confidently lead the GND to a clean, comfortable hotel. Unfortunately, finding our way didn't get any easier once we were off the bus. According to the map, if we turned right and followed a sandy path we would come upon the Paradise Vacation Hotel, a neat and clean hotel within our modest price range. Our problem was locating the correct sandy path in the dark. Each one I tried petered out after a few metres or, worse, led to a stinking pile of rubbish. In the end the GND suggested we follow the shoreline. It was a clear night and the moon was fullish, so the walk along the sand among the palm trees was not unpleasant.

Sensing my frustration, the GND tugged on my arm and smiled. 'This is beautiful,' she cooed. 'I think I'm going to like it here.'

By hugging the shoreline we found the Paradise Vacation Hotel easily – it was only ten metres or so back from the water – and, while modest, the room we were given was on the second floor, facing out over the veranda with deck chairs and hammocks and over the water. It was also blissfully quiet, so that night we went to sleep lulled by the gentle lapping of water on the shore.

The next morning we took a stroll through Placencia, and, if anything, it was more charming than we had expected. Not so long ago the only access to Placencia was by boat, so the village was set around a single concrete path that cut through the sand close to the sea rather than the road, which was a relatively new interloper. The path was lined by wooden houses on stilts, many with tiny flower gardens, and the few shops and restaurants in the village, clustered around the Belize Telecommunication Limited (BLT) telephone office. As we walk along the length of the path, people smiled, said hello and stepped aside for us to pass.

We had been told that we could get on the Internet at the Sea Spray Hotel, so we dropped in there to check our e-mails. The computer was in a room behind the hotel reception desk, and was the responsibility of a large cheery woman called Hatty. Judging by the number of people who dropped in for a chat, Hatty was also the village gossip.

'When did you folk get in?' she asked cheerily, pulling out the phone and plugging in the modem. She seemed alarmed when we told her that we had arrived the night before.

'On the Z-Line bus?' she cried. We nodded.

'Hey Peggy,' she called out to her friend in reception. 'These people were on the Z-Line bus that crashed.'

'Our bus didn't crash,' I said.

'It crashed this morning on the way back to Dangriga,' Hatty explained as she dialled into her ISP. 'The driver was still drunk from a big one last night.'

'Oh my God!' said the GND. 'Was anyone hurt?'

'Only the driver,' she said. 'He died. The bus was empty.'

Hotmail was the default homepage so we tapped in our username and password and we were in.

'Just disconnect when you're finished!' she smiled before going back out to reception to swap more gossip with her friend.

The rest of the day we did what we couldn't do on Caye Caulker – walk along a white sandy beach, sit under palm trees, lie in the sun for a while, all without being eaten alive by sandflies. When Santa came to the village that night as part of a radio station promotion, throwing gifts to screaming, laughing children from the back of a pick-up truck, it felt like we had found a little piece of paradise.

When we returned to our hotel that night, the only other guest was sitting on the veranda. He introduced himself as Voh, and he was the temporary manager of the local BLT office. It was a job that would see him staying at Placencia for three months altogether, and like most married guys living away from home in a hotel, he walked around in a singlet and ate his dinner from a can.

Voh was from Corozal, a town in northern Belize, close to the Mexican border, and like most people we'd met, felt that the country was going to the dogs. 'It is okay here,' he said, looking out across the palm trees at the platinum sea. 'But in Belize City it is lawless. Even Dangriga is dangerous.'

He knew from first-hand experience, he said. His son had played in the football youth championships there, helping his team to victory in the final with two goals. His son didn't get to enjoy the victory, though. The medal presentation ceremony was called off when supporters of the losing side invaded the field with guns. 'He got the medal in the post two weeks later,' Voh said, disgusted.

Periodically Voh would go to his room and bring us back BTL merchandising – BTL pens, BTL sunglasses, even BTL water bottles. When we got up to go to bed, he returned with a BTL T-shirt for the GND. It was green, the BTL colour, and celebrated '10 years of service' and the fact that BTL was 'crafted with Skill, Pride and Customer Satisfaction'.

'I think he's taken a shine to you,' I said to the GND.

'Well, it's lucky you've been in a better mood lately,' she joked. 'I might have been tempted to run off with him.'

I nearly joked, 'Lucky for who?', but in a rare moment of good judgement didn't.

◼   ◼   ◼

After a few days we decided to actually do something. The local dive shop offered lots of activities – snorkelling, diving, night diving, deep-sea fishing. But after scouring the list the GND decided she didn't want to do anything quite that active. The Manatee Sunset Cruise appealed to her though. It entailed a leisurely barbecue lunch at the Soulshine Resort followed by a cruise at sunset – beer and cocktails supplied – to search for an elusive manatee. The manatee is a huge slothful sea creature like the Australian dugong, and is quite retiring. The blurb for the cruise made it quite clear that despite the tour's name, there was very little chance that we would actually see a manatee, and the guy at the dive shop felt compelled to reiterate the point before he took our money. The GND didn't care. It was the 'sunset' part that had appealed to her.

The Soulshine Resort was on the lagoon side of the island, at the end of a long sandy road and on the other side of the channel. When we reached the end of the road we were instructed to yell out and someone from the resort would come and collect us. I had an uneasy feeling. The resort, lovely as it was with its thatched huts, looked deserted. Still, we yelled, for ten minutes. We didn't stir a soul.

I spotted a fibreglass paddleboat, the sort usually seen on artificial lakes, and decided to use that. The fact that the paddling mechanism was largely rusted away and the thing went in a crab-like fashion meant that it took several attempts to reach the pontoon on the other side, backing away and trying again like a pensioner trying to parallel park on a busy street. The upshot was that the journey took seven minutes instead of seven seconds.

As we pulled up to the other side, a stocky Englishman called David came out of the main building and waved. 'You must be the Australians,' he said. 'Do come in!'

It was quite a set-up: inside a wood-panelled restaurant and bar with satellite TV and a collection of board games; outside a pool and a timber deck. The place was one of the swishest we had been in, and it seems we weren't alone in that judgment. David showed us a fax he'd just received from his brother. 'Apparently we've just been named one of the top ten resorts in the Caribbean by *Travel & Leisure* magazine,' he said proudly. 'As you can imagine, we're quite chuffed!'

From what David said, it was just what they needed. Hurricane Mitch had scared off a lot of tourists. 'This is our busy season,' he said motioning towards the empty pool. 'God help us! Still, mustn't grumble.' He started to light the barbecue. 'At least Mitch didn't hit here. It just hovered offshore and all we got was rain. No major damage.'

After a delicious meal of barbecue chicken, we swam in the pool and had ice cold drinks brought to us. At four, a local man called Bertie came along with his plywood catamaran and we set off in search of a manatee and a spectacular sunset.

We spent three hours sailing around the bay, chasing leads that turned out to be nothing but Hurricane debris. Over the course of the afternoon we saw the remains of a shop sign, a broken window frame and what was left of a particularly beaten up life buoy. As the sun began to set, we turned to head back. Then a manatee swam right under our boat.

'He be a big one!' cried Bertie, obviously excited, as the sky turned an unnatural shade of pink and orange like in a bad Hollywood movie. It was an agreeable end to a perfectly agreeable day. Our sighting of the manatee convinced the GND that luck was on our side.

'That was an omen,' she said optimistically. 'I reckon we're going to get all the way through Central America after all.'

After our one day of action – if you could call it that – in Placencia, we fell back into a relaxing, blissful routine. We'd stroll along the beach, take a dip in the calm Caribbean Sea and get a snack at the Flamboyant Restaurant. Then we'd retire to the Paradise Vacation Hotel and kick back in the hammocks. We had been in Placencia for five days, and although we were only seven weeks into our six-month journey, it was tempting to jettison our plans and just stay there. We were disagreeing less, and the GND admitted that for the first time in a long time she wasn't secretly craving a cigarette.

We spent one afternoon dipping into a box of old paperbacks that had been left behind by previous guests, then lying in the hammocks reading them. Most of the books in the box were dreadful, written by authors I'd never heard of and published well before I was born. The only one that held my interest was a slim volume called *Cheerleaders – The Tryout*. It was the first in a series of Cheerleader books to be published once a month, each volume continuing the story and developing the characters.

Not that there was much developing to do. The characters were pretty much fleshed out in the first book. There was Kirsty, the beautiful blonde, whose mother had been head cheerleader and saw her daughter's selection as a birthright. Val, the dark, beautiful new girl, who was intelligent but wanted to get on the team to make friends in her new school, despite her doctor father's disapproval. And Pip, the happy, chirpy girl, who was everyone's friend and held the team together despite all the internal bitchiness. I finished it in an hour and ferreted through the box to see if there were any more from the series. Unfortunately, *The Tryout* was the only one.

I began to wonder if Pip got into the team or if Biff, the captain of the football team, asked Kirsty out. The next time we went to the Sea Spray to check our e-mail, I even dropped in on Amazon.com to see if you could order the rest of the Cheerleader series on their site. (In case you're wondering, you can't.)

I think it was then that I realised that it was time for us to move on.

CHAPTER ELEVEN

Copán

(Honduras)

Annoying habit >>> Stubborness
Culprit >>> Peter

The next morning we caught the *SS Hokey Pokey* across the lagoon and through mangrove swamps to Mango Creek, a small settlement on the mainland. I had hoped to see another manatee – the trip took us across the same stretch of water we had spotted our first one – but the boat was going so slowly that even a crippled one would have been able to avoid us. We arrived in Mango Creek an hour later – a ridiculous amount of time considering how short a distance we covered – and walked from the dock down a dusty road to the 'town', a collection of houses. Here we waited under a tree for the bus to Punta Gorda which arrived, eventually, coated in dust and with half the windows broken.

The highway south was as corrugated and potholed as the rest in southern Belize, but here the mountains in the south loomed larger and the countryside began to look more like the backblocks of Guatemala. The road was still lined by citrus farms, with their neat lines of trees and the latest irrigation technology, but now they were interspersed with traditional Mayan villages of thatched huts, rooting pigs and naked children, struggling to hold the jungle at bay.

About forty kilometres outside of Punta Gorda the road became a flattop of smooth bitumen. Roadside signs proclaimed that this stretch of highway had been paid for by the government of Kuwait. As I wondered whether the road had been a gift for Belize's support during the Gulf War – had they supplied the troops with orange juice, perhaps? – the tarmac ended and with it the Southern Highway. We had reached Punta Gorda, the southernmost town in Belize.

To describe Punta Gorda as sleepy, as our guidebook did, was an understatement. The bus made its way along the seashore to the centre of town without passing another vehicle. About halfway through the town, at King Street (just before Queen and Prince Streets) the bus driver stopped the bus and pointed us towards the dock for the boats to Puerto Barrios in Guatemala. We hadn't told him that was our plan, but he was probably a local and knew that there was no reason for us to stay: the International Rainforest Festival, an attempt by the town fathers to pursue the eco-tourist dollar, was still two months away.

The boat office, customs and immigration were all conveniently located at the docks on the imaginatively titled Front Street. We were able to buy our boat tickets to Puerto Barrios, get our exit stamps from immigration and have our baggage checked by customs without venturing more than 500 metres. The boat wasn't leaving for another hour so we sat outside a small general store – also within the 500 metre radius – and spent the last of our Belizian currency on chocolate-coated bananas. Unfortunately, our funds would only stretch to one, so the GND suggested we change some more money.

'But we're leaving in an hour,' I said. 'Why don't we just wait until we get to Guatemala?'

'But I'm hungry *now*!' she moaned.

I bridled. Changing money minutes before leaving a country goes against all my travelling ethics. I get a pathetic thrill out of budgeting so that I leave a country with little or no money left. If that means going hungry, so be it.

The GND thought this was stupid and my argument that we'd be stuck with excess Belize currency made her angry. 'We change the money, we spend it,' she reasoned. 'There's no Belize dollars left.'

Now to my mind that was just being wasteful. I think I must have been Amish in a previous life, because this idea of spending money for the sake of spending money upset me just as much as the idea of getting stuck with excess Belizean dollars. As far as I am concerned, in these circumstances you go without. You make sacrifices. It is character-building and you end up a better person for it.

But the GND took a much more short-term view. 'If I'm hungry, I'm hungry,' she said. 'I'll worry about the consequences when we're really low on money.'

I still didn't agree.

'What's the worst that can happen?' she argued. 'We go home early. We're on holidays, not a prison sentence!'

There was no reasoning with her. We changed another $US5 and the GND ordered herself a plate of chicken, beans and rice to go with her choc-coated banana. Out of spite, I refused to eat. I did have a cold Coke – under sufferance, of course – but I didn't enjoy it. Really.

Just as the GND was contemplating whether she'd ever be able to have children with a guy with an almost evangelical belief in the beneficial side-effects of suffering, a boat arrived from Guatemala. One of the passengers, a Swede, had just travelled through Nicaragua and Honduras, two of the countries most affected by Mitch. I was keen to speak to him and hear first-hand what the situation was. To this point most of what we had heard was wild speculation from people back home on the basis of a two-minute report they'd seen on the evening news.

'Most of the bridges are washed out,' he said. 'But where the rivers were too deep for buses to cross, there are boats to ferry people across to the other side. They are really determined to get people through.'

I asked him about the cholera vaccinations that Amanda, the American girl we had met in San Christóbal, said the Guatemalans insisted travellers had.

'That's crap!' he said. 'No one checks anything! It's too chaotic.'

I was strangely heartened by the news. Our plan had been to head straight down to Antigua, the beautiful old town just west of Guatemala City, but after hearing this news I was tempted to pop into Honduras and visit the other major Mayan site of the region, the ruins at Copán. They were just on the other side of the Guatemalan–Honduran border, and if the roads hadn't been too damaged by Mitch, we may well be able to pop across and still be in Antigua for Christmas. The GND, content with a belly full of food, agreed that it sounded like a good idea. The Swede wished us luck and continued on his way.

The boat he had arrived on was returning to Guatemala so the captain indicated for us to get on board. It was three metres long with rows of seats and a canopy for protection from the sun and was powered by an outboard engine. It skimmed across the sea, powering towards mountains in the distance that were layered – light, dark and darkest. The engine was too loud for conversation, so the GND and I sat silent, looking at the horizon. I hoped that she wasn't too angry with me. The time we had spent at Placencia had been good for us, washing away the tensions that had been building slowly. I'd hate to think that our spat over changing money had destroyed that. Distracted, I dangled my hand in the water. It caused a spray of water that drenched the passengers behind me.

The boat roared along the north coast of Guatemala, passing empty beaches or small settlements with fishing boats drawn up on shore. Soon, Puerto Barrios appeared on the horizon, and even half an hour out we could make out the container ships, docks and cranes of the huge port.

Puerto Barrios was a company town, built early in the twentieth century by the United Fruit Company as part of a deal it did with the Guatemalan government of the time. In return for vast amounts of land in the fertile Río Motagua valley, the company agreed to build the port, the city and the railroads that transported the bananas grown on the plantations to the port. The bananas were taken to America in the company's distinctive 'Great White Fleet' of transport ships, one of the largest private navies in the world. Courtesy of this beneficial deal, the United Fruit Company became the largest employer in Central America. The importance of Puerto Barrios as a port also meant that it effectively controlled all of Guatemala's international trade.

Despite the jobs and infrastructure it brought to the region, the United Fruit Company had not been popular in these parts. Local journalists had referred to the company as El Pulpo, The Octopus, feeling that it corrupted government officials, took advantage of workers and had more of a hand in the workings of the government than they thought a foreign company should. Others bridled at company rules that insisted that native Guatemalans were to 'give right of way to whites and remove their hats when talking to them'.

Following its boom days from the thirties through to the late fifties, the company, and the town, fell on hard times. The United Fruit Company merged with United Brands in the sixties, which collapsed in the early seventies before selling off its interests in Guatemala to the Del Monte corporation in 1972. A new modern port has been built a few kilometres to the southwest at Santo Tomás de

Castilla. Puerto Barrios has been in decline ever since.

That Puerto Barrios was once a company town was immediately apparent. The town was built on a grid pattern, with everything generously spread apart – a feature, I've found, of every town built in the developing world to service a primary industry. The immigration office was a good couple of blocks away from the port. The cheap hotels and the centre of town another four blocks in. And even though Puerto Barrios was now in effect a secondary port, huge semitrailers hauling shipping containers made up most of the traffic.

We got a cheap room in a hotel overlooking the markets, and ate at a restaurant with a balcony overlooking the streets. It was dusk – a hazy, dusty dusk – and after the south of Belize it seemed noisy and busy, frantic almost. Later we went for a walk in the balmy evening air, essentially to find an ATM that would accept my Visa card – the 'issue' over changing money in Belize was all but forgotten – but also just to have a look around. It was the week before Christmas and we stumbled upon a neighbourhood Christmas party. The street had been blocked off, tables and chairs dragged out and a band played from the back of a truck. As the adults ate and drank, their children, freshly washed and in their best outfits, got up on stage and sang Christmas carols.

It was a wonderfully festive gathering and I immediately thought of my nieces and nephews back in Australia. Although I grew up in Sydney, our family had undergone the usual diaspora – one of my sisters still lived in Sydney, but the others, as well as my parents, had moved to

Queensland. This year everyone was spending Christmas in Queensland, the first time in a long time that the whole family would celebrate the festive season altogether. All my nieces and nephews in the same room ripping open their Christmas presents, running around chasing each other and getting a little crazy, and I wouldn't be there. That night, watching the laughing and singing children of a tiny street in Puerto Barrios, I wished that I could be back in Queensland to see it. I kept those feelings to myself, of course. I didn't want the GND to think I wasn't equally excited about us spending our first Christmas together.

●   ●   ●

There was nothing to keep us in Puerto Barrios, so the next morning we caught a bus to Chiquimula, a mining and tobacco-growing town where we would find buses to El Florido and the Honduran border. The bus was an old fifties-style aluminium Greyhound, the kind you see in old American movies, but with a dreadfully uniform red vinyl interior and 'God is my Saviour' written across the front window. It wouldn't have survived a Belizian road, but thankfully the road from Puerto Barrios south, Carretera al Atlántico, was the main trade artery for the country and hence in good condition.

For much of the way the highway followed the Río Motagua, the Sierra de las Minas high and dry on one side, the agricultural plains on the other. The river was still high with the rains from Mitch, but judging by the amount of debris in the surrounding fields the water level had dropped from what it had been. It was an uneventful trip, livened up only when we picked up a clown at Los Amates. He wore your standard-issue clown gear – colourful striped shirt and baggy pants with braces, with a red nose and a badly painted smile.

'Look at this clown,' I said to the GND.

I was relieved when she laughed. I figured our relationship was in pretty good shape if she still found my bad jokes funny. The same could not be said for the clown's routine. We couldn't understand his jokes – they were in Spanish – but judging by the reaction of everyone else on the bus, it didn't matter. He had a can full of stones that he used to punctuate his jokes, a portable drum roll if you will, and it was thanks to this can, rather than raucous laughter from the other passengers, that we were able to tell when he had delivered his punch lines. He shuffled through the bus, a colourful cap extended, but nobody gave him money. In the end he gave up and spent the rest of the journey to Río Hondo (Deep River) sitting up the front of the bus talking to the driver.

At Río Hondo the clown got off and the bus turned off Carretera al Atlántico and headed south towards Chiquimula. This road followed a river too, and judging by the twisted remains of iron bridges, the flooding here had been worse. The farmland on either side seemed to have survived undamaged, with row after row of tobacco plants growing unaffected.

'*Hmmmm*, tobacco!' said the GND. It had been the first time she had mentioned smoking for a while.

Chiquimula was a quaint town of low houses, shops and narrow roads surrounded by dry barren hills. It was hot and, like the lower parts of Mexico, dusty. It was market day, so it was bustling with farmers and Indians from the surrounding districts. When we found the bus to El Florido, the town closest to the border, it was already teeming with passengers and the roof laden with goods bought at the markets, including a fridge. It was an old American school bus and was so packed with people and produce that the door at the back of the bus couldn't be shut properly. When the bus took off the door swung open, a small boy hanging from the handle. His father reached out, grabbed his son and pulled the door shut as if it was the most natural thing in the world to do.

It was only 58 kilometres to El Florido, but the road was so bad that it took us over three hours to get there. The bus chugged up steep dry mountains, averaging less than 20 kilometres an hour, struggling under the combined weight of the passengers and the products of their Saturday morning market spree. In places the road had fallen away, slowing progress even more as the bus crawled along what was left, the driver being careful not to plunge over the huge ravine on the side.

Most of the passengers, including the lady with the refrigerator, got off at El Florido. The rest of the passengers, Hondurans mainly, continued to the frontier a few kilometres further on, chatting excitedly about going home. It was a pretty spot in a valley, the border nothing more than a striped pole with offices on either side and a couple of small restaurants. The GND and I crossed from Guatemala to Honduras without too much trouble. The border officials on both sides extracted the usual couple of dollars for exit and entrance taxes and we found a small Japanese pick-up truck waiting on the Honduran side to take people the rest of the way to Copán.

We clambered into the back of the pick-up, throwing our packs on the floor and standing precariously on the edge of the tray with all the other passengers. The road to Copán was almost vertical, climbing up through pine forests and fields that were alpine in appearance. The air grew crisper and the other passengers laughed and joked among themselves. I felt like we were on an adventure again – we hadn't been in the back of a pick-up since our side trip to Chacahua – and stood with the cold wind whipping my face, exhilarated. We arrived in Copán just as the sun was setting over the mountains, the last of its golden rays falling agreeably on the colonial town and the green valley surrounding it.

Copán was a misty highland town populated by guys in boot-cut jeans and white cowboy hats. At its heart was a scruffy park where locals sat on benches chatting and old ladies sold steamed corn on the cob from battered metal trolleys. The cobbled streets were deserted by seven o'clock – a light rain was falling – the only sound the occasional clip-clop of horses' hooves. It was magical and delightful and the GND and I found a room in a cosy hotel where the water for the shower was heated by a live electrical wire.

The next morning we ventured out to the Copán archaeological site. It was on the southern outskirts of town, on the other side of a stone bridge that had been partially washed away by the flooding caused by Hurricane Mitch.

Nestled high in the mountains, these ruins had an altogether different feel to the other great Mayan sites we had visited at Palenque and Tikal. Here the grounds were more park-like – neat grassy areas dotted with pyramids and platforms and the occasional carved stela rising like a gaudy headstone. There was even a cool breeze that should have made our visit very pleasant indeed.

Unfortunately, the GND and I had long reached ruin overload. In the Mayan world, it is the equivalent of cathedral overdose in Europe or temple burnout in Asia. We had seen more stone pyramids that you could poke a stick at in Palenque and Tikal, and impressive as the grand plaza was here at Copán, with its Mayan ball court and all, to us it was just another scenic bunch of rubble.

Having said that, two things about the site at Copán did impress us. The first was the hieroglyphic staircase, the handiwork of King Smoke Shell. It was 63 steps high and bordered by ramps on which the history of the royal family of Copán was told in intricate carvings, reliefs and glyphs. The other was the three-metre-high stelae, again intricately carved, that had been put up by King Eighteen Rabbit. They told the story of his reign, although there were some featuring Chac, the rain god, quite telling considering it is believed that it was the city's inability to feed its citizens due to drought that caused its downfall.

As usual, it was the names the rulers of Copán chose for themselves that made the biggest impression on me. As well as King Eighteen Rabbit and King Smoke Shell, Copán was also home to such other Mayan luminaries as King Mat Head, King Waterlily Jaguar and the impressively monikered Great Sun Lord Quetzal Macaw. Only the second-last ruler, First Dawn, had a disappointingly weak name. Once again, I suspected that his name was the real reason behind the decline of the city. I mean, how can you respect a guy who sounds like he was named by a pair of ageing hippies?

That night we ate at the Tunkul Bar, a charming restaurant in an old colonial house run by Pedro, a Honduran guy with a strong American accent. It was a lovely place, with a bar and outside barbecue, and normally it would have been well out of our budget. But business was slow, and they were offering Mitch Specials that we could afford.

'Business is down 99 per cent,' moaned Pedro when I asked him about the specials. 'People see the damage caused by Mitch on TV and think that all of Honduras is like that. If it keeps up like this we may as well close down for the season.'

Out at the ruins I had picked up a copy of *Honduras This Week*, the English-language newspaper, and it told a similar tale. Ninety thousand people had visited the Copán ruins in 1998 before Mitch. After, there was only a handful each day. Copán, it claimed, was being tossed aside for temples in Thailand, bullfights in Madrid and, interestingly, the Great Barrier Reef of Sydney!

The sad thing is that the Hondurans had such great plans for this season. Political stability had come to the region and tourist numbers had been steadily climbing. In his column for the Summer–Fall issue of *Honduras Tips*, the official travel guide of Honduras, the editor had written that 1998 would become 'a landmark year in the development of the tourist industry in Honduras'. Mitch had certainly made sure of that.

I asked Pedro if it was possible to travel through the rest of the country.

'Most of the bridges have been washed away but the buses are still going,' he said. 'It just takes longer.' Then, remembering some of the footage he'd seen on television, he added, almost as an afterthought, that there were some places we 'wouldn't want to go to'.

Our meal was delicious and cheap and it was tempting to stay and help Pedro drown his sorrows during the generous 'three-for-one' Mitch Hour. But we had decided to pop into the old movie theatre around the corner to see *The Mask of Zorro*. And besides, the only other patrons, two German guys, were trying to teach the restaurant's parrot to say 'scheisse'.

The Mask of Zorro is a Saturday afternoon matinee kind of movie and the movie theatre in Copán was a Saturday afternoon kind of theatre. It had a balcony, wooden floors and a heavy velvet curtain scalloped across the screen. The patrons were all men, in town for Saturday night in their best boots and jeans. As the only woman there, the GND excited a lot of interest, so we sat in the more expensive balcony seats to escape any unwanted attention. The men sat below us, a sea of white cowboy hats, occasionally looking back to catch a glimpse of the GND.

The Mask of Zorro was such a rollicking good yarn that the men below us soon forgot about the GND. They were particularly impressed by two scenes in the movie – the spectacular horse-chase sequence and the sword fight between Catherine Zeta-Jones and Antonio Banderras. As horsemen themselves, they admired the level of skill involved in the horse-chase sequence and 'oohed' and 'aahed' at the trickiest manoeuvres. The sword fight that saw Antonio strip Catherine down to her undies with his sword simply appealed to them as men. As they streamed out, chatting excitedly amongst themselves, I wondered how many horses and wives would be injured when they tried the tricks they'd just seen at home.

We left Copán the next morning, heading back the way we came in on the back of a pick-up. The mountains were shrouded in a heavy mist, so we arrived at the border with damp hair and rosy cheeks. The border proceedings on the Honduran side were perfunctory – our passports were stamped and we were sent on our way. But on the Guatemalan side a teenage boy of about 14 was officiating as immigration that day, and after glancing at our passports insisted on a 100-quetzal 'entrance fee'.

I refused to pay and he became flustered. Now I don't want you to think that I make a habit of refusing to pay government fees, but by this stage we had entered Guatemala twice before, once at El Naranjo from Mexico and the other time at Puerto Barrios from Belize. Neither time had we been charged an entrance fee. The kid was trying to rustle up a bit of pocket money, so I snatched my passport back, and finding the previous entrance stamps, began to harangue him in broken Spanish.

'El Naranjo,' I said stabbing the appropriate stamp with my finger, 'Gratis!' (free). 'Puerto Barrios, gratis! El Florido, 100 quetzals – mucho corruption!'

The kid panicked and mumbled something about dropping the fee to 60 quetzals.

Unimpressed by his offer, I continued my tirade. 'Mucho corruption!'

The Hondurans waiting behind me joined in, hoping that if I didn't pay the fee they wouldn't have to either. 'Si!' they cried, punching the air with their fists. 'Mucho corruption!'

The boy was really nervous now. His eyes darted around nervously, looking for an escape route should events turn even nastier. But still he insisted I pay.

By now the bus to Chiquimula had arrived and the GND went ahead with our bags to get a ticket. Sensing that he had the upper hand now the boy refused to budge, and when the bus was ready to go, our bags on its roof, we still didn't have an entry stamp. The choice was simple. I could either back down and pay the money or stand my ground and miss the bus. In the end I waved to the GND and indicated that we were staying. Our bags were taken down and the bus drove off.

I was furious now and demanded to see the comandante (the boss). The boy pointed to a small restaurant, so I snatched back our passports and stormed off towards it. The comandante was eating breakfast and after I gave him my spiel, he shrugged his shoulders and said okay. I had stuck to my principles and won. We got our entry stamps without having to pay. But the next bus to Chiquimula wouldn't leave for another two hours. The GND didn't say anything, but I suspected that all the fence mending of the past two weeks had been undone.

Like all return journeys, the bus trip back to Chiquimula seemed longer and dustier than the one going the other way. When we hit the main highway, however, the bus driver stopped and waved down an express bus heading to Guatemala City, saving us the hassle of changing buses or waiting in Chiquimula. It was a nice gesture, something that was becoming more common now that we were in Guatemala.

The conductor of the express bus was called Marcos and he had lived in America for two years. He gave us front-row seats, supposedly so he could practise his English, but it was already very good. In fact it was excellent, and I told him so.

'If you didn't speak English in America', he explained, 'you didn't exist.'

Soon we were back on Carretera al Atlántico and making good progress. The bus stopped occasionally to pick up extra passengers, who stood in the aisles with their bags and sacks. 'We shouldn't really pick them up,' explained Marcos. 'This is a luxury bus, so by law we can only carry seated passengers. But the extra money helps.'

I looked at the bus and tried to figure out why it had been given such a lofty rating. Noting my perplexity, Marcos explained that any bus that wasn't an old US school bus was regarded as a luxury bus in Guatemala. And judging by the number of passengers Marcos and his driver were squeezing in they would be able to retire within a month.

The scenery was straight out of a spaghetti western, dry and barren and dotted with cacti. I noticed that the oncoming drivers were flashing their headlights and making a scribbling movement with their hand, rather like the universal hand signal used by patrons in restaurants to call for the cheque.

'Policía!' said Marcos. He muttered something in Spanish to the driver, who sped up to catch a 'non-luxury' bus ahead. By flashing the headlights and making a series of frantic hand gestures he was able to make it pull over and transfer all the standing passengers onto it. As a gratuity, Marcos handed the other driver 20 quetzals. Twenty kilometres later, after we passed the police roadblock, the buses stopped again and the standing passengers were transferred back onto our bus. Marcos spent the rest of the journey warning other buses by pretending to write cheques.

◼   ◼   ◼

Guatemala City was another busy, crumbling, dusty city in the classic third-world mould. The buildings were low, in deference to the high number of earthquakes, and the city set out on a grid pattern. It was founded in 1776 after the former capital, Antigua, was destroyed by an earthquake. Colonial administrators thought that the ravines surrounding this new site would absorb the shocks of earthquakes, thus protecting it from the fate that had befallen their previous capitals.

About halfway through the city and still a good couple of blocks from the main bus station, Marcos stopped the bus and pointed up the street. 'The buses to Antigua are four blocks that way,' he said pointing up a street that was a jumble of overflowing market stalls. 'Enjoy your stay in Guatemala ... and Merry Christmas!'

The bus we caught to Antigua was distinctly non-luxury and packed to the ceiling with people who had come to the city to do a year's worth of shopping. In fact, if I hadn't been in Guatemala, I may have suspected that they were stocking up early for the Y2K bug. Every passenger was loaded with enough canned food, plastic tubs and bags of washing powder to sit out any apocalypse.

The driver, on the other hand, thought he was playing Gran Turismo, and was making up for being assigned the worst-specced vehicle (Old American School Bus, Third World Edition) by driving at the peak of his abilities. He flew out of the city centre, past the Americanised outskirts with their drive-thru McDonald's and shiny new malls and up the steep, windy road into the mountains as if he were on a time trial. He raced past other buses and hunted down smaller, nippier vehicles. With large trucks, he waited until a sharp bend would approach, and then took the corner with them, side by side, as if this dangerous manoeuvre would gain him extra bonus points. The GND surmised he was on a suicide mission – his family had left him and he was spending Christmas alone. Now he had snapped and he was taking us all with him.

Then, after the top of the mountain was tamed and we descended into cool pine forests on the other side, the bus driver mysteriously slowed down. Maybe he had come to his senses, a flash of his child smiling, or a memory of Christmas past. Or maybe he had been soothed by the sight of the old colonial capital of Antigua Guatemala, in all its charm, nestled among a ring of volcanoes below us.

It certainly soothed my troubled nerves.

CHAPTER TWELVE

Feliz Navidad

(Antigua Guatemala)

Annoying habit >>> Smoking
Culprit >>> GND

Antigua lies in the Valle de Panchoy at the base of three volcanoes: Volcán Agua, Volcán Fuego and Volcán Acatenango. While they add immeasurably to the town's charm – a picturesquely conical peak is visible from virtually every corner – they also ensured an element of unpredictability in the lives of the city's inhabitants and administrators. In the 230 years that Antigua served as the capital of the Spanish colonial realm, hardly a decade went by without an earthquake, volcanic eruption, or both.

It must be said that the Spanish were not particularly good at picking their colonial capital cities. Founded in

1543, Antigua was originally known as the Very Noble and Loyal City of Saint James of the Knights of Guatemala, and was their third attempt at a Central American HQ. Their first, a city founded near the Mayan city of Iximché, was hastily abandoned after the local Indians rebelled over exorbitant demands for gold. The second, called Ciudad Vieja, and only 5.5 kilometres from Antigua, sat at the foot of Volcán Agua and was washed away by a mudslide. Antigua, while putting in a respectable 230 years as the capital, suffered three major quakes before being abandoned after the most devastating, the great earthquake of 1773.

For a city that has had such a hard life, Antigua didn't scrub up too badly. We found a fantastically rustic hotel down near the markets with exposed wooden beams in the ceilings and a central courtyard with flagstones and a pretty fountain. A brief reconnaissance to the centre of town to find an ATM revealed that the city streets were still cobbled and most of the old colonial houses had been tastefully restored and painted in an appropriate shade of terracotta, mustard or mauve. There was a suitably grand monastery or church on every corner, and just enough crumbling plaster and general neglect to take the colonial Disneyland edge off the place and give it an authentic feel.

In many ways, Antigua is the Prague of Central America. It has escaped the ravages of slipshod redevelopment through the vagaries of history and now presents itself as a complete jewel, a snapshot of a time past. It's a look popular with tourists and, like Prague, Antigua was crawling with them. They sat in courtyard cafes sipping on lattes or browsed through antique stores looking for a genuine

Spanish colonial candlestick holder. Others wandered the cobbled streets taking photos of the villagers or had their shoes shined by young boys with smudges of polish on their noses.

You'd find them in their greatest numbers down at Parque Central, a beautiful park with trees and a large ornamental fountain that featured a topless woman squeezing her breasts and water shooting from her nipples (imagine the council meeting when that one was discussed!). The park was quite literally the heart of the city, surrounded by some of the most beautiful buildings in Latin America – Santiago Cathedral, the stately double arcade of the capital building, the town hall. It was also the major habitat of the stocky, brightly outfitted Mayan women in town to sell handicraft to tourists.

The women operated in groups of three. They'd spot a tourist sit down on one of the park benches, and after giving them enough time to relax, would circle and trap the tourist behind sacks of shirts, shawls, wall-hangings, purses, belts, tablecloths and wood carvings. The shoe-shine boys, knowing their quarry was trapped, used the opportunity to show off their brush skills. Tourists would invariably leave the park with shiny shoes and a new outfit that Dame Edna Everage would eschew for being too over the top.

The large number of tourists didn't bother us. (Nor did the packs of iridescent women. They seemed to innately sense that we weren't in the market for an embroidered waistcoat – the GND had already blown her budget for inappropriate ethnic clothing in Oaxaca – and gave us a wide berth.) We had suspected that Antigua would be like this, in fact, we had counted on it. We wanted to be somewhere with a large tourist population so that a) we could be sure of finding a phone to ring our families for Christmas and b) we could be sure of finding a place serving a traditional Christmas lunch. And in Antigua, we found both.

We also found the good folk of Antigua celebrating Christmas in their own indomitable fashion. In the few days before Christmas the streets literally echoed with the crackle of fireworks. Sometimes it was a string of bungers exploding, setting off car alarms and sending skittish cats clambering up trees. At other times it was fizzing rockets, ricocheting of shop windows and very nearly taking the eye out of a passing shopper. Every shop had pine needles scattered on the floor and was decorated with tinsel and fairy lights that played Christmas carols using annoying electronic beeps.

'That smell reminds me of Christmas back home,' the GND said wistfully, the scrunch of pine needles underfoot. 'We always had a real Christmas tree.'

It was the stone fruit down at the market that reminded me of Christmas back home. In Australia, fruit like peaches, apricots, nectarines and cherries are at their best at Christmas and a bowl full of them was always a centrepiece on our Christmas table.

My favourite part of Christmas in Antigua, however, was the rapping Santa at the appliance shop across from our hotel. He played a tape of Christmas carols in a ghettoblaster at levels that could still be heard over the incessant fireworks and would dance to them in an inappropriate hip hop manner. During the Spanish version of 'Jingle Bells', he would lean back with his arms folded. When someone walked past he would point at them like he was Puffy Coombs. During 'Santa Claus is Coming to Town' he would try and do that dance where your arms form a rubbery wave. My favourite, and a dance he only attempted rarely, was when he tried spinning on his head. His hat and his beard would end up tangled.

When it was Christmas Eve in Antigua it was already Christmas back home in Australia. So after watching the Antigua Christmas Parade, a collection of wagons bearing statues of the Virgin Mary lit by fluorescent tubes powered by noisy generators hidden in hay bales underneath Mary, we went to the phone office to call home. After a few attempts, Guatel not being one of the world's most efficient telcos, I got to speak to all of my nieces and nephews and hear who got the Tickle Me Elmo and who got the rollerblades when they really wanted a Nintendo. They were all excited about spending Christmas together and were still hyper from ripping open presents. After reassuring my mother that we didn't have cholera and our Christmas dinner wouldn't be Hurricane Mitch ration packs, I hung up, a little sad. It was beautiful here in Antigua, but for a moment I wished I was back in Queensland with my family.

The GND called her family too. They were all together as well – her mother, father, brother, grandparents – sharing a big Christmas lunch in Wollongong. Her brother had lived in Spain for a year, so he wished us a merry Christmas in Spanish – Feliz Navidad. Her mother asked if she was eating properly and her father, no doubt aware of his daughter's spendthrift ways, asked if we had enough money. The GND, a little teary, assured them she was fine on both counts.

Our spirits were raised when we cut through Parque Central on the way back to our hotel. The park was lit with fairy lights and the giant Christmas tree that sat outside the cathedral seemed brighter and cheerier. Couples strolled by, rugged up against the cold, stopping occasionally to smooch or to listen to the mariachi band that had set up near the fountain. The band looked brilliant. They all wore black suits and white frills, like in *The Three Amigos*, and each and every one of them had a wispy moustache. They took requests, and didn't mind a group of people from Guatemala City singing along and dancing in front of them.

The GND and I stopped and watched them for a while. 'This is what I imagined Christmas would be like here,' said the GND, taking my arm. It was what I had hoped it would be like too.

❖　　❖　　❖

We spent Christmas morning opening the presents we had bought each other and listening to a tape that we had bought together. The GND gave me a new wallet, a Mayan surfer-style one, with Velcro strips for easy opening. (I took this to mean that the GND felt my wallet wasn't opening fast enough.) In turn I gave the GND a Che Guevara T-shirt – a sly dig at the fixation she had developed with Che since hitting Central America. The tape was by Shakira, a Latin Alanis Morissette, whose song 'Ciega,

Sordomuda' we had heard on every bus we had travelled on and in every restaurant we had eaten in.

On listening to the entire Shakira tape it was probably a rash purchase. I should have known better really. I have an entire shelf of cassettes from my travels that I played once and never played again. Cassettes that I had hoped would take me back instantly to where I'd bought them from but instead have me vowing never to go back again. Kanda Bongo Man's *Greatest Hits* from Zaire, *20 Dangdut Hits* by various artists on the Blackboard Label from Indonesia, *Pump up the Bangra* from India and a tape by Ajda Pekkan, a Turkish chanteuse, that I had bought purely on her cute picture on the cover. (I never got past the first song on that one.)

We were having Christmas lunch with a middle-aged Canadian couple called Pat and Barb we had met a couple of days earlier in the Connexion Internet Cafe. Antigua was dotted with Internet cafes, and apart from Parque Central and a few of the bars popular with Spanish language students, they were the places you were most likely to come across fellow travellers. Pat and Barb were travelling through Central America for three months and had only discovered the joys of e-mail since hitting the road. A young American guy they had met in Oaxaca showed them how to sign up for a Yahoo! Mail account and they were hooked. They wrote to people back home, pestering them for their e-mail addresses, or swapped e-mail addresses with people they met on their travels. They used e-mail to organise drinks with us at the Macondo Pub, and used it again to give us the details of Christmas lunch at Masala Cafe – 12 o'clock sharp, Christmas Day. Bring an appetite.

Christmas lunch would be the first time we had been 'out' on our trip, so the GND decided to celebrate the occasion by doing her hair and putting on some makeup. For convenience – and because it didn't really matter what she looked like in Central America – the GND had taken to just pulling her hair back into a ponytail and stepping out sans makeup. So when she emerged from the bathroom on Christmas Day, the transformation was quite startling.

'What do you think?' she asked, obviously rather pleased with how she had scrubbed up.

After two months of seeing her without makeup, I thought she looked like a Russian prostitute. My appearance-filtering device (the one that instinctively tells guys to answer 'No!' when asked 'Does my bum look big in this?', no matter what the 'this' is) must have short-circuited that day, because that's exactly what I told her.

'Gee thanks!' she said. 'Remind me to be as sympathetic the next time you ask me if I think your hairline is receding.'

In retrospect, Russian prostitute was probably a bit harsh. I simply got the same feeling seeing the GND wearing makeup after two months as I did every time I saw a picture of JonBenet Ramsey, the six-year-old beauty queen who was murdered. The makeup and big hair just looked wrong. Of course, no good would have come of that comparison either. I should have simply said she looked lovely.

Needless to say, Christmas lunch ended up being a little strained. The GND took every opportunity to remind me of my tactless comments. 'You don't think it's a little overdone, do you, Peter?' she'd say as the turkey was carved and placed on our plates. 'And this plum sauce, the colour doesn't startle you, does it?' I smiled weakly, trying to pretend it was all part of an in-joke, but Pat and Barb sensed the tension. As soon as they had finished their traditional plum pudding they made their excuses and left. We couldn't even tempt them with our offer of genuine Guatemalan apple champagne back at our room.

Perhaps that was why the GND didn't look favourably on my idea of climbing Volcán Pacaya the next day. Pacaya was an active volcano close to Antigua, and many of the travel agents offered walking tours to the crater. What concerned the GND, however, was that Pacaya had erupted only a week or so before – nothing serious, spitting up just enough ash to close Guatemala City airport for a couple of days – and was a popular hangout for bandits keen on liberating a few cameras and camcorders.

'So let me get this right,' the GND said when I suggested it. 'You want to climb a volcano that erupted only a few days ago and is a well-known haunt of thieves. Are you crazy?'

I tried to rationalise with her. The fact that the volcano had erupted recently made it less likely to erupt when we were climbing it. And if we climbed the volcano as part of one of the tours organised in Antigua, not only would we get a lift straight to the top of the trailhead, we would also be accompanied to the crater by an armed guard.

'An armed guard?' she cried. 'That just means that if the thieves attack there'll be shooting. We'll probably get caught in the crossfire.'

As a last resort I told the GND that she was just being lazy. I knew that was hitting a raw nerve and only ever used it in emergencies. She didn't talk to me for the rest of the evening, but only after agreeing to climb Pacaya the next day.

Our group was driven to the trailhead at the tiny village of San Francisco in a beat-up transit van by a guy who looked like he'd had one too many brandy schnapps at the office Christmas party. He dumped us at a small cantina where our guide, Miguel, a thin wiry man in a similar state to the driver, led us to a path that started behind a chicken coop, and disappeared ahead into thick forest.

To the GND, it looked like prime bandit country. 'Where's our armed guard?' she asked Miguel.

'The policeman is just having a beer,' he said. 'He'll catch up with us.'

The first part of the climb was a pleasant walk through farmland and then forest. As it got steeper, and the forest thicker, we would occasionally come into a clearing where we could spot the perfectly conical Volcán Agua to our right. After an hour the forest cleared and we came to the base of Pacaya's cone and a valley of grey slag and skeletal tree trunks. It was eerily quiet, the air filled with an oppressive silence that seemed to muffle any sound we made.

'See that patch over there,' Miguel said, pointing to a grey river of cooled lava. 'It's from the eruption ten days ago.'

From here the climb became a torturous scramble through loose black scree in a haze of sulphuric fumes. A sign marked the beginning of the steepest and most difficult stretch. 'Warning!' it read. 'From this point forward you

could be exposed to harmful gases and falling rocks that
can cause injury.'

I was surprised that the warning wasn't followed by the
usual disclaimer that climbers proceeded beyond this point
at their own risk. I suspected that the Guatemalan National
Volcano Authority were woefully underfunded, and figured
that no one would bother suing them for 35 quetzals and
an old typewriter ribbon. Instead it finished with cheerful
news that 'the approximate climbing time to the crater is
30 minutes' – a statement more likely to deter would-be
climbers than threats of rocks and poisonous fumes. It
certainly had that effect on the GND.

'I don't see the sense in doing this,' she moaned. 'What's
at the top anyway? Just smoke by the look of it.'

It didn't help that there weren't any firm footholds now
and that for every step we took we'd slide back three. The
GND grabbed a rock for support and was startled to find
it was hot.

'That's it,' she said. 'I give up!'

I didn't say anything and kept going. This was my first
active volcano and damn it, I was going to get to the top.
In my determination to reach the crater, I lost my footing
and slid back down to a point I'd been at ten minutes
before.

Just below the summit, the volcano changed again, this
time into something like the pictures you'd expect the
Voyager to send back from Jupiter. Now I picked my way
through rocks coated with a yellow sulphuric crust and
through fumes that rushed down from the summit in such
density that I could only see a metre or so ahead. Just as I

was beginning to worry that I may inadvertently stumble over a ledge and into the crater, a strong gust of wind cleared the fumes to reveal our guide sitting on a rock, warning people not to walk to the right of him. I asked him how far it was to the summit.

'Dos minutos mas', (two minutes more), he said, pointing to a thin path among the rocks. He was fibbing. It was still a good ten minutes away.

The summit was a tiny ledge that overlooked the crater. Well, I guessed it overlooked the crater. Thick plumes of noxious fumes billowed up from below the edge, blocking my view and leaving a sickly taste of sulphur at the back of my throat. Not only that, the wind seemed determined to blow me into the crater. Momentarily, it turned its efforts on the gases, clearing the fumes, and for a second I was presented with a magical vista across to Volcán Agua. But then Pacaya would belch again and I couldn't see my hands.

It was a fantastic feeling, all the same, looking into the mouth of an active volcano, if only for a split second, and I was annoyed that the GND had given up so I easily. I turned to leave, determined to say something to her, and insist that the next time we climbed an active volcano she was to accompany me to the top. Then, five metres or so down the path, I came across the GND sitting with our guide. He was digging below a rock with a stick to show her some lava.

'Cool view, eh?' she said, pointing back up at the ledge. She'd been standing right beside me and I hadn't even seen her.

◙ ◙ ◙

A couple of days later we packed our bags and caught a bus to the resort town of Panajachel on Lake Atitlán. We had missed the only direct bus to Panajachel. It left at 7.15 in the morning, a time the GND had declared too early. Instead, we caught a bus to Chimaltenango and the Interamericana and waved down a bus heading west to the lake. The bus had originated in Guatemala City, and in the fine tradition of third-world bus services had not left according to timetable, but only when it was physically impossible to squeeze any more people on. By the time we waved it over it had picked up a few more passengers, a pig or two and the entire output of a craft village. Somehow, somewhere, we were expected to get on.

Being a blonde, and an attractive one at that, the GND was able to get a seat, albeit between two Guatemalan hippies. One was long and thin, with dark hair down his back, a pointy beard and enough amulets around his neck to sink a ship. His friend, a chubby round guy, wore a large flowing caftan. They passed a bottle of wine between them and snickered in that Beavis and Butthead manner that anyone who has had half a dozen cones invariably falls into. But at least the GND was sitting. I was jammed in a solid wall of humanity.

Eventually I was offered a tiny bit of space on a seat. In all honesty, it would have been more comfortable to stand, but an Indian family had squeezed together to let me sit and it would have been rude to refuse their generosity. I sat down – well, a small portion of my right buttock did –

and spent the rest of the journey painfully balancing and squatting.

Every now and then, when an entire family alighted or a standing passenger shifted onto another foot, I was able to catch a glimpse of the scenery outside the window – maize fields up mountain sides, corncobs drying on tin roofs, people wandering around in outfits in retina-searing colours. It was like we had been sucked into a Discovery Channel special on the Mayan world.

Just after Los Encuentros we turned off the Interamericana and wound down a steep mountain road towards Panajachel and Lake Atitlán. Now the road went through pine forests, with occasional glimpses of the lake and the volcanoes surrounding it. Finally, we came upon Panajachel.

The Guatemalans have nicknamed Panajachel 'Gringo-tenango', Place of Foreigners. During the sixties and seventies it was a hangout for hippies, a Central American equivalent of Kathmandu. And like Kathmandu, it still trades off that legacy with hundreds of ethnic clothing stalls and restaurants lining Calle Santander, the road leading down to the lake.

As we walked down the road looking for a room, Indian women, wearing the stunning blue huipiles (blouses) native to this area, flashed textiles at passing tourists, all the while delicately balancing bundles of cloth on their heads. A tourist, his hair dyed the same blue and wearing heavily embroidered clothes, rollerbladed past us. It was a weird juxtaposition, but typical of Panajachel.

We found a room, nothing flash, but cheaper than any other room we'd had in Guatemala, and made our way down to the lake to watch the sunset. The GND stopped at an ice cream shop and bought herself a cone with two scoops of ice cream. I didn't buy one – I didn't feel like one at the time – but as we walked down the street and I watched the GND devouring hers, I changed my mind and asked if I could have a bite. I was astounded when she refused.

'I asked you if you wanted one,' she slurped. 'If you wanted one you should have bought one.'

I was flabbergasted. This was the same argument I had used every single day of our journey when she asked me for a sip of my drink. I would ask the GND if she wanted a drink, she would say no and I would buy a drink of a size suitable to my thirst. Without fail, before I finished that drink, the GND would ask for a sip. When I asked her why she didn't buy a drink, she would say she wasn't thirsty enough for a whole drink and just wanted a sip.

My friend Sean has long contended that the major soft drink manufacturers should release 'sip' size versions of drinks. He argues that every guy is sick of his girlfriend or wife asking for a sip and would buy one whenever they bought a drink together. It's a good idea and, needless to say, not one currently in vogue in Central America. That aside, what astounded me most were the double standards. Whenever I refused to give the GND a sip of my drink I was called all manner of names, selfish bastard with intimacy problems being perhaps the only printable one.

'An ice cream is different,' argued the GND. 'You don't take a sip, you take a bite. And you've got a big mouth.'

She slurped on the ice cream all the way down to the lake, making murmurs of delight right to the bottom of the cone. I made a promise to myself then that she would never get another sip of my Coca-Cola ever again.

The sunset over the lake was spectacular. Like Antigua, Panajachel is surround by volcanoes and they turned every imaginable hue of blue and mauve as the sun set. The restaurants down near the lake had terraces where the more wealthy visitors could sit and drink cocktails, but the GND and I sat with the rabble on a low concrete retaining wall. Our hippie friends from the bus had set up a small table and were selling trinkets. They smiled and waved their ever-present bottle of wine at the GND.

'You know what would be perfect right now?' the GND said, gazing across at the setting sun. 'An ice cold bottle of beer.'

I went to a stall just up the hill and bought two.

◼   ◼   ◼

We spent the day of New Year's Eve on a boat trip around the lake. The trip started early so the lake was still, the volcanoes reflected in the platinum sheen of the water. Fishermen threw nets into the lake from canoes. And up on the slopes of the volcano we could spot the tiny figures of farmers planting maize. The maize fields clung to the steep slopes at impossible angles and I felt sorry for those whose task it was to plant and harvest. I hoped that the soil was fertile or why would you bother? When the boat departed I went up the front, and like everyone who has endured *Titanic*, hammed it up by putting my arms out and yelling 'I'm King of the World'. Usually these antics made the GND laugh, but that morning she just gave me a weak smile. I'd like to think that it was because she was tired – cruising colourful ethnic clothing stalls *can* be physically draining – but I suspect that the ice cream incident may have annoyed her more than I had thought.

Our first stop was San Pedro, a tiny village of tiny houses and cobbled streets that wound up a hill. Groups of Mayan women went about their business, squatting beside the road haggling over chickens or bundles of carrots, ignoring us as we passed. For some reason the place was also popular with 'cool' world travellers, who wandered around looking very disaffected. One couple, incredibly brown and looking like they'd just stepped out of a mid-sixties commune, strolled by, he with a guitar, she with a book entitled *Spiritual Literacy*.

From San Pedro the boat followed the shore line to Santiago Atitlán, a village where the traditional lifestyle of the Tzutuhil Maya survives. The road up from the dock, a pretty spot with wooden boats drawn up under weeping willows, was lined with stalls selling carpets, textiles and huipiles. The stalls were run by pushy girls with American accents and a fine line in sales techniques and, in particular, obligation. 'Okay, when you come back,' they'd say when I indicated that I wasn't interested. 'My name is Maria. I'll give you a good price.'

Further up the hill, the tourist stalls gave way to an untidy town of muddy lanes, market stalls and grubby shops. The town was dominated by the church, a huge whitewashed edifice surrounded by cloisters. The walls of the church were lined with wooden statues of saints, all looking rather spiffy in clothes knocked up for them by the local women. One, in a spandex, spangley outfit and a quif, looked uncannily like Elvis during his Vegas period. Rather imaginatively, I christened him Saint Elvis. Up front, just to the left of the pulpit, was a Christmas nativity scene that hadn't been pulled down yet. It was draped with Christmas fairy lights that also played Christmas carols. Somehow, a tinny rendition of 'Rudolph the Red Nosed Reindeer' didn't seem so appropriate.

At every turn – in the church, in the courtyard, in the street – a small child appeared, snot invariably running from their nose, tugging on our clothes and offering to take us to see Maximón. Maximón was Santiago's most famous resident and stayed in a different house each year. We eventually succumbed to the pleading of a young girl who had snot dribbling from both nostrils and let her lead us through narrow twisted lanes to the place he was staying in that year. It was a modest mud-brick place, like the others around it, except for the colourful streamers and bunting. We were told to wait on the veranda while other visitors paid their respects. Then, finally, we were ushered in to meet the great man himself.

Maximón sat on the floor, a huge smouldering cigar hanging from his lips and a bright yellow scarf draped around his shoulders. Before him, the faithful prostrated themselves, lighting candles, giving him money and begging him to help them with their problems. And all the while he sat there motionless, seemingly oblivious to their pleas. We knelt before him too, lighting a candle and asking for his blessing on our trip.

'It's a wooden statue!' hissed the GND.

The GND thought we were coming to visit the town elder, not the wooden effigy of a local deity believed to be a blend of ancient Maya gods, a particularly fierce conquistador called Pedro de Alvarado and the biblical Judas. Worse, she got pissed off that I found it was funny that she had made such a mistake. 'You did that on purpose!' she said angrily. 'You wanted to make me look like an idiot!'

I hadn't. I thought she knew Maximón was a statue – a statue that got to live in a different house each year, smoke cigars and be showered with rum and beer. Perhaps she was upset that he bore such an uncanny resemblance to Michael Jackson.

That night was New Year's Eve and we returned to find Panajachel full of rich kids from Guatemala City driving Dad's new Toyota Camry with a boot full of beer and dance music pumping from the car stereo. They all wore baggy shorts and sat on the bonnet of their cars drinking beer and watching their mates attempting to breakdance. And in the finest Central American tradition, they carried enough fireworks to blow a safe. It was barely sunset, yet already the air was heavy with smoke and the constant crackle of fireworks. Elsewhere, rockets fizzed past with the accuracy of errant Scud missiles, sometimes exploding into the night sky but more often than not ploughing into the door panel of a brand new Japanese car or an unsuspecting gringo's head.

After showering and putting on our best clothes (I had bought a new red striped shirt from a roadside stall especially for the occasion), we stepped back into the fray and battled our way up Calle Santander to the Circus Bar on Calle Los Arboles. We'd found the Circus Bar on our first night in Panajachel. It was dark and smoky, pokey and crowded. The walls were covered with black and white photos of circus performers, and ventriloquist dolls hung from the ceiling. There was always a buzz in the place and on that New Year's Eve it was no different. The tables were full, so we sat at the bar, eating pizza, drinking tequila and clapping along to the two guys playing guitar and belting out Gypsy Kings-style tunes. It was a great raucous, celebratory evening with people dancing between the tables and beside the bar.

The GND decided to have a cigarette and got angry when I tried to talk her out of it. 'It's New Year's Eve, for Christ sake!' she said. 'I'll stop smoking again in the new year.'

She had done so well to stay off the cigarettes so far. I was proud of her and worried that having a cigarette would only give her the taste for it again. When she ignored me and bummed a cigarette off the barman my heart sank, bitter with disappointment. Instead of handling the situation maturely, I took a coaster from the bar and drew a caricature of the GND puffing on a cigarette. I entitled it 'The Incredible Smoking GND' and gave it a voice bubble saying, 'But it's only one puff!' The GND responded in kind, snatching the pen off me and drawing a picture of me brandishing a cross and a bible and saying, 'I am a wowser!'

The evening didn't really pick up after that. We went to a disco across the road where the only other gringo, a guy from Melbourne, was wearing the exact same shirt as me. I sat at a corner table drinking beer, the GND got up on the dance floor, sashaying with an El Salvadorian couple and having exaggerated drags on a cigarette whenever she caught me looking. I would have bailed out well before midnight except that the management had pulled down the security roller door to stop merrymakers from lighting fireworks and throwing them in the middle of the dance floor.

When midnight – and the New Year – finally came, I think I was just staring out onto the street, occasionally distracted from my misery by the 'dink' sound of rockets hitting the window. The GND was getting kisses from her new friends and every other guy on the dance floor, and taking drags on all their cigarettes. In my bad mood I considered going up to her and reminding her that the new year had begun and she should put out the cigarette. Instead I looked out the window at the chaos of celebration. Among it all, one guy, one of the young rich Guatemalans in baggy clothes and a baseball cap on backwards, lit a whole string of fire crackers and danced over the top of them. He danced in that hunched, simian style favoured by rappers, each explosion acting like a strobe light, exaggerating the jerky movements. I had a sinking feeling that things weren't really working out as I'd planned.

CHAPTER THIRTEEN

Quetzaltenango

(Guatemala)

Annoying habit >>> Farting
Culprits >>> GND and Peter

The GND's new year's resolution was to give up smoking again. Mine was to learn Spanish. For over two months now I had been stumbling around Central America aggravating everyone I attempted to speak to with both my simplistic questions and an inability to understand their replies. And that's not to mention the hundreds of people I had unwittingly insulted through a garbled mispronunciation or slip of a twisted tongue.

I had rather hoped that by travelling through countries where Spanish was the mother tongue I would be forced to pick up a little bit of the language along the way. But

English being the international language that it is, the GND and I were able to get by with only a handful of stock Spanish phrases. If a bus driver couldn't understand a word we said, the fact that we were gringos on a bus with a sign that read Panajachel on the front gave him a pretty good idea of where we wanted to go. Similarly, when we turned up at a hotel with our packs on our backs and dripping with sweat, the manager could be pretty certain that it was a room we were after and not a postage stamp. After two months my Spanish language skills amounted to little more than 'Una cerveza, por favor' (One beer, please) and the complementary phrase 'Dónde estan los baños?' (Where is the bathroom?).

Most people who came to Guatemala to learn Spanish studied at schools in either Antigua or Quetzaltenango. Antigua, where every second immaculately restored building seemed to be a Spanish-language school, offered a greater range of courses. Quetzaltenango, a city in the western highlands, had fewer schools but a world-wide reputation for excellence. As we had already been to Antigua and noticed the many opportunities to indulge in a little illicit English-speaking, we decided to take the more extreme approach and brush up our Spanish skills in Quetzaltenango.

Realising that my resolutions have the same life expectancy as a March fly, the GND and I packed our bags and headed off for Quetzaltenango on New Year's Day. It was something I was loath to do – it is never a good idea to try and catch a bus on a public holiday – but I knew that if my dreams of speaking fluent Spanish were ever to be realised I would have to act immediately.

'We've always been lucky with buses,' the GND reasoned as we walked to the bus station. 'We'll probably get one straight away.'

I looked around for wood to knock. It may well have been the case that we were lucky with buses – it did seem like we had been able to stroll up any time of the day and find a bus going where we were going – but the GND was silly to say it out aloud. Those were the kind of thoughts you kept to yourself, especially in Guatemala and especially on a public holiday. I must have found my piece of wood, a tiny sapling beside the road, too late. We spent the morning of New Year's Day waiting for a bus that only took us as far as Los Encuentros, the crossroads town on the Interamericana, only 20 kilometres away.

It didn't get any better at Los Encuentros. As the meeting point for roads heading north to the mountains, east to Guatemala City and west to Mexico, it is normally one of the busiest crossroads in Guatemala. But that day it was quiet and the shanty restaurants that would usually be doling out rice and beans to passing passengers were shuttered. You could embroider an entire huipil in the time between buses. And every one of those buses was going somewhere we didn't want to go.

As if waiting wasn't bad enough, a drunk stumbled up and sat beside me, determined to help me pass the time. Worse, he spoke very good English. 'I like that!' he slurred, pointing at the GND's legs.

The GND had insisted on wearing shorts, despite the chilly highland weather and the fact that every other woman was wearing a thick ankle-length skirt. She wanted to show off her tan – to whom exactly, I wasn't sure – and wouldn't listen to me when I told her that her outfit would be regarded as risqué. She had argued that I was jealous that I didn't tan as well as her, which was true, but only part of the story. I had warned her that wearing shorts would cause problems, and here, in the freezing highlands of Guatemala, I'd found my proof: a drunk guy who thought that leering at my girlfriend would help squeeze $3 out of me.

'It's not much to you,' he argued, still sizing up the GND's legs like a prime cut of meat. 'But it will get me home.'

When I refused to give him the money he asked me where we had been and where we were going.

'You are going to the wrong places,' he pooh-poohed. 'You should come to my village. We have everything you could ever want there. Onions ... broccoli ... potatoes ... '

I made the mistake of interrupting and telling him that if I'd wanted to see a selection of fruit and vegetables I could have saved the airfare and simply wandered down to my local supermarket.

'No, no!' he argued. 'We have twelve things to eat that you don't. I swear.'

If I could have been sure that the guy would have used the $3 to buy a bus fare I would have given it to him. But I suspected that he would simply buy some more maize moonshine and then stumble back to annoy us some more.

'We have apples, pears, cabbages,' he continued, unperturbed. 'And cauliflower, carrots, beans, peas and brussel sprouts.'

'That's only eleven,' I said, counting the first three vegetables he had listed. 'And besides, we have them back home too. Every one of them.'

He looked at me blankly, as only drunks can, and then stumbled off for another drink.

An hour later he returned. He'd had a few more drinks and wanted to get something off his chest. 'I have been in your country,' he slurred, trying to poke me in the chest but missing. 'Your people treated me very bad.'

He thought we were from the US, where he'd spent three unhappy years working as a kitchenhand in a Dallas restaurant. When I told him we were from Australia, his mood lightened considerably. 'Ahhh! Kangaroos!' he cried, putting his hands in front of his chest like paws and jumping about. I thought he was going to claim that they had furry marsupials in his village as well, but instead he continued with his Skippy impersonation by pretending that the front of his trousers was his pouch. Miraculously, the bus came and, ever the kangaroo, he waved us goodbye with his shortened paws.

The bus, like all of the buses we had caught in Guatemala, was a seething mass of humanity. But unlike most of them on this one I actually got a seat. Sure, my thigh only barely touched the seat, but the bus was packed so tightly that I was held suspended above the aisle. Of course, there was always the chance that I would be shaken loose and left sprawled indelicately among the feet of other passengers when the bus hit a pothole. But on the whole, the other passengers acted as a giant shock absorber and I had one of my most comfortable bus rides on the journey so far.

Like Antigua, Quetzaltenango is built under the shadow of volcanoes and is prone to earthquakes. In fact, in the late nineteenth century, at the height of a coffee boom that had brought great prosperity to the city, it suffered the indignity of both an earthquake and volcanic eruption at once. The boom ended and the city was devastated. Only its position at the crossroads of the Pacific Slopes, Guatemala City and Mexico has ensured its continued existence.

Having said that, I liked Quetzaltenango immediately. It was an old colonial town of low buildings and cobbled streets, like Antigua, but it was scruffy and down at heel. Instead of cafes and antique stores it had shoe stores and shops selling second-hand clothes from America. While Antigua's livelihood depended on tourists, in Quetzaltenango they were incidental. And because the town sat high in the Western Highlands it was cooler and, in the mornings, mistier than anywhere we'd been in our travels so far.

The heart of Quetzaltenango is the Parque Centroamérica, a pretty park where the city fathers exhibited grand ambitions via countless neo-classical pillars and pointy obelisks. It is surrounded by grand squat buildings built during the boom times – the town hall, the museum of natural history, a cathedral – and in the south-eastern corner, a bustling market. On the west side of the park was Pasaje Enriquez, a tattered shopping arcade that had once been as elegant as any of the finest arcades in London or Paris. Now it was dusty and largely deserted, home to litter blown off the streets by the cold mountain air, the less than salubrious Tecún Bar, and the Utatlán Spanish School.

The Utatlán Language School had been suggested to us

by an American guy we'd met in Panajachel. He had studied there for a week – the same amount of time we had allowed – and claimed that he was now able to order food in restaurants and converse with locals fluently and with confidence. He wrote a list of the teachers at the school he personally recommended and the families he had heard were the best to stay with.

The list in the end proved useless. When we met with the director of the school to discuss the various courses, we discovered he could only speak Spanish. Preferred teachers and families being beyond our Spanish skills, we listened instead to a no doubt eloquent but to us incomprehensible monologue that may or may not have been about the school, the quality of the teaching staff and its first-rate facilities. Although we were unsure exactly what the various courses he presented us with offered – there was no mention of either beer or baños – we signed up for the 'total immersion' option. For only $US100 (about $A160) each, we would get five hours of one-on-one instruction for five days plus seven days' full board with a local family. After a few phone calls on an old Bakelite phone, the director found a family who could take us both.

Within ten minutes the matriarch of our family arrived. Her name was Catarina and she was a matronly woman in her middle years with a friendly but slightly austere manner. After a few words with the director and the discreet exchange of a plain brown envelope, she led us through the cobbled streets of Quetzaltenango to her home. The entrance wasn't anything special, just another door among a few in a long white wall. But behind it was a maze of warm, cosy rooms, including a huge kitchen with a long table that served as the familial meeting place. Here we were introduced to the rest of the family – the teenage son Carlos, Wilma, the wheelchair-bound aunt, and Rocky, the family Rottweiler – and shown Catarina's Smith Corona Competency Certificate (1956) which had pride of place on a wall covered with family photos.

After dumping our bags in our room – a homely space with separate beds topped with padded quilts and a bedside lamp you'd buy in a kitsch second-hand store – we were immediately served a delicious lunch of spicy vegetable stew. When I asked for the salt in English and I was promptly scolded by Catarina who said that as long as we were under her roof we were to speak only in Spanish.

When we retired to our room for an afternoon nap, the GND came and sat on the edge of my bed. 'I'm not sure that this total immersion thing is such a good idea,' she hissed. 'Unless I learn a few more words I'm going to starve!'

The GND didn't say anything more for the rest of the evening. She was afraid that Catarina may have been lurking outside. The next day I started a journal of our time 'immersed', hoping it would trace our rise from destroyers of the Spanish language to graceful speakers. I present it to you in its entirety:

Day one: Sunday

A special treat today – pancakes for breakfast! After months of subsisting on the Central American staple of rice, chicken and beans, it's like manna from heaven. Catarina and her family off to church – unless hands pressed together have a different meaning in these parts. The GND and I are off on our first extra-curricular activity – a trip to the hot springs at Fuentes Georginas, high in the mountains surrounding Quetzaltenango.

We find that we are the only ones going with Juan, a teacher at the school and designated expedition leader. Juan speaks English fluently, but as we are on total immersion, refuses to speak anything other than Spanish. Already my head feels as though it is about to explode.

Luckily, the route is spectacular and leaves us all speechless. We hitch a ride on the back of a pick-up truck past mountain-side fields tended by women in incredibly colourful embroidered clothes. As it gets steeper and higher, the fields give way to lush jungle, hidden in clouds. A sulphur smell alerts us to fact that hot springs are near. We arrive to find the whole of Quetzaltenango camped there for the day, sitting in the pool and on the rocks around it like the monkeys at the start of the movie *Baraca*. I sit in the pool but am disturbed by the sensation of hot water bubbling under my bum.

We return for a light dinner – a delicious stew and tamales. After we tell our hostess that the day was 'bueno', the table descends into silence. We excuse ourselves and have an early night. School starts tomorrow.

Day two: Monday

We are assigned teachers. Mine is a young university graduate called Mayra. The GND notes that she is the prettiest teacher in the school, but I say I hadn't noticed, I am here to learn.

I spend my first day pronouncing the alphabet and expanding my vocabulary to include most household items, parts of the body and anything else visible from desk.

Today's activity is a visit to Almolonga, a small village in the hills just behind Quetzaltenango. Juan takes us through market gardens pointing out carrots, radishes and cauliflowers and then telling us their names in Spanish. The fields are owned and worked by entire families – from grandmas right down to toddlers – and are irrigated by hand by scooping water with a wooden shovel from nearby canals and flinging it across the field. Everyone stops working to listen to our lessons and laugh at our poor pronunciation.

The excursion ends in medicinal hot baths nearby. I begin to wonder if Juan has a thing about seeing foreign language students in bathers.

My plan to impress our host family by naming every vegetable on the dish at evening meal is dashed when we are served chicken, beans and rice. I am tempted to recite alphabet but decide instead to eat meal in silence. Retire to room and break wind. The GND says none of her other boyfriends farted in front of her. I blame the beans.

Day three: Tuesday

Mayra greets me with a smile and then proceeds to grill me on my vocabulary before moving on to regular verbs in the present tense.

The afternoon activity is a visit to the tiny village of San Andre. Classic Mayan terrain – maize fields up steep mountains, orange corn still on the cob, drying on roofs, and a bright yellow church. At the back of the town Juan points out Mayan 'temple' where a shaman is waving burning incense and a chicken over a small child. Presumably the child is sick and the chicken will soak up the illness before being sacrificed. Either that or the chicken is sick and the child will be sacrificed. Regardless, the absence of Coca-Cola in the ritual does not augur well for the recovery of either.

Day four: Wednesday

More verbs, all regular (thank goodness), all in the past tense. I feel better now that I can form sentences about what I have done rather than what I am doing.

I sneak out to the Internet cafe across the hall and discover that my youngest sister has had another ultrasound. I don't tell Mayra, but not because she'll punish me. It's just that the whole concept of giving birth is way beyond my Spanish at the moment. Besides, it would entail expanding my vocabulary to include parts of the body I'm not sure I could use at the dinner table.

Lunch with our family, however, is unusually chatty. I'm able to say that I received an e-mail from my sister and studied regular verbs. The afternoon activity is watching Jeremy Irons speaking dubbed Spanish in *The Mission*. I feel a little sorry for the native Indians he was trying to convert. I didn't understand a word either, and I'd had 15 hours of Spanish lessons.

Day five: Thursday

A brisk, cold morning, on which we walk to school in mist

and I decide I like Quetzaltenango a lot. The tiny square, the cobbled streets, even the old American school buses, look quaint. Mayra begins the lesson by giving me a piece of fruit called a granata, which she had tried to describe the day before. Turns out to be a passionfruit – I decide not to tell the GND.

Back to the Internet cafe and find another e-mail from home, this time entitled 'It's a boy!'. I'm an uncle for the sixth time. I tell Mayra and we put aside regular verbs in the present tense for a moment to discuss our families . . . in Spanish. It is fun and enlightening, and for the first time felt I was communicating with a Guatemalan about their life. Unfortunately, Mayra spoils it all by telling me I have an exam tomorrow.

Dinner goes cold as I entertain the hosts with a long and detailed discussion of my sisters, their children and my childhood. Catarina looks on with a matronly smile. I would bask in glory of effortless communication but I have an exam tomorrow. I am distracted from my studies by the GND breaking winding. Despite her best efforts she is no longer able to keep them in.

Day six: Friday

Mayra spends the first part of morning reviewing what I have learned. I skip the Internet cafe and use my half-hour break to study. It pays off. The exam is a cinch and I get 100 per cent. Mayra tells me I am very intelligent, but I suspect that she deliberately made the exam easy. I enjoy a chatty lunch with the family before retiring, exhausted, for an afternoon nap.

Day seven: Saturday

Our week of Spanish lessons concludes with a special dinner at the school, prepared and served by our teachers. The director gives a long and rambling speech and I'm surprised by how much I understand, considering how many Gallo beers I've had. I accept my certificate with a tear in my eye and make a speech in Spanish thanking the school, my teacher, my family and – like American performers at the Grammy Awards – Dios (God).

We adjourn to the Tecún Bar and party with our fellow students from Denmark, Holland, and Switzerland, talking Spanish under the misapprehension that we are being understood. Things must be better between me and the GND because two Dutch girls insist they are coming to our wedding, which they say can only be a couple of months away. The night ends when I pass out in corner of the bar, clutching my certificate, muttering in Spanish.

CHAPTER FOURTEEN

Guatemalan Highlands

Annoying habit >>> Skewed priorities
Culprit >>> GND

With our competency certificates tucked securely under our arms, the GND and I decided to put our new found language skills to the test with a long hard trawl through central Guatemala to the Caribbean Coast at Lívingston. We had been dawdling in Guatemala, celebrating the festive season and learning Spanish, hoping that in that time the worst of the damage caused by Mitch would be repaired. Now it was time to see if it had been.

Studying Spanish had given us a break from each other as well. Before we reached Quetzaltenango we had been with each other 24 hours a day, seven days a week. But studying had given us a precious five hours a day apart. As a result, the GND seemed less irritated with me. It would be interesting to see if the détente lasted.

My language skills immediately fell apart at Quetzaltenango's sprawling bus station. Drivers were revving their engines, huge bundles were being lifted onto the top of buses and touts were running from one new arrival to another, trying to get them on their bus. We were heading to Chichicastenango, a mountain market town only 94 kilometres away, and now that I had learned Spanish grammar I wanted to ask a perfectly formed question, in the correct tense.

The words for bus (autobús) and Chichicastenango (Chichicastenango) were easy enough. And I knew the word for where (dónde). But I struggled on the form of 'is'. Was it está? Or están? The tout I had collared was getting agitated, watching potential passengers being taken by other touts, as I mumbled in Spanish, trying out each alternative to determine which one sounded right. He gave me the kind of look that said, 'This is costing me money, you silly gringo.'

'Just ask him!' said the GND, a little annoyed.

For the sake of expediency and our relationship, I abandoned a week of total immersion and slipped back into pidgin Spanish. 'Autobús. Chichicastenengo. Dónde?' I blurted out.

It wasn't very elegant but it worked. The tout understood what I was saying and pointed us towards an old school bus already incredibly packed. I vowed then that next time I would have my questions formed well before I asked them.

Chichicastenango is the most famous market town in Guatemala, a charming place of winding streets, white houses and red-tiled roofs that wander over a little hill set in a cup-shaped valley. It is named after the chichicaste, a purple prickly plant that grows there profusely, but it is best known for its Thursday and Sunday markets, when the plaza is overrun by Indians from the mountain villages surrounding the town keen to sell their wares.

We arrived the evening before the Sunday market. It was cold, smoky and quiet, but there was a gentle buzz in the air around the town plaza as villagers from the surrounding hills set up stalls, laying out their goods before bedding down underneath them.

One guy selling wooden figures waved us over and tried to sell us a crappy carving of Saint John. 'Tomorrow two 'undred dollars,' he said in stilted English. 'Tonight only two 'undred quetzal.'

We thanked him and moved on. To be honest, after Antigua and Panajachel, wooden effigies of saints and brightly coloured huipiles had lost their appeal.

It wasn't any better the next day, market day. We wandered the cobbled streets in a daze, among the hundreds of stalls selling bags and statues and shawls, looking at things more out of obligation to our duty as gringo tourists than from a real desire to buy anything.

Having said that, a few things did spark our interest that day in Chichicastenango. The evangelist running the Christian karaoke out the back of the markets was good for a few laughs. And the flower sellers on the steps of Santo Tomás church, the colour of their flowers and huipiles muted by the smoke of burning juniper bushes, were suitably picturesque. And the GND was particularly taken by the kitchens in the middle of the markets, huge cauldrons surrounded by bench tables, doling out basic tucker for the villagers who had come to town for the markets.

Not that the locals had to worry too much about our disinterest in their handiwork, anyway. A constant stream of coaches arrived throughout the day bringing in willing consumers on day trips from Antigua and Panajachel. They wandered around with their video cameras and zoom lenses, and a seemingly unending supply of deutschmarks, francs and dollars. We did a circuit through the markets, soaking up the colour and movement before heading back to our room, on the way stepping over the inordinate number of men who had come to town specifically to drink heavily and then pass out in a pool of their own vomit.

Our room didn't have an attached bathroom, but it did have cable – the manager looping a wire from his room along the balcony, poking it under our door and then into the back of a television. We spent the rest of our time in Chichicastenango watching a succession of crappy movies – *Chaplin, Frantic, Florida Straits,* and *The Assassin* – and catching up with the latest news about Hurricane Mitch.

At last, the news was good. Shocked by the horrific images on their TV screens, the international community had responded with billions of dollars worth of aid. The UN World Food Program announced it was sending more than 100,000 tons of rice, corn, fish and oil to the region. The Paris Club of Creditor Nations said it would grant debt relief to Honduras and Nicaragua, allowing funds that would otherwise be used to pay loans to be diverted towards rebuilding infrastructure. Doctors from Cuba had brought a dangerous cholera epidemic under control in Nicaragua. The Americans had sent in the marines to repair roads and bridges in Honduras and Nicaragua. Elsewhere, the CNN reports showed people shovelling mud, picking through belongings, and getting on with their lives. It was time for us to get a wriggle on too.

The first part of our journey towards the Caribbean – the 19 kilometres to Quiché – went smoothly enough. It was a half-hour journey down a winding road to a valley where a river passed through pine trees, beside grassy picnic spots blighted by rubbish left by families. Quiché itself, despite its alluring name, was just another dusty town with a muddy bus station.

It was here that our plans – and our new period of détente – started falling apart. The bus to Uspantán, the next port of call on our trawl, didn't leave for another three hours. We wandered through the markets looking at tools made in China and cheap watches from Taiwan. There wasn't a carved mask or bright shirt in sight, just cheap shampoo and a handcream with the unfortunate name of 'Outbreak'. We returned to the bus station 40 minutes before the bus was due to leave, only to find that enterprising locals had reserved all the seats by either sitting in them or roping them off with clothes – jumpers or jeans.

The delay had put the GND in a bad mood and left her disinclined to stand up during another Guatemalan bus journey. I undid a pair of jeans tied from one bench seat to another and motioned for her to sit down.

'But it's been reserved,' she said, looking anxiously around. 'You might cause an international incident!'

Frankly, I didn't care. The thought of standing up on a bus with its suspension shot didn't appeal to me either. If our seat robbery caused too much of a commotion, we could get up and beg off as dumb tourists. When the guy who had reserved the seat returned he complained to the driver but the driver just laughed. With that laugh relations between Guatemala and Australia were saved and, more importantly, we got to spend the trip on our bums, not our feet.

It is only 90 kilometres from Quiché to Uspantán and the first 50 kilometres north to Sacapulas went quickly and comfortably. At Sacapulas the bus stopped at a small food stall, just on the other side of the Río Negro, where everyone got off the bus and stocked up with drinks, food and biscuits. The GND asked why they were stocking up when Uspantán, the bus's final destination, was only 40 kilometres away. If the bus continued at the rate it did to Sacapulas – 50 ks in just over an hour – we'd be in Uspantán before they'd get a chance to eat it all.

'Must be cheaper here,' I said, watching one woman stockpile enough food to see her through the millennium bug crisis.

Four hours later, when the bus finally staggered into Uspantán, we were tired, cranky and hungry. Lying as it does at the end of one of the worst stretches of road we had come across in Guatemala, Uspantán does not have a lot going for it. Rigoberta Menchú, the 1992 Nobel Peace Prize laureate, grew up in these parts and her award-winning autobiography describes the hardships growing up here and the atrocities committed against her people by the Guatemalan military. She was currently in the news in Guatemala for supposedly making up parts of her autobiography, and that day I wondered if it was a section that described her home town as charming and delightful. When we arrived in Uspantán a cold grey mist had descended on the town, muffling sound and deadening our spirits.

There was a pick-up truck waiting to take passengers on to Cobán, the capital of the Alta Verapaz district, and still a good distance away. Even though we'd just spent the good part of a day travelling just over 100 kilometres, I was keen to keep going. Cobán was a large town, so I figured we'd get the hard travelling done and then take a break in a place big enough to have hotels with hot water and a Campero Fried Chicken outlet. Sure, we'd have to sit in the back of a beat-up Ford F100 among bags of onions and unprotected by the elements, but in six hours' time we'd be tucking into some southern fried chicken.

The GND refused to continue. 'I don't mind travelling on the back of trucks, but not when it's cold, raining or too uncomfortable,' she said. 'And besides, I'm hungry.'

From what I could gather the only other way to get to Cobán was on a once-a-day bus that left at three in the morning. We'd found a truck going to Cobán – right here, right now. It has been my experience that you don't refuse those sorts of offers. 'You don't want an adventure,' I spat. 'You want a *Women's Weekly* discovery tour.'

I don't know whether it was because I was hungry and tired too, but the GND's refusal to go any further made me furious. 'What are we going to tell people when they ask about our trip,' I continued. '"When the GND was hungry, she ate. When she was thirsty, she drank. And when she was tired, she slept."'

When the GND still refused, I suggested a compromise. 'How about we find the bus and sleep on it?' I asked. 'That way we save on accommodation and we don't have to worry about sleeping in and missing tomorrow's bus.'

But the GND wasn't having a bar of it. She wanted a room. She wanted food. And she wanted it now. After checking into a basic hotel that didn't have hot water, we found a small restaurant, Comedor Kevin's, and ate in silence. Usually I would have pointed out all the calendars on the wall, made a crack about the owner's wife being a real calendar girl. Normally I would have said something about how good and cheap the food was, and would have suggested we bought one of the delicious Madeira cakes to take with us. But I didn't. I was too angry.

The GND wasn't in the best of moods either. I have a photo of her that afternoon, standing in front of the concrete music bowl in Uspantán's Central Park, the mist shrouding the whitewashed church behind her. She looks tired, irritable and like she's about to strangle me. It pretty much sums up how bad things were that afternoon.

It wasn't any better at 2.30 the next morning when we were waiting on a street corner beside the bus, hugging ourselves against the cold, waiting for the driver, who we could see sleeping, to stir. The GND and I stood silent, refusing to talk to each other, as a small crowd of passengers gathered, shuffling from one foot to the other, talking in muffled tones, greeting each newcomer with a bright 'buenos días'. Finally, there were a few clunks and shuffles on the bus and the driver settled behind the seat and started the engine. He opened the door and we clambered aboard.

The bus drove through the dark streets of Uspantán, picking up people who stood under streets lamps waiting. I've always loved journeys that start before dawn. When I was a kid we started our holidays by being bundled into the back of a car at three or four in the morning. Dad had said it was to miss traffic, but I think it was because he knew that after bickering a little we'd all fall back to sleep and give him a good four hours of peaceful driving without plaintive cries of 'Are we nearly there yet?' It was the same that morning. I spent most of it sleeping fitfully, waking occasionally when the bus stopped to pick up passengers, most of whom had lit fires beside the road to keep themselves warm.

When dawn came, so too did a different Guatemala. In the darkness we had passed from chilly highlands to a more tropical, fecund mountain environment. This was coffee country now – neat, green and dotted with huge estates or fincas. Towns like Santa Cruz Verapaz buzzed like they had just enjoyed a morning long black, bustling with the energy that money brings. The roads were better, the houses neater. Coffee had bought affluence. So too had cardamom, the reed-like stuff with white spiky flowers, that lined the road and in which Guatemala was the world's largest exporter. When we turned onto the main road coming up from

Guatemala City, it was smooth and freshly tarmaced and lined with billboards.

Cobán was a large bustling town nestled in pretty mountains and with a hints of Germanic architecture that were more in keeping with Bavaria than Guatemala. The Teutonic influence came from the German immigrants who moved here in the nineteenth century and founded the huge coffee plantations that surrounded the town. Many were Nazi sympathisers and were kicked out after pressure from the US during the Second World War, but there is still more than a little touch of the lederhosen in Cobán.

Nowhere more so than the Café El Tirol where the GND and I had breakfast that morning. Set in an old finca, with views over the back of the town towards the plantations, you could imagine the plantation commandant keeping a close eye on his Indian workers, barking out orders when they slackened off. The GND spoiled herself with a western breakfast and was delighted when it was served in the order she liked – granola first, toast second and coffee last.

While the GND had a full belly and was still in a good mood, I suggested that we keep on going rather than stay in Cobán. I argued that the night in Uspantán had put us behind schedule (that we had a schedule was news to the GND but, to her credit, she didn't comment). After checking our e-mail we headed to the bus terminal to tackle the next stage of our grand journey, a six-hour bus ride to Fray Bartolomé de las Casas.

It was a journey that took us through the coffee plantations of the mountains, dotted with grand homesteads at the end of long driveways lined by palm trees, down to the hot plains below, where the villages were little more than a collection of wooden shacks. We stopped at one such village for lunch, and when the GND inquired where the toilet was, she was startled to discover that the village didn't have one and she would have to use the banana plantation out the back. I remembered visiting the Big Banana at Coffs Harbour on the New South Wales north coast when I was a kid and the guide telling us that snakes liked to hang out under fallen banana trees and would nip the heels of the banana pickers.

'Great,' she said. 'Not only do I have to worry about someone walking in on me, I might get bitten on the bum by a snake as well.'

I am happy to report that neither happened and the bus was able to continue on its way without having to wait for an embarrassing snakebite treatment to be performed. The countryside now looked like that around Tenosique in Mexico. The plains had been cleared for cattle and were dotted with swamps popular with white egrets that flapped lazily away as we passed. But where we had passed the odd pick-up truck or a lone horseman beside the road in Mexico, here the land was largely deserted.

Fray Bartolomé de las Casas wasn't much livelier. It wasn't quite a town – just a road, a park and a collection of shacks – and its existence was totally reliant on a cross-road where another road branched off and headed north to Poptún. We stayed in a dilapidated hotel with small airless rooms looking onto a courtyard that was muddy and bare. A deer was kept in a miry enclosure out back and guinea pigs skittered about wherever they damn well pleased. It wasn't the most salubrious of places, but it was the best that Fray Bartolomé de las Casas offered. And besides, we where only staying until the next bus left for Modesto Méndez, the next step of our journey.

When we asked the owner if he knew when the bus to Modesto Méndez left he said 2 am in a questioning tone that suggested he wasn't altogether sure. As we left the hotel in search of a second opinion he called after us again, this time proffering 7.30 am as the right answer.

Over the course of that afternoon we asked the same question of a number of the citizens of Fray Bartolomé de las Casas and, alarmingly, each of them gave a different answer. The constable down at the local police station was sure it left at 7 am and pointed out the spot where he thought it left from. The shopkeeper at the shop closest to that spot said it left at 8 pm. The priest from the church at the end of the road was certain the bus left at 8 am. That night, as we ate in one of the town's restaurants – the GND regretting she ordered beef when she saw the cook walk in with a slab of meat covered in flies – we got a different answer from each of the staff. In the end we decided to get up at dawn and wait beside the road. By midday we were still waiting.

'This bus is never coming,' whined the GND. 'And I'm dying for a cigarette. I don't know why we came this stupid way. It's not like we've seen anything interesting.'

I bit my tongue. It's true, it hadn't been postcard vistas and we'd had to endure some of the worst bus rides of our journey so far. But it had been an adventure. We'd seen parts of Guatemala that most travellers, quite sensibly it would seem, avoid. I'd hoped that the GND would have seen it the same way, and got the same feeling that I did – that we'd actually achieved something. Instead it seemed that she felt I'd just been throwing up unnecessary obstacles.

'I hadn't even thought of smoking before we came to this crappy town,' she said. 'I hope you're happy with yourself.'

After that little outburst, we sat beside the road in silence, leaning against our packs, afraid to go and find something to eat just in case the bus came along.

Around 2 pm we spotted a gringo stumbling up the road. He was a burly Irishman, unshaven and wearing a grubby Guinness T-shirt. He was a volunteer worker in these parts, a mechanic, and drove the local school bus. I asked him if he knew when the bus left.

'The bus to Modesto Méndez, you say,' he said scratching his ginger growth. 'I'd 'ave thought that would be past by now.'

He sat down beside us with a look on his face that suggested he was either concentrating or suffering from indigestion. Suddenly he broke from whatever it was and jumped to his feet.

'There it is,' he said, pointing to a cloud of dust only 200 metres away. 'Wave to it! Stop it!'

I jumped out and the bus came shuddering to a halt a further 300 metres down the road past us.

'You're lucky ones, to be sure,' he grinned, helping us with our bags. 'It only comes once a day.'

Indeed we were. Another day in Fray and I'm sure only one of us would have walked away alive.

The bus had started its journey in Sayaxché, over 100 kilometres away, but didn't have a single passenger on board. Every single seat was broken, most reclined fully, and many of the windows were missing or replaced by plastic sheeting that had since become tattered and torn. Any window that was left was cracked and the whole vehicle, including the driver and his conductor, was covered in dust. The good news, however, was that the bus was going beyond Modesto Méndez and all the way to Río Dulce, the town where we hoped to catch a boat up to Lívingston and the Caribbean coast.

It didn't take long to see why the bus was in the state it was. Just outside of Fray Bartolomé de las Casas the road deteriorated into the worst stretch we'd seen in our journey so far. It was corrugated, potholed and dusty and shook my fillings loose. When we came upon stretches where it had rained recently, it was muddy and boggy. By the time we finally hit tarmac at Modesto Méndez the GND and I were shaken, stirred and basted. The road was a pussy now, winding gently past huts with neat gardens and startling tropical flowers, and the GND stared out the window in a catatonic state. When we finally reached Río Dulce she had to be physically shaken from her funk.

There are two Río Dulces – the dusty, chaotic town also known as Fronteras and the spectacular waterway it backs onto. Our plan was to catch a boat up that waterway to Lívingston, a tiny settlement on the Caribbean Sea. Our problem was that the only way we could get there was to take a 'tour'. Río Dulce was once home to pirates who marauded throughout the Caribbean, and the ruins of a

Spanish fort they destroyed is only three kilometres away at San Felipe. The pirates' legacy, it seems, lives on in the motor boat owners hanging around the docks of Río Dulce.

The 'tour' wouldn't leave until there were enough passengers to fill the boat. The GND didn't mind. The boats left from the Hollymar Restaurant, a place popular with the yachties, who moored around these parts because the chef's culinary repertoire extended beyond the customary beans, chicken and rice.

The GND ordered a pizza and nearly passed out in anticipation. 'God I'm looking forward to this!' she said licking her lips. 'If I had to eat another plate of beans and rice I would have really been in a bad mood.'

As is the way of things, the pizza arrived at precisely the same time that the boat captain decided that there were enough people to fill his boat and ensure a US college education for his children. The staff at Hollymar kindly put the pizza in a box and we took our spot on the speedboat. It powered off majestically, and soon Río Dulce, the dusty, crappy town, was a spec behind us.

The boat clipped along at a fair rate of knots, scaring birds and fishermen alike. Its velocity made it difficult for the GND to eat her pizza. Each time she lifted a slice to her mouth, the wind would whip it into her face and then snatch it out of her hand, leaving only a greasy blob of mozzarella on her nose. It was hilarious, but I dared not laugh.

The GND was close to tears. 'All I want is to eat my pizza,' she said, aggravated. 'Is that too much to ask?'

Luckily our 'tour' included stops at various points of

interest along the waterway, so the GND was able to munch on what was left of her Super Supreme as the boat captain slowed to point them out. These included such 'must-see' spots as Bird Island, a clump of mangrove smack bang in the middle of the lake that was a popular resting spot for all the birds making the long flight across the waterway, and the Hot Springs, a current of hot water that mysteriously appeared close to shore. The GND was able to scoff down most of the pizza before the boat powered off again and passed through the magnificent limestone canyons towering above the lake.

It really was beautiful here and most of the passengers 'oohed' and 'aahed' appropriately. The GND and I probably didn't appreciate the 'tour' as much as we should have – by this stage we just wanted to get to Lívingston. We had been travelling solid for three days, staying in hotels that were lucky to have water, let alone warm water. Having said that, when we finally came through the canyon and into the bay, palm trees tumbling down to the water, my heart leapt a little. We were back on the Caribbean again. But this time we were barely speaking to each other.

CHAPTER FIFTEEN

Caribbean Coast

Annoying habit >>> Seasickness
Culprit >>> Peter

When we arrived in Lívingston a funeral procession was
making its way along the narrow street leading up from
the dock to the cemetery that sat on a hill overlooking the
town. It was a New Orleans-style funeral, with a brass band
leading the way, first playing sombre tunes and then bursting
into more up-tempo numbers, like 'When the Saints Come
Marching In'. The coffin rode in the back of a Japanese
pick-up truck with the closest members of the family sitting
around it on the lip of the tray, sobbing or staring forward
blankly. The other mourners followed, women in dark
dresses and hats, men in their best black suits, shuffling

respectfully. I asked the guy standing next to me, a Spanish-looking fellow, if it would be all right for me to take a photo.

'I don't know, man,' he said. 'These black people have their own culture.'

That culture was Garifuna, and Lívingston was one of the few Garifuna communities in Guatemala. The Garifuna (or Black Caribs) trace their roots back to the Africans brought to the New World by the British as slaves. After the Garifuna revolt of 1795 on St Vincent, they were forcibly resettled on the Honduran island of Roatán and from there they spread out all around the Caribbean coast of Central America, from the Corn Islands of Nicaragua to Belize.

The community in Lívingston was a particularly vibrant one and was reflected in the brightly painted clapboard houses, the markets, the reggae music playing in the bars and in the funeral procession that was passing by. The Garifuna eked out an existence fishing and, from what we had heard, spent their spare time drinking rum and dancing the punta, a sensual and rhythmic dance, believed to be crucial for fertility. Apparently, one would be hard pressed to watch the punta and not have one's mind turn to all things horizontal.

Everyday life in Lívingston was just as lively. Large black women, swathed in colourful dresses, balanced huge plastic bowls full of freshly caught fish on their heads. In the bars and restaurants, rasta boys hung around laughing and joking, dragging on hand-rolled cigarettes of generous proportions and unspecified contents.

This was a different kind of Guatemala, a little bit of the

West Indies in Latin America. It was certainly a Guatemala the GND felt more comfortable in. She ditched the padded jacket she'd bought in Quetzaltenango and put on her little blue swing dress. She was back on the beach and her mood lightened accordingly.

'If I'd known it was going to be like this here I would have caught that truck to Cobán in Uspantán,' she said that night, as we watched a group of kids dancing on the street from an open-air restaurant. 'I don't know why you gave up so easily.'

Thankfully, I noticed the teasing smile before reacting.

■   ■   ■

The next morning we set out for Las Siete Altares, the Seven Altars, a series of freshwater falls and pools about five kilometres north of Lívingston along the coast. It was a pretty walk under palm trees beside the azure water. We passed Garifuna villages of thatched huts and dodged dugout canoes dragged onto the beach and fishing nets that were hanging between trees to dry. In one village we came across the Happy Fisherman Bar. On the outside wall was a mural depicting a fisherman with a fish hanging off his penis. The GND laughed out loud for the first time in a long time. The sun, the sand, the relaxed ambience of the place, was all having a positive effect.

It was quite a walk. Halfway along we had to ford a waist-high river that escaped into the ocean, and at the end of the beach the jungle tumbled right down to the water, forcing us to leave the sand and pick our way along a muddy path and among gnarly tree stumps. It was in here that we found the falls, a collection of pools of extremely chilly water. We swam and laughed and splashed. It was as if the hardships of Central Guatemala had never happened.

We walked back along the beach rejuvenated. Just after we crossed the river, we met a rasta. Like most rastas, he looked like Bob Marley and wore a knitted beanie to keep his dreads out of his eyes. He had been fishing and the fish he had caught were threaded through the gills onto a single strand from a palm leaf. His name was Steve, but his friends, for reasons he didn't elaborate on, called him Lobster Rasta. To prove this fact he pointed out that on his rasta beanie was the word 'lobster' knitted in white. It had been knitted by his girlfriend, a Canadian.

'You wanna buy a fish, mon?' he asked.

We explained that we didn't have anything to cook it on.

'You wanna come up to my place?' he asked. 'I'm clearing a block of land. I'm gonna plant bananas and maize but I won't kill the birds. It's going to be a bird sanctuary.'

We declined, but that wasn't going to stop the Lobster. Being a rasta, it seems, was a multi-skilled profession. 'You want me to play drums?' he continued. 'How about I paint you a picture? There must be something I can do for you.'

I asked if I could take his photo and he readily agreed. After a shot of him on his own, he suggested I take one of him and the GND. At last there was something he could do for us.

'Lay some Qs on me!' he said after posing.

I said there wasn't anything I wanted to know.

'Not questions!' he replied. 'Quetzals! Give me some cold, hard quetzals.'

A rasta, it seems, has to eat.

■   ■   ■

The GND and I spent just over three days in Lívingston doing, well, pretty much nothing. We'd have breakfast at the Happy Fish, their waffles making a pleasant change from the rice and beans of the rest of Guatemala, before spending the day on a palm-fringed beach that overlooked the Caribbean Sea. At night, we'd wander down to the El Malecón or the African Place and enjoy a meal of fresh fish or a local delicacy like tapado, a tasty stew made from fish, prawns, crab, coconut, plantain, banana and a dash of coriander.

After nine weeks of travelling together it finally felt like we were getting to know each other better as well. I knew that the GND liked to spend a couple of hours a day on the beach. And she knew I could handle that as long as we did something energetic, like walk to the waterfall, first. Our time in Lívingston had been wonderfully relaxing, but as tempting as it was to stay there, recharging our batteries and perhaps even taking a shot at learning the punta, it was soon time for us to head off again.

Our destination was Utila, one of the Bay Islands off the Caribbean coast of Honduras. The islands had borne the brunt of Hurricane Mitch, but apparently it was still possible to visit them. There were two ways of getting to Utila from Lívingston: hitching a ride with a yacht from Lívingston or heading back to Puerto Barrios following the notorious 'jungle trail' into Honduras.

The jungle trail seemed to be the preferred option of all the other travellers we met in Lívingston. Lars and Lars, two Swedish guys who camped out the back of a restaurant to save money, were going that way. So were an American couple who seemed to be constantly bickering. Even three Australian medical students heading into Honduras to help out after Mitch had their hearts set on crossing into Honduras along the jungle trail.

I've got to admit, it did sound exciting. The name alone – 'The Jungle Trail' – conjured up all sorts of images of slashing through tangled vines with a machete, monkeys chattering overhead and porters refusing to go any further in fear of upsetting some ancient God. What's more, it involved a boat ride through a marshy swamp. The GND, however, had other ideas. Her heart was set on a yacht trip. 'We've done the river crossing thing back in Mexico,' she argued. 'I'd rather go sailing.'

The idea of a sailing trip in the Caribbean was a terribly romantic one, and if I were to be honest, it was the travel fantasy I had worn out most in my mind all those months ago when the serotonin levels were still high. But now that it was a serious option – and the only option as far as the GND was concerned – reality kicked in and I began to panic. Despite sharing the kind of intimacies that most married couples take 20 years to reveal, there was something I hadn't told the GND, a dark secret that I had hoped I would be able to skilfully conceal. I was extremely susceptible to seasickness.

Mothers tell their children that getting seasick is nothing to be ashamed of, but believe me, 30-odd years of patronising contempt has taught me that it is. Society does not regard seasickness as an illness but rather as a personality flaw. Get struck down by a virus or a bug and it's just bad luck. Start chundering the moment the water gets a little choppy and there's something wrong with you. People say, 'You don't get seasick, do you?' with a little sneer of superiority. Worse, on office harbour cruises, people take photos of you in your pathetic state and stick the photos up on the noticeboard for everyone to laugh at.

It shouldn't be that way. There should be a Garvin Institute for Seasickness or, at the very least, a Seasick Sufferers Anonymous. In fact, let me start one here and now. My name is Peter Moore and I get seasick.

Having said that, I was still concerned how the GND would react when she discovered the awful truth. She saw us arm in arm, our legs dangling over the side watching a Caribbean sunset as dolphins frolicked at our feet. I saw myself, my head over the side, losing what little respect the GND still had for me. I was still pushing the cause of the 'jungle trail' in the Bahía Azul Restaurant one morning when the GND spotted a sign that read, 'Come Sailing with Russell'. It had been created on a computer and featured a crappy clip-art picture of a yacht, a palm tree and a sunset.

'It's an omen!' she exclaimed excitedly.

From that moment my idea about the jungle trail, and hiding my seasickness habit, was dead in the water.

Russell was an Australian and, as luck would have it, he was very easy to track down. The manager of the Bahía Azul Restaurant told us to look for a guy with a red bushy beard and blue eyes who walked up the street saying

'Howdy' to everyone. Within twenty minutes we had found him, in the Café-Bar Ubafu checking his e-mail, and told him we were interested in sailing with him to Utila. Russell had a no-nonsense manner and explained the route – along the north coast of Honduras, mooring in a small bay overnight along the way – and told us the price. Seventy dollars each, all meals included. The price was dependent on getting a few other passengers.

'I've got two other people interested,' Russell said. 'But they're a bit strange. I think they're on something.'

In the short time we'd been talking to Russell, it was clear he thought every one was strange and 'on' something. I asked him what he thought these particular people were on.

'Mushrooms,' he said, leaning forward conspiratorially. 'Magic mushrooms.'

We arranged to catch up with Russell later that afternoon and when we did, the news wasn't good. He had tried to find the mushroom people, but they'd left town, deciding to try their hand at the 'jungle trail'. He'd hit the streets again, wandering up and down the length and breadth of Lívingston saying 'Howdy' to everyone he met and trying to talk them into a two-day Caribbean yacht trip, but hadn't had any success. He was a little brusque – I wouldn't have been surprised to find out he had been brought up in the country – and I suspected that may have had something to do with his lack of success.

'I wonder if there are any people of the gay variety in town,' he mused. 'Last time I was in Key West they told me I should be chasing the pink dollar.'

I asked him how much he would charge if he took just me and the GND.

'Ninety dollars each,' he said. 'But we'll be making an early start, so you can save money by sleeping on the boat the night before we leave.'

We agreed and made arrangements to meet Russell at the municipal docks, down by the park surrounded by concrete turrets, later that evening at seven. When we found him he was loading provisions into a dinghy in the dark. The dinghy would take us out to Russell's yacht, the Annie Rose, moored 500 metres offshore. As we clambered in a man emerged from the shadows and asked Russell for money for watching his boat. Russell told the guy – a dishevelled, angry-looking drunk – to bugger off. The guy in turn threatened Russell by telling him that he had a big knife.

'Yeah, well I've got a bloody big oar,' said Russell, unconcerned.

With that the guy backed off and disappeared into the shadows again. The GND was astonished.

'Happens all the time,' said Russell. 'Just wants drinking money.'

Russell rowed out to the boat. The harbour was still and quiet, the only sounds the clank of the oars, the splash on the water and the muted sounds of music on shore in Livingston.

The GND shivered with excitement. 'I can't believe it,' she said, clutching my knee. 'We're going sailing!'

Now I don't know much about yachts, but Russell's seemed okay. It was a 36-footer and had a double bed up front and some seats that converted into beds in the galley. He'd bought it up in Florida and sailed it down to Río Dulce and now made chartered trips to Belize, Honduras and sometimes back to Florida. Like everyone else in the region, he was doing it tough after Mitch. Normally he would charge $130 per person for a charter of six people for this trip. We bunked down for the night glad to have what little space there was to ourselves.

At three in the morning, just as the tide turned, Russell started the diesel engine and motored out of the bay towards the ocean. The depth sounder indicated that there were fish about, so Russell tossed a line over to trawl behind us just in case. 'Not that I expect to catch anything,' he said. 'I reckon those fish pictures have been programmed in.'

I went back to sleep, hoping that I could stave off my seasickness for a while longer that way, and woke to find the GND behind the wheel while Russell made breakfast. He pointed to the compass, floating in a ball in front of her.

'Keep it between east and north east,' he said. 'That will keep us away from the reef and we might be able to pick up a bit of a breeze.'

The GND jumped to it. She didn't say, 'Aye, Aye, Captain,' but she might as well have.

I declined breakfast, even though it was toast and Vegemite, a rare treat for Aussies in these parts. I had so far managed to keep my seasickness under control and wanted to keep it that way. It hadn't been too rough, it was overcast and there was a light breeze to cool my sweaty brow. I was able to stare off at the horizon and keep my stomach quiet. I was doing so well that by lunch I was convinced I could eat.

I was wrong. Lunch was a simple sandwich, but as soon as the first bite hit my stomach, I felt the immediate urge to throw up. I clambered up on deck, desperate not to plaster the galley with poorly chewed bread and diced carrots, and projectile vomited over the rail. With that, all my hard work and concentration was undone. I had broken the seal and there was no stopping it. I found a spot, just to the right of the mainsail, where I could lie in the shade and lazily put my head overboard to throw up.

I was like that for the rest of the day. Every now and then the GND came to check on me and express alarm at how pale I was. She'd ask if there was anything she could do, but apart from turning around or dropping me off at some part of the deserted coastline, there was nothing that could be done. This was how I was going to spend the rest of the journey. I told her to go back to the wheel, which she did with what I regarded as indecent haste. She could have at least pretended that my wellbeing meant more to her than the thrill of piloting a yacht through the Caribbean.

Soon I got myself into only a marginally uncomfortable position where I was able to watch the world go by and throw up into the water with a minimum of effort. The ocean was littered with debris from Hurricane Mitch and I whiled away the hours watching it float by – palm tree trunks, fragments of doors, windows and other pieces of houses, as well as clothes and personal effects. I spotted the occasional flying fish, and once, to the absolute delight of the GND, a pod of dolphins swam beside us. For the GND, it was heaven on earth – sailing a yacht in the Caribbean with dolphins frolicking in the wake, the troublesome boyfriend lying prone and impotent on the deck. It was probably the happiest moment for her on the trip. For me it bordered on being the opposite.

Just when I thought it couldn't get any worse, or I couldn't look any more pathetic, it started raining. I was more than happy to lie on deck and get drenched, letting the rain wash the vomit off me and the deck around me, but Russell wanted me below. I might get washed overboard and with the reduced visibility he wouldn't be able to see me. He pulled out a tarp and rigged it up over the steering wheel, so he could steer without getting wet. The tarp had painted handprints all over it, and names in childish scrawl. It had been 'attacked' by his nieces and nephews before he left, he said. Beneath his gruff exterior, Captain Russell was really a big softie.

As Russell rigged all this up, the GND took over the wheel. She was in her element. She loved sailing, and all the skills she'd learned sailing Sydney Harbour with one of her previous boyfriends – a rich guy who owned his own yacht – paid off. She looked off into the horizon, peering through the squall like an old sea-dog. She didn't even acknowledge me as I shuffled past and went below.

Just before sunset, the rain cleared and we motored into a small bay. It was a beautiful spot, where the jungle and the ocean met on the points of a crescent of white sand lined by palm trees, many of them knocked onto their side by Mitch. The GND and I swam as the sun set and Russell cooked dinner. It was perfect.

The swim invigorated me. I felt clean and fresh and my mind was cleared of its seediness. I could even eat. The meal was delicious, with a satay sauce that was Russell's own recipe. We'd already sampled his pineapple tea and his secret recipe maple syrup and were convinced that with the right marketing Russell could be onto something.

We joked that he should bring out his own range of condiments with his face on the jar, like Paul Newman, but called 'Captain Russell's'.

■   ■   ■

The next day passed in a similar fashion. The GND spent most of it behind the wheel, while I spent it with my head over the side. By mid-afternoon, Utila appeared as a dot on the horizon. An hour later, Russell was manoeuvring the Annie Rose alongside a dock belonging to one of the dive shops. We had arrived in Honduras.

A tanned gringo stripped to his shorts waited on the dock to catch the ropes. 'G'day Russ!' he called. 'How's it hanging?'

Another Australian! After two months of seeing very few of our fellow countrymen they were popping up everywhere. Russell said Utila was full of them. The island was the cheapest place in the world to get your dive certificate and most of the dive teachers were Aussies. It also helped that a large proportion of the people on Utila were descendants of the early British settlers and spoke English. This had been the first time Russell had been back to Utila since Mitch and he was surprised at how quiet it was.

'This time of year it's usually packed,' he said. 'You'd see travellers wandering up and down the street begging people to let them camp in their front yard.'

It was hard to imagine. Utila was somnolent, a one-road town that made the cayes in Belize look like bustling metropolises. It was a dive town, yet most of the dive shops were closed, or only had a few students who watched instructional videos or listened to dive instructors in silence. Many of the buildings were still shuttered up, wood nailed over the windows, their American owners having still not arrived or not coming at all. Elsewhere, it was difficult to tell what was hurricane damage and what was simply neglect. We found a room, showered and had a nap, and then ventured out again just as night fell.

Saturday night was obviously the big night in Utila. Everyone in town sat on a low retaining wall opposite the Bottom Up disco and restaurant, freshly washed and wearing their best clothes. In the vacant block beside the restaurant, some of the town matrons had set up stalls selling cakes and plates of food. It had the feel of a church social, no doubt helped by the fact that the ministers of each religion on the island stood on opposing corners with microphones and small amplifiers, preaching. Young girls walked by arm in arm and giggled as boys called out to them.

We ate dinner at the Bundu Café. It was run by a South African guy called Steve. 'You the guys who came in with Russell?' he asked.

We nodded. News travelled fast in Utila, which was not surprising when you considered how short a distance it had to travel.

'You know, you caused quite a stir,' Steve said. 'We had to reward the tourist sweepstakes.'

The Bundu Café ran a sweepstake where regulars tried to guess the number of tourists arriving that day. It was a game they had devised to take their minds off just how few tourists were coming to the island. A contact down at the municipal dock would count the number of tourists getting off the once-a-day ferry from the mainland and report back to Steve, who would then announce the winner. We had thrown a spanner in the works by arriving unannounced and unnoticed at a different dock.

'Yep, there was quite an uproar,' he continued. 'Dave from Gunter's Dive Shop reckons that the sweepstake only covered the people arriving on the ferry. But he'd won, so he would, wouldn't he? In the end we all got together and it was agreed that you counted. After all, you arrived on the island, didn't you? Dave's still pretty pissed off, though.'

I asked how much was at stake. By the sounds of things it must have been pretty high stakes.

'Twenty-five limps [lempira, the Honduran currency] – about two bucks,' he said. 'You staying for the movie tonight?'

The Bundu Café had a small cinema – basically a room to the side of the cafe with a TV and a video player – and that evening they were playing *Fear and Loathing in Las Vegas*. As a special treat, it would be preceded by an amateur video about Hurricane Mitch, filmed by a guy who lived on Roatán. He obviously fancied himself as a TV reporter, because it began with him holding a microphone as the wind howled, bending palm trees and ripping off tin roofs, speaking earnestly about the destruction and the number of lives lost.

Unfortunately, he ended up looking like an entrant in Hondura's 'Funniest Home Videos'. His balding head and spectacles gave him an earnest, bookish appearance rather than the dashing image he was hoping for and the wind was so strong that it distorted the sound and shook the camera. Worse, he favoured the sweep-over to conceal his baldness, leaving a length of hair 20 centimetres long dancing from the side of his head at a 90 degree angle.

When he was off-camera and simply filmed what was going on, the footage, though poor quality, was sobering. He followed villagers as they picked their way through what was left of their houses, zooming in on a photo album or a muddy, tattered child's toy. He followed rescue workers to a beach where five corpses had been washed ashore, not sparing us the horrific sight of their blue, bloated bodies. Then, he filmed a helicopter ride to Guanaja, the worst hit of the islands. What had once been lushly forested now looked like a stripped cob of corn. It was barren, its trees bare, and the settlements were totally destroyed. According to the reporter, the hurricane had hovered over Guanaja for six hours, unleashing all its fury on this speck in the Caribbean Sea.

On Roatán he came across some English tourists who had been trapped on a resort for four days while Mitch attacked. One guy, a stocky East End barrow-boy type of chap, broke down as he told of his relief when the British rescue boat arrived. The tape ended with a slow-motion montage of destruction, misery and heartache. The final shot was our reporter gazing on the destruction and shaking his head.

The tape finished and the room was silent. Although it was amateurish and had been spoiled by the reporter's Sixty Minutes ambitions, it had been a sobering experience. *Fear and Loathing in Las Vegas* felt a little flat.

The next morning, as we ate breakfast at Thompson's Bakery, I noticed with alarm that most of the locals all looked the same. They had pasty skin and eyes that were a little too close together and spoke a patois that was a little broader and simpler than we'd heard in either Belize or Lívingston. They also had a penchant for a tipple. None more so than Jake, the old town drunk. He staggered past, calling out to the waitress to bring him a drink. She asked him why he wasn't at home. Jake looked up, pondering the question slowly. It seemed as though he was about to answer when a woman rode by on a bike, distracting him.

'Come here, you whore!' he yelled, before staggering, hunched forward, down the road a little, shaking his fist after her as she rode away. He turned back and staggered into the restaurant. The waitress must have been expecting this turn of events, because she had a plate of scrambled eggs ready for him. He wolfed down the eggs in a manner only a drunk can.

He must have sensed us watching him because he looked over at the GND and me. 'I'm lucky I can even eat!' he slurred. 'I drank lime once, burned my lower intestines. Look what it did to my tongue.'

Under the scrambled egg, his tongue was badly mutilated.

'Jesus saved me,' he continued quietly. 'A man in white robes and sandals injected me.'

He mumbled a bit further and then asked me what religion I was. I told him I'd been brought up as a Seventh Day Adventist. He looked up wildly. 'It was your Jesus that cured me!' he cried. 'Not your pastor though. He's a whore monger!'

The waitress looked at us and rolled her eyes. We finished our breakfast and left.

Our days in Utila progressed along in a leisurely manner. We'd walked from one end of the island to the other, from the airport to Blue Bayou, the sad 'aquatic park' that lay abandoned after the hurricane. We snorkelled with gear hired from Dick, the big burly American who rode around town on a bike with a fantastically bright red macaw on his shoulder. We had walked across to Pumpkin Hill Bay and checked out the cave that had supposedly been the hideout of Henry Morgan, the pirate. We were as happy as we had been – it's hard not to be when you're living this kind of lifestyle – but I wondered what it would be like once we left the island for the Honduran mainland. It was one of the areas worst-affected by Mitch and travelling through it would be hard work.

One evening we bumped into Lars and Lars, the two Swedes we had met in Lívingston. They'd come to do some diving and had arranged an all-you-can-dive deal with one of the dive shops desperate for customers. I asked them about the jungle trail.

'There is no trail anymore,' the short one said. 'They've built a new bridge and the roads are better than Guatemala.

We got pick-up trucks all the way. It was very disappointing!'

To her credit, the GND did not saying anything. She simply gave me one of those enigmatic smiles that women give when they've been proved right.

On our last morning we had breakfast with Russell at the Bundu Café. He hadn't been able to find passengers to go back to Lívingston and was toying with the idea of heading back anyway. He had a block of land in Río Dulce and was thinking of clearing it. Steve asked us if we wanted to go in the Tourist Sweepstakes, but as we were leaving and wouldn't be able to collect, we gave it a miss. Russell, feeling a tad optimistic, bet on seven.

We were going to miss Russell. Despite his gruff exterior he had a dry sense of humour and was full of ideas on how he would make his millions. Unfortunately, he wouldn't be making them that day. Later, as we waited for arriving passengers to disembark from the boat taking us to the mainland, we counted just four tourists getting off.

CHAPTER SIXTEEN

Honduras

**Annoying habit >>> Tourette's Syndrome –
baggage-related
Culprit >>> Peter**

The air-conditioned Galaxy II was the best boat we'd seen
on our journey so far, the kind of sleek vessel you'd expect
to see full of supermodels on the Côte D'Azur, not inbred
islanders in northern Honduras. It took 50 minutes to get
to the mainland, just long enough to reach the end of 'The
Three Stooges' episode playing on the on-board TV. As the
boat made its way up the mouth of Río Cangrejal, it became
apparent that Hurricane Mitch had done a pretty good
impersonation of Larry slapping Mo about the head on the
hills La Ceiba. The breakwater was littered with trees and
what was left of the tin roof on the port building flapped

in the breeze. The bridges along the road leading out of the port were still too damaged to support the weight of buses, so taxis were ferrying passengers into La Ceiba, 20 kilometres away.

We didn't stop at La Ceiba. Our plan was to travel west to Tela, and then south to San Pedro Sula, the second-largest city in Honduras. The bus we caught to Tela was another former American school bus, but instead of the obligatory glowing neon Jesus above the driver it displayed notices from its previous incarnation. 'Don't lose your riding privileges. Follow the rules!' read the largest. It was a maxim the La Ceiba bus company lived by. The timetable said that the bus to Tela left at ten, and although the bus was full, the driver refused to leave until the clock reached that time exactly.

While we waited, a collection of hawkers took the opportunity to sell food, drinks and personal grooming items. One guy was selling digital wristwatches and Brut 33, items I wouldn't have thought would be in big demand after a killer hurricane had swept through your district. After I declined the Brut, he demonstrated how the watch face of one of his watches flipped open to reveal a calculator. He obviously thought that this was a big deal – perhaps it was this feature that had convinced him to carry this particular line of watches – and seemed certain that the demonstration would have me reaching into my pocket for money to buy maybe a dozen. He seemed genuinely shocked when I indicated that I wouldn't even be buying one and started the demonstration all over again, thinking that I must have missed something the first time. Thankfully, the clock just then reached ten and we were on our way.

Before Mitch, the 103-kilometre journey from La Ceiba to Tela was a simple and straightforward one, a one and a half hour journey along excellent roads built to transport the fruit that was grown along this fertile coast. But the topography of the north coast of Honduras that makes it so fertile also makes it an easy target for passing hurricanes. You see, this part of Honduras is a thin strip of land cut by rivers that run from the dramatic mountains behind. The mountains impeded Mitch's progress long enough for it to lash the coast with 300-kilometre-per-hour winds and a year's worth of rain. The rivers swelled, washing over the flat farmland, destroying everything in their path. What had once been one of the most dramatically beautiful regions in Central America was now a wasteland.

The damage was horrific. Vast fields of pineapples, stretching as far as the eye could see towards the mountain, had been turned to brown mush. Grey tree trunks lay scattered across the fields, looking like matchsticks spilt from a giant box of matches. Elsewhere, they lay in piles, dragged there by tractors now coated with thick grey mud. Most of the farmhouses had been destroyed too, the ones that survived now coated with mud. We passed one house, the entire rear section twisted and torn, and spotted its owner sitting on a chair on the front veranda, still in shock, gazing dull-eyed across the fields of mush that had once been his livelihood.

It was the bridges, however, that had suffered the most damage. Some were patched temporarily, waiting for the next decent rain storm or the rivers to rise to start the problems all over again. Most however, were beyond immediate repair, and waited silently for international aid to arrive and help with their reconstruction. Until then, vehicles simply followed tracks beside them down to the river and forded the rivers. The rivers were low now – it was the dry season – but even so, progress was slow, with trucks and buses and cars lining up either side to take their chances in the swirling water.

But at Río Bonito that mode of river crossing was impossible. Here the damage had been too severe – only the concrete pylons of the bridge remained – and the banks either side too steep for vehicles to attempt a river crossing. Instead, a suspension bridge had been built, strung up from one pylon to the other. Buses from either direction pulled up at either end, dumping their passengers to cross on foot to the other side, where another bus would take them the rest of their journey.

It was a slow and tedious solution. The bridge could only support a certain amount of people at a time, and even then they had to cross in single file. Armed soldiers stood on either side, limiting the number of people crossing and stopping them altogether when it was time for people to cross from the other side. When the bridge twisted slightly as we crossed and the GND shrieked, they laughed.

Down on the river, about ten metres below, teams of American marines were busily rebuilding the bridge. The suspension bridge had been their handiwork, thrown up quickly in the first days after they arrived. Now, with bulldozers painted in Gulf War camouflage brown, they were tackling the more daunting task of rebuilding. We lined up for another bus and soon we were on our way again.

We saw teams of American soldiers periodically over the rest of the journey. At Caracas, another graveyard for trees, they were using chainsaws to cut the trunks into a more manageable size. At Río Perla, they were busily repairing the approaches to the bridge, covering huge concrete drains, which they poured and created on the site, with soil and tarmac.

The scope of the destruction we saw that day was staggering. It was hard to imagine that these fields of mush, where tractors were now plowing the soggy carcasses of pineapples back into the soil, had once been the vast gardens of multinational fruit growers. We had seen some of the damage on Caye Caulker. And the video on Utila. But nothing on this scale.

'It's unbelievable,' said the GND, shaking her head. 'Nothing has been left untouched.'

Almost as if to prove her point, we spotted a huge slab of tarmac, a piece of road complete with lane markings, lying, quite bizarrely, in the middle of a field. It certainly put into perspective our own small problems. Our bickering about things like smoking and money paled into insignificance in the face of this kind of destruction.

It was night when we finally pulled into Tela. A journey that usually took an hour and a half had taken us the good part of a day. A heavy rain was falling and made Tela look greyer and more depressing than it really was. We stayed in a drab hotel with voracious mosquitoes, down by a temporary aid distribution centre that worked all through the night, and ate at a Mexican restaurant where we were the only customers and the waitress breastfed her baby between courses.

Tela's main attraction, apparently, was its beaches, so when it dawned bright and sunny the next morning we decided to check them out. They turned out to be grey and grubby, the restaurants and cabins lining them abandoned and derelict. The town is also famous for its Garífuna Museum, which our guidebook described as 'interesting' and 'cultural', but it was closed and, according to the caretaker, there were no plans to open it again in the foreseeable future. We had given the town a chance. It was time to head on to San Pedro Sula.

The journey was slow and depressing, broken only by a stop in El Progreso, a lively, dusty market town that was going on as if nothing had changed. It was a facade though. On the outskirts of town, just where the road to San Pedro Sula became a multi-laned highway, we passed a huge expanse of mud that had once been a banana plantation. Tractors were pulling trailers loaded with dark banana bulbs that workers, knee deep in mud, were pulling from the soil. A foreign TV crew followed them, filming. In La Lima, a small town by a river, the roads were still slick with mud, the slightest rain shower turning the roads into a smash-up derby. The GND spotted one house surrounded by mud a metre high, with a path to the door carved into the mud as if it were snow.

As we got closer to San Pedro Sula the roads were better and the physical effects of the hurricane less pronounced, but the social effects of the disaster became more apparent.

Families from surrounding areas seeking refuge had set up makeshift communities on the median strips, sheltering under plastic tarpaulins and cooking over charcoal fires. Their children ran among the tents playing, in effect, between two lanes of busy traffic, under a billboard with a picture of a flame-grilled burger and the caption 'A Whopper from Burger King is only 15 kilometres away'. In the distance, a huge bottle of Coke topped one of the hills surrounding the town.

San Pedro Sula is a big, dirty town with nothing really to recommend it. It is surrounded by factories, many of them foreign-owned, attracted by tax breaks and cheap labour. It had that grey-brown concrete look that seems to go hand in hand with excessive noise and diesel fumes, and has the dubious double honour of being the most heavily polluted town in Honduras, and the AIDS capital of Central America.

We stayed in the eponymous and crappy Hotel San Pedro, beside the railway tracks, but close to Parque Central and the cathedral. The hotel had once had grand pretensions – you could see that in the impressive reception desk and mahogany message box – but the prices, about $2.50 a night, indicated that they had long been given up. Now it was home to shonky businessmen, hookers and, as luck would have it, the three Australian medical students, Dave, Tina and Alison, who we'd met in Lívingston. They had put the disappointment of the jungle trail behind them and were helping out at an Anglican Mission on the edge of town.

'We could do with the extra hands,' said Alison, the tall,

thin one. 'When the containers come in we're struggling to get by.'

At 7 am the next morning we were in a taxi heading to the Iglesia Episcopal Honduras Church compound on the northern outskirts of town. My first job as an International Aid Worker was to break into the building where the clothes were stored. Some of the boxes the clothes were in had tumbled during the night, blocking the inward opening doors and effectively denying access. It wasn't hard. Calling upon the skills I have honed after years of losing my house keys, I simply took the glass slats out of the louvered windows of the toilet and climbed in. Still, such acts were obviously out of the everyday experience of the good church folk, and I was looked upon with a mixture of appreciation and apprehension.

Otherwise, the church had quite a slick operation going. They hired drivers and semitrailers to pick up the containers full of aid as soon as they arrived in Puerto Cortés and bring the stuff back to the compound in San Pedro Sula immediately. From here it was distributed to villages throughout Honduras using a fleet of pick-up trucks. It was a classic example of the 'hub and spoke' distribution network favoured by major aid organisations, but it also had the added benefit of effectively taking the Honduran government out of the loop. Honduran port officials were notoriously corrupt and the church wanted to make sure that as much of the aid as possible reached those who really needed it.

The muscle power needed to unload the containers was provided by volunteers who had come down to Honduras from churches in America, or people like us who turned up out of the blue and wanted to help. When it got particularly busy they would use locals, paying them in food and clothing from the containers. Hopefuls would stand outside the barred gate, and were picked and allowed in only when one of the larger semitrailers arrived.

The day soon settled into a distinct pattern. A semitrailer would arrive, back into the compound and we would all help to unload it. Goods were divided into three sections – food and water, clothing and medicine – and put in the appropriate piles. The day the GND and I helped out, most of the containers were full of food and water.

'Good, no clothes,' said Dave. 'I think they've already got enough Jurassic Park T-shirts.'

Obviously someone in the states thought that the victims of Hurricane Mitch didn't have enough personal grooming products, because the GND discovered a box of Clinique foundation. 'This is good stuff,' she cooed. 'Each one of these tubes would cost $50 back home!'

While the GND, Tina and Alison ferreted around excitedly to see if there was any matching mascara or lipstick in the box as well, I wondered what had possessed someone in America to send a box of makeup to Honduras. I imagined it had been a woman, probably from the southern states somewhere, moved to help after watching the reports of Hurricane Mitch on the six o'clock news. 'Gee, that Hurricane Mitch can't be doing much for their skin,' I heard her saying. 'Hey I know, I'll send them some makeup.' The women of Honduras might have lost their homes and their families, but hey, at least they'll feel good about themselves.

The semitrailers came in twos and threes and after they were emptied, we barely had enough time to catch our breath before the smaller pick-up trucks from surrounding villages started arriving. They distributed the aid to where it was needed and we piled on boxes of clothes, food or medicine according to the needs listed on their clipboards.

'This is the good part,' puffed Tina. 'This is when we know it's actually getting to someone.'

Just after lunch, a film crew turned up. They were from an NBC affiliate in Virginia and they spent half an hour filming us unload containers. 'Makes the people feel like their stuff is getting through,' said the cameraman, stepping aside as we passed. 'Especially to see you guys helping. I don't think your average American trusts your average Honduran, if you know what I mean.'

The camera crew were staying in the best hotel in San Pedro, and after they finished filming spent another half an hour trying to convince the GND, Tina and Alison to go back to it for a swim in the pool.

The GND looked tempted. 'Well, it would be nice!' she exclaimed. 'I haven't sweated so much in my life!'

It was hard work and there had hardly been a let-up. It seemed that there was always another semitrailer to unload or a pick-up truck to load. At the end of the day we were soaked with sweat and completely buggered. But we could venture south the next day knowing that in some small way we'd done our bit to help and without feeling totally like ghouls.

■   ■   ■

We caught a bus south the next day to Santa Rosa, our muscles still aching. The bus was leaving the terminal when we arrived – after spotting the Clinique the GND had decided that she had neglected her skin and insisted on applying Vitamin E lotion on every exposed part of her body before we left. I waved it down and handed my pack to the conductor who had scampered up onto the roof to take it, and I let out a string of expletives as I lifted it up to his waiting arms.

'I wish you wouldn't do that,' the GND said.

'What?' I asked, thinking that perhaps the careless way I had handled the bag offended her.

'You swear every time you pick up your bag,' she said. 'It's embarrassing.'

To be honest, I hadn't even noticed I was doing it. I knew I was annoyed by the weight of my pack (it was currently coming in at just under 25 kilos). And I was aggravated by a nagging suspicion that the GND had deliberately brought a small bag so she wouldn't have to help lugging guidebooks (which made up most of the weight). But I thought my cursing was internalised. I didn't realise I was questioning the parentage of my bag and its loose sexual proclivities out loud.

'There's nothing I can do about it,' I said as we got on the bus and found our seats. 'Besides, it gives me the energy to pick the fucker up.'

'Well, I think it's unnecessary,' she said. 'It's like you've got Tourette's Syndrome, that swearing disease.'

'But I only get it when I pick up my pack,' I argued.

'Well, okay, it's baggage-related Tourette's Syndrome.'

Two Honduran cowboys sitting in front of us wearing white cowboy hats turned around and watched us open mouthed. At first I thought they could understand English and were listening in on our admittedly bizarre conversation. They couldn't, they were just fascinated by the GND. Everything she said and everything she did was a source of constant wonder to them. The GND opened a pack of biscuits and offered them one, hoping that the offer would make them realise that we were aware they were watching us. Unperturbed, they took a biscuit, put it to their mouths and ate it, all without taking their eyes off the GND's face. They sat like this all the way to La Entrada, one and a half hours away, where, to their undying disappointment, they had to get off.

'I've still got it,' said the GND, flattered by the attention.

Yes, I thought. But do you really want it?

After La Entrada, the scenery changed, transforming from green rolling hills and farmlands to pine forests and misty mountains. Women sat beside the road with neat piles of vegetables – carrots, potatoes, turnips – piled into little pyramids. Men rode by on horses, going nowhere in particular. Soon we reached Santa Rosa de Copán, a small Spanish colonial town with a distinctly brisk climate.

There's not a lot to do in Santa Rosa. It's just a pretty little town with a gentle atmosphere. We stayed a couple of days, just soaking up the atmosphere down at the tiny central park and eating at the Rodeo Restaurant, where the heads of the bulls that gave their lives so that we might eat were mounted and displayed on the walls. The highlight of our stay was a visit to the La Flor de Copán cigar factory.

Honduran cigars are regarded as second only to Cubans, and La Flor de Copán cigars among the finest. In fact, many of their cigars are repackaged and sold under the Davidoff brand in Europe.

We were shown around the cigar factory by Anabel, a sweet girl who was also the only English speaker in the factory. Happy to be given the chance to abandon her desk, she led us through the factory explaining the different tasks involved in creating a cigar. She pointed out the Blender, the person responsible for choosing the mix of tobacco to be used in each type of cigar, and the Buncher, who took that tobacco and made it into rough, cigar-size bunches. The Wrappers and the Rollers, the men and women whose skills turn that rough bunch of tobacco into a smooth, fine-drawing cigar, sat at desks, like school children, busily doing their tasks. I asked Anabel if I could roll one.

'Sure,' she said.

Let me just say that it is harder than it looks. Someone in Switzerland is probably cursing a Davidoff that looks like a dog shit and is drawing badly even as you read this.

We had two options from Santa Rosa, both seeing us pass through Nueva Ocotepeque. We could head straight south from Nueva Ocotepeque, crossing into El Salvador at El Poy, heading along Highway 4 straight to the capital, San Salvador. Or we could head west, crossing briefly into Guatemala at Agua Caliente, before looping through Esquipulas then crossing back into El Salvador at Anguiatú.

I favoured the latter option. It gave us the chance to visit Esquipulas, a town whose great white church was home to a black Christ and had been compared by previous visitors to no less worthy structures than the Church of the Holy Sepulchre in Jerusalem and the Caaba in Mecca. And it would put us in the east of El Salvador, allowing us to visit Santa Ana, a supposedly pretty town that we would miss if we took the other route. The GND expressed her concerns at entering Guatemala for the fourth time, just to see a black Christ, but she reluctantly agreed.

We had hoped to catch an express bus to Agua Caliente at 9 am, but by 10 am it still hadn't materialised. A big guy in a knee-length leather coat, looking all the world like a Miami Mafia hitman, who was also waiting for the bus, was clearly agitated. 'I am tired of this,' he huffed, partially to vent his frustration but mainly to show he could speak English. When I looked up, he introduced himself. 'I am Marvin,' he said. 'I am from Denver. I am sorry I am angry but I need to get to Guatemala.'

Marvin worked in Denver, but was originally from Santa Rosa. He had been in town to visit his family. 'Denver is bewdiful,' he said. 'Snow five feet deep. I work at Sam's. You know it?'

He was surprised when we said we were from Australia, and a little disappointed. It hadn't been a good Christmas for Marvin. He'd had to have a 'stomach operation'. 'I needed surgery,' he said, lifting his shirt to reveal heavy strapping around his waist. 'But they wouldn't operate until I gave them the money.'

I said it couldn't have cost much. I was wrong. They had charged him $4000.

'In the US they let you pay in instalments,' he said. 'Here they would let me die unless I paid.' Marvin was catching a bus to Guatemala because airfares to the States were cheaper there.

Eventually a bus came, not the directo but heading towards the border all the same. Marvin asked me to help him with his bag – he was still too sore after the operation to lift it – and when we arrived at the border he asked me to carry it to the customs office for him as he hobbled along behind me. The GND caught up with me and asked if I'd taken leave of my senses. 'What if it's drugs?' she hissed.

I guess it could have been. It was a canvas carry bag. And it was pretty heavy.

'What can I do?,' I asked. 'I can't make him carry it. Look, he's suffering!'

The GND wasn't convinced.

'It could be just other stuff,' I said. 'Clothes, maybe even cigars. He might think it's less likely that I'll get checked.'

In the end, I compromised. I carried the bag to the border post, but made it quite clear to the immigration officer, the customs officer and the guy sweeping the gutter that it belonged to Marvin, not me. I placed the bag at his feet when we lined up to get our passports stamped and at customs, where the guy just waved us all through anyway. I did the same at the Guatemalan border.

Marvin was catching a bus to Guatemala City, we were catching a minivan to Esquipulas, ten kilometres away, so we said our goodbyes. Marvin repaid my kindness by haggling with the driver of a minivan to make sure we got charged the local price.

'Don't pay him any more that ten quetzals,' he called

out after us, waving as best he could. 'For both of you!'

Esquipulas sat in a valley at the bottom of a winding mountain road. The first thing we saw was the basilica, a massive, blindingly white edifice that dwarfed the ramshackle town around it. Built in 1758, the basilica has withstood earthquakes due to its imperious sturdiness and, thanks to the Black Christ it houses (carved by Quirio Catano in 1594), it continues to draw pilgrims from all over Central America.

We arrived on a Saturday, so Esquipulas, the town, was packed solid with pilgrims and sightseers. The streets were jammed with cars with Guatemalan, Honduran and El Salvador number plates, as well as the odd Mexican one. Wandering mariachi bands serenaded families huddled over plates of beans in restaurants or picnicking in the park in front of the cathedral. The streets were chaotic, a tumble of neon signs advertising hotels, restaurants and shops, all with distinctly biblical names, most alluding in one way or another to El Christo Negro, the black Christ. The hotels were all full, so we had to make do with a small room, usually used as a storeroom, at the top of a hotel packed with young noisy families.

The heart of Esquipulas was the basilica, a twin-domed cathedral that sat at the back of a pretty park, where every man and his dog was lining up to see the Black Christ. The line snaked its way from the front of the park, doubling back on itself at least half a dozen times before entering a door to the left side of the basilica. We joined it – there was no way we could come to Esquipulas without having a squiz at the Black JC – and queued patiently in line with the devout. Three hours later we reached the door, and another half-hour later we began to wind our way along the ramps to the glass case that housed the carving. We had 30 seconds in front of the Black Christ – 15 seconds each – and then we were hustled back out the door.

I have spoken to other travellers since who visited Esquipulas on a week day and discovered that they were able to stroll straight up to the door, wander past the carving and be back out on the streets in the same time it takes to boil an egg. Sometimes I made the mistake of telling them that I was glad that we had to queue for three and a half hours – they usually backed away worried that my insanity was contagious. But there was a real camaraderie in that line, a sense of community. People offered each other food, or minded a spot when someone had to take an essential toilet break. It was happy, joyous and celebratory. In the end, it was the line, not the Black Christ, that I remember most fondly.

Of course, to the locals it was more than just a day out in a queue. They had made a pilgrimage especially to see the Black Christ, and gazing upon it was a life-defining moment. The little old lady in front of us, a black shawl over her bony frame, knelt before it, crossing herself and after staying much longer than her allotted 15 seconds, had to be dragged away by a guard, tears streaming down her face.

After viewing the Black Christ, the pilgrims immediately retired to the stalls surrounding the basilica to pick up a souvenir of their visit. Here they could find shirts, hats and dresses, proudly embroidered with Esquipulas. There were tiny Black Christ trinkets – even a Black Christ snowdome – as well as baskets with candy, cakes and Black Christs topped by colourful cellophane. Some chose Black Christ towels, necklaces, key rings and rugs. For the children, there was popcorn and a Black Christ lollypop (I felt the latter bordered on being blasphemous). Our favourite souvenir was a poster of Jesus, sitting behind a desk, his hands clasped in front of him, with an earnest-looking face. The GND and I christened him Job Interview Jesus.

At the back of the souvenir stalls there was a carnival. It was like carnivals at holiday spots the world over – a little tattered and run by people who look like they are on the run from the law. It had a ferris wheel, dodgem cars and the mandatory spinning ride guaranteed to make people like me throw up. It also had the various games of skill that involved throwing basketballs through hoops, knocking tins down with a tiny sack of beans, or shooting battered targets. One of the shooting galleries had a distinctly Latin American flavour – the targets were on top of dioramas where Barbies and Kens were dressed as mariachi singers. If you hit the target, music started and they moved. I found myself paying for more and more turns, just to see them dance. Without trying, I won a Black Christ key ring.

As we walked back to our room arm in arm, I gave the key ring to the GND. She said it was beautiful and gave me a peck on the cheek. It was like a bad American movie, where the shy farm boy takes his sweetheart to the country fair. Only instead of winning my girl a cuddly toy, I'd won her a tacky piece of religious junk.

Nevertheless, things were good again.

CHAPTER SEVENTEEN

El Salvador

Annoying habit >>> Laziness (again)
Culprit >>> GND

It's never a good idea to arrive in a country on a Sunday. Transport to and from borders is not always reliable and if the border is busy enough to have a bank it will be closed. Any official you deal with is pissed off at having to work weekends and less inclined to believe your story about your excess duty-free. That day, when the GND and I crossed the lonely border in the north-west of El Salvador at Anguiatú, most of the money changers had decided to take the day off as well.

If I'd had any sense I would have changed more money at the border with the one moneychanger I could find. He was a shady-looking character in a grubby polyester shirt, the top shirt pocket bulging with dirty notes from four different countries and a calculator with all the numbers worn off the keys, but he was there and he was willing to take US dollars. The GND certainly thought I should have. When I reluctantly did a deal with the guy, at the rate of eight colónes to the dollar, she was shocked that I was only changing a fiver.

'Five dollars!' she said incredulously. 'That won't even get us dinner. Why don't you change $50?'

While things were undoubtedly good again between the GND and me, the issue of money always threatened to cause problems. I don't think the GND had realised that I was such a skinflint. All the flowers and chocolates I showered upon her before we left probably made her think I was of a more extravagant bent.

Anyway, I wasn't changing $50 because I had absolutely no idea how many Salvadoran colónes I should get to the dollar. Worse, the guy changing money at the border knew that I had no idea. He could have told me that a single colón was worth $8 and I would have been none the wiser. By only changing $5 I was limiting the amount I could possibly be ripped off. Then, when we reached Santa Ana, I would find an ATM, get cash out at a favourable rate and we'd have more than enough for a decent hotel and a slap-up meal. When that didn't sway the GND, I told her that I only had a limited supply of US cash, which I wanted to keep for emergency.

'This is an emergency,' whined the GND. 'It's a Sunday, there are no banks open and I'm hungry!'

'Look!' I said. 'This is how I've always done it and it's how we are doing it now!'

What I conveniently forgot to tell the GND were the times when this way of doing things had left me well and truly stranded. Like the time I arrived in Kigoma in Tanzania without any shillings and had to leave my passport as collateral at a hotel so I could eat their buffet meal. Or when I misjudged how long it would take to go from Bucharest to Istanbul by train and was left penniless and hungry for 26 hours.

'What if they don't have ATMs in Santa Ana?' she asked.

'It's the second biggest city in El Salvador,' I said with what I hoped was only a slight quaver of uncertainty in my voice. 'They'll have ATMs.'

Of course, I couldn't be absolutely certain of that fact. El Salvador had only recently emerged from a long and debilitating civil war. Its infrastructure and economy were in tatters. Two-thirds of the population were classified as living in poverty and it had one of the lowest standards of living in the world. Unemployment was high, exacerbated by ex-combatants from both sides of the civil war who were looking for a new line of business. Only one in 32 people had a telephone. Perhaps providing the convenience of 24-hour banking wouldn't be high on the new government's agenda.

I certainly wasn't cheered by our arrival in Santa Ana. It was a quaint place, but on that Sunday it was deserted and a chilly wind whipped through, tossing rubbish about. The few people who were on the streets were clearly mad, shuffling around in circles and yabbering to themselves, and obviously not au fait with the city's cash machines. In the end we found half a dozen ATMs, including one for the Salvadore Fertiliser Bank, but not one of them accepted my Visa card or the GND's Mastercard. The GND's mood, already dark, was not helped when the loonies stopped to watch us. Tourists were a rare sight in El Salvador, ones sticking cards into walls even more so.

Luckily, we were able to find a hotel that would let us pay after we had been to the bank the next morning. The hotel was popular with truck drivers, who would back their trucks through a narrow passage and parked them in the courtyard onto which the rooms faced. They sat about reading the sports pages or washed their shirts and hung them out to dry. As we walked to the room one truck driver began strumming a guitar and sang a mournful song that seemed to float on the night breeze and linger. It was a lovely moment and I would have commented on it, but the GND wasn't talking to me. She was hungry and cranky, and that night she fell asleep with her back to me.

Our first point of business the next morning was a visit to the Banco Salvadoreño. It smelled of floor wax and paperwork and had the feel of a fifties bank, but for the security guard frisking customers at the door. We were clean, but other customers had to check their machetes, knives and small handguns in a small wooden cabinet to the left of the entrance. The guard pointed us towards a scrum of people I suspected was supposed to be a queue.

The bank only had one computer, an old beige terminal like the ones you see at most government schools. A harried-looking woman picked at the keyboard hesitantly, as the scrum of people shouted and thrust scraps of paper at her. She ignored them, except for a bunch of slick guys wearing Calvin Klein jeans and Lacoste shirts, who she served immediately. They carried huge wads of US dollars and were obviously the big shots, the movers and shakers of Santa Ana. No one, not even those at the head of the queue, questioned their right to be served first. Frustrated at getting nowhere, I followed their lead, leaving the queue and coming up the side, two $50 notes and my passport thrust forward at the teller. The woman took them from me and processed them immediately.

We ate breakfast at a cafe nearby. The GND feared that she would faint from hunger if she didn't eat immediately and attacked a plate of pupusas (small corn tortillas stuffed with meat or cheese) with the gusto of a shipwreck survivor. Between mouthfuls she agreed that we could visit Cerro Verde, a nearby national park, that day. Cerro Verde is regarded as one of the gems of El Salvador, a national park on top of an old volcano, with fantastic views of Lake Coatepeque below it and Izalco Volcano beside it.

The bus we caught wasn't going directly to Cerro Verde – it was continuing on to Izalco and Sonsonate – so the driver dropped us off at the turnoff, still 14 kilometres from the national park gates. A group of people stood on the corner, waiting for a truck or bus to take them the rest of the way or to the coffee plantations that lined the steep, winding road. I asked when the next bus was due and they shrugged their shoulders. The GND sat down beside them, prepared to wait too.

'Why don't we start walking,' I said. 'It'll be good

exercise. And if a truck or bus comes along we can wave it down.'

The GND reluctantly agreed and we set off up the hill. It was fantastic – the sun was out, but we were high now, so it was cool as well. We passed small settlements and massive coffee plantations where workers were picking beans and loading them into giant wicker baskets on their backs. Every now and then we would catch a glimpse of the lake, a splash of stunning blue, or, ahead, the forested slopes of Cerro Verde. It was invigorating and I strode forward purposefully. But the GND's heart wasn't in it and soon she began to fall behind. When she had lagged a couple of hundred metres, I stopped and went back to her.

She was not in a good mood. 'This is stupid,' she puffed. 'We should have waited.'

Just as the GND started to say how much she wanted a cigarette – an urge which often surfaced with the possibility of physical exercise – a pick-up truck drove by with all the people who had waited at the corner clinging desperately to the back. Despite the frantic waving of arms by both the GND and I, or maybe because of it, the truck didn't stop.

The GND declared that that was the final straw and with a huff said that she was turning back immediately. I told her that I wanted to keep going. She listed the reasons for her decision, including the very convincing 'We still have a long way to go and the only vehicle to pass that afternoon just drove straight by us'. And I listed the reasons for mine, including the admittedly less convincing, 'It's a nice day and the walk will do us good'. Soon the discussion broadened to encompass me not changing more money and the GND's constant refusal to do anything the least bit strenuous. From that point, it wasn't long before our tiff degenerated into the sort of nonsensical shouting match that invariably ends with both parties saying, 'Well, fine then!' Such was its intensity that neither of us noticed that a car had pulled up beside us, and its driver, a man in his thirties, was smiling at us.

'Would you like a lift to Cerro Verde?' he asked in lilting, accented English when we stopped to catch our breath.

The GND and I turned and looked at him, open-mouthed, and nodded our heads dumbly.

The guy's name was Miguel and he was from San Salvador. He had brought his wife, Maria, and their daughter Frida, on a drive to the countryside. Maria sat in the front passenger seat smiling, unable to understand English. Frida sat between the GND and me, playing with her doll.

As we wound our way up the hill, stopping briefly at a viewpoint over the lake, I realised how foolish I'd been to think we could have walked the 14 kilometres from the turnoff to the national park gates. The higher we got, the steeper the road became, the ordered rows of bushes of the coffee plantations giving way to thick forest that clung precariously to the mountain side. Miguel's beat up Nissan Skyline struggled to make it up the hill and around mud and rubble that had slid onto the road. He dropped us at the gate and turned around. Miguel hadn't planned to come this far, but had done it so we didn't have to walk. 'Enjoy your stay in my country!' he called.

What Miguel didn't realise was that his generosity probably saved my relationship with the GND from ending on that mountain that afternoon. Or perhaps he did. As they drove off down the mountain, Miguel gave Maria the sort of smile that suggested he remembered when their relationship was young and fiery and she refused to climb volcanoes.

Cerro Verde is 2030 metres above sea level and the lookout point near the park entrance affords fantastic views across southern and eastern El Salvador. Our guidebook warned to arrive early, as thick fog often enveloped the area making it impossible to see anything. It seemed our luck was in – it was three o'clock in the afternoon and the sky was as clear as a bell. El Salvador is the smallest country in Central America, a mere 21,041 square kilometres, and that afternoon I felt as though I could see all of it. The Pacific Ocean was a silver crescent to the south. San Salvador was only 60 kilometres away, a brown smudge to the west. Volcán Izalco, a perfect cone of black rubble, was just to our right, almost close enough to touch.

Before 1770 there was nothing where Volcán Izalco now stands. It was just an empty field with a hole that smoked and spat occasionally. Then in February 1770, about the time Captain Cook was discovering the east coast of Australia, a cone began to mysteriously form where the smoke had fumed, and grew, courtesy of a series of violent eruptions, to its present height of 1910 metres. The last serious eruption was in 1957, but prior to that the explosions had been so regular and so spectacular that sailors knew Volcán Izalco as the lighthouse of the Pacific.

The GND wasn't at all comfortable with the idea that a volcano could just appear out of nowhere and even less enamoured with my idea of clambering down a jungle path to its base. 'What if it erupts again?' she said.

I argued that if the volcano was about to blow, the park warden wouldn't have taken our money for the park entrance fee. In fact, I suspect that he would have had the good sense to abandon his post.

'What will I see that I won't see from here?' she argued.

Grudgingly, I admitted 'not much'. But the next bus heading back down the mountain – and the last of the day – wasn't leaving for another two hours. The round trip to the base of Izalco Volcano took just over an hour, making it, I argued, the perfect way to kill the time. Admittedly, it was probably not the wisest choice of words to use with someone worried about the possibility of being showered with red-hot magma, but I was still annoyed when the GND refused to do it. I told her she was just being lazy and plunged down the path, suddenly alarmed by how sharply it descended.

An hour later, I staggered back up the path and collapsed on the road panting like a dog. The GND had been right – all I had seen was volcanic rock, the sort of stuff they break up into tiny pieces and sell at gardening shops. But I didn't tell her that. I clambered onto the bus, my clothes clinging to my sweaty skin, adamant that it had been one of the most breathtaking sights I had ever seen.

■   ■   ■

That night we ate at the Regis Hotel, a tiny local bar a couple of blocks from our hotel. We had spotted it as we walked the streets, a scruffy place that was a cross between a cafeteria and a sports social club. It had a scattering of laminated tables and chairs and a big old television tuned to satellite sports stations and was run by a big cheerful chap. He showed us to our table, talking excitedly in Spanish in the same manner as the loonies wandering the streets did. When he realised we couldn't understand a word he was saying he called over his son, Jaime.

Jaime was 16 and he could speak English fluently. 'My father welcomes you to his humble restaurant,' he said. 'What would you like?'

We ordered a couple of beers to start and Jaime asked if we wanted bocas. Not altogether sure why anyone would want something that sounded like an infectious disease, the GND asked Jaime what a bocas was.

'They are small snacks,' explained Jaime. 'Like soup, enchiladas or pupusas. You get one free with every beer.'

Not altogether sure why Jaime felt he needed to ask, the GND nodded her head enthusiastically. Jaime brought our beers and bocas over and asked if he could join us and practise his English. When we agreed, he waved over his two friends Luis and Victor, who sat at a nearby table awaiting our approval.

'Our English teacher tells us we should practise our English with every foreigner we see,' he explained.

I was interested to talk to these young guys. They had grown up during the most turbulent period of their country's history. They were born in the same year that right-wing President D'Aubisson created the notorious death squads that terrorised and slaughtered trade unionists and anyone remotely connected to the left-wing call for agrarian reform.

The year they started primary school, the US-sponsored military murdered six Jesuit priests and launched an offensive against the FMLN guerrillas that saw over 4000 people killed. As they entered high school, peace negotiations between the government and the FMLN began, a peace accord was signed in New York and the legislature approved a general amnesty for all those involved in criminal activities during the war. Now, as they were finishing school, their country was struggling to come to terms with the demands of a market economy and the problems of ex-combatants, both FMLN and military, trying to reintegrate into society.

I was surprised to hear that they were enthusiastic and optimistic about the future. All three boys were bursting with ideas – not all of them good, most of them Internet-related, and creating a website about a rabbit with flashing eyes called 'Funny Bunny' being perhaps the most sensible of them. (The site hasn't come to fruition – I just checked www.funnybunny.com and there's nothing there.) I asked them what they wanted to do when they left school and they were equally ambitious. Jaime wanted to be a scientist, Luis wanted to be a computer engineer, and Victor, the best looking of them and easily the most confident, wanted to be an actor.

'I know it's a wild and crazy idea,' Victor said rather dramatically. 'But it is what my heart is telling me to do!'

He was certainly dedicated to learning his craft. He had talked his way into a part-time job at the local video store so he could spend time watching movies and practising his lines. His goal now was to go to an acting academy in Mexico City. 'They make lots of soap operas there,' he said enthusiastically. 'You know, Salma Hayek started in a Mexican soap opera!'

I didn't have the heart to tell him that Salma had a few assets that he didn't!

As the evening progressed, Jaime's father brought us more beers and more bocas. Each time he placed them on our table, he smiled broadly, proud that his son was speaking with us. Like all fathers, he was determined that his son would have what he couldn't. We left the Regis a little tipsier, with three new e-mail addresses, and a little more confident about the future of El Salvador than when we went in.

That confidence evaporated the next day when we left Santa Ana for the coastal town of La Libertad. The GND was attacked on the way to the bus station by one of the local loonies – an old hag punched her on the arm as she passed, for no apparent reason – and the 72-kilometre trip proved to be a complex process that involved changing buses at Sonsonate and Santa Tecla. Worse, La Libertad turned out to be a sad, desolate, depressing seaside town. It was, quite literally, a shithole.

It hadn't always been that way. An abandoned warehouse down near the dock, a cavernous empty place with railway tracks running through it and down to the wharf, suggested that once La Libertad had had something the world wanted. Now the warehouse, and others that sat neglected on the tree-lined street, were littered with the cardboard nests of squatters and piles of human shit in corners.

It was the same at a small park beside the beach. It had broken tables and chairs where families must have picnicked, and an empty concrete pool where the rich must have once swum. Now the pool was used as a communal toilet, an example of the lack of community pride in the town. La Libertad reeked of neglect and decline. It was depressing.

The beach was no better. It was an ugly stretch of black sand where boys in shorts played soccer amidst litter and fish heads. They'd stop occasionally to take a puff on a communal cigarette and pick out the rubbish from between their toes.

The only thing that added any charm was the long wooden pier where fishing boats were winched up after a day of fishing. The pier was in effect a communal dry dock and hauling the boats up to it was a long-winded and laborious process. Once the boats were hauled from the water, they were put on trolleys and wheeled into parking spaces. Thin, taut trolley boys moved them around with the dexterity of a valet in New York to accommodate the constant stream of vessels. The outboard motors were taken off and put onto trolleys and wheeled home by the owners. I figured that the fishermen didn't drag their boats up on the beach because they were afraid they would be stolen.

We stayed at the Pensión Amor y Paz (Hotel Love and Peace), a semi-abandoned establishment right on the beach. It had panoramic views to the wharf and the headland beyond it, but looked like it had been thrown together out of stones and driftwood found washed up on the beach. The bars on the window and the doors had been rusted through by the salt air and when we went for a swim, hoping a dip would lift our spirits, I trod on a fish head and a condom wrapped around the GND's leg. When we returned from a crappy meal at a restaurant up the road that night, we discovered our towels had been stolen and that there was a drunk woman out front making herself an alcoholic slurpee by pouring moonshine into a cup of shaved ice.

'I just want to get out of this place,' said the GND as we settled into our tatty camp bed for the night. 'It gives me the creeps.'

The next day, as we lined up to get on the crowded bus to San Salvador I caught a little girl trying to open my canvas camera bag slung over my shoulder. When she smiled sweetly as I lifted her arm away it dawned on me that that was the first and only time I'd seen anyone smile in La Libertad.

❉   ❉   ❉

If we thought it was going to get any better in San Salvador, the capital of El Salvador, we were wrong. The city centre was as depressing and rundown as the rest of the country, the internal migration of the rural poor to the city giving it the feel of a giant squatter camp. Every second man seemed to be undoing his fly and taking a leak against a crumbling building, or sometimes straight into the broken gutters already littered with cans and rotting vegetables. A blind guy, complete with white cane and dark glasses, had an arm wrapped around a street sign for support as he peed. Walking the streets around the crowded market was an exercise in dexterity, although one of the compulsive urinators thoughtfully redirected his stream of piss to let the GND pass.

We caught a taxi out to the more exclusive suburbs around the University of El Salvador, near Boulevard de los Héroes. This was a different San Salvador, a place of neat houses, tree-lined streets, American-style shopping malls and drive-thru McDonald's. During the civil war FMLN supporters living here turned their houses into guesthouses for people who wanted to learn more about the organisation and their leftist ideologies. I had hoped to stay in one of these places and talk to its owner, who I imagined would be a battle-hardened veteran. I wanted to know what it had been like during the civil war and find out if the ex-combatants were as optimistic about the future as the young guys we had met in Santa Ana. Unfortunately, when we eventually found one – most of the guesthouses listed in our guidebook had been closed – it was run by the wife of an ex-FLMN combatant who was more interested in making pirate copies of *Armageddon* than chewing the fat on agrarian reform.

Despite the affluence of the suburbs around Boulevard de los Héroes – or maybe because of it – there was still a palpable sense of unrest and tension. The laundromat where we had our clothes washed, just around the corner of our guesthouse, insisted that we pass our dirty washing, item by item, through a security grill rather than risk opening the door. The pizza restaurant up the road had a security guard posted on the door who wore body armour and carried a pump-action shotgun. And you were as likely to hear the wail of sirens as the chirping of birds.

Our attempts at sightseeing in San Salvador followed the pattern of our attempts elsewhere in the country – a lot of effort for very little in return. The Teatro Nacional, once the gem of the city, with ornate golden boxes and plush velvet seats, was now shuttered and covered in grafitti. The Metropolitana Cathedral, the largest cathedral in this strictly Catholic country, was neglected and dowdy. And Teleférico de San Jacinto, an amusement centre in the south of the city with a gondola ride that our guidebook said was 'a must', was closed because of lack of funds.

Our day trip to Lago de Ilopango, the largest lake in El Salvador and only 15 kilometres out of the city, was equally uninspiring. The bus ride from the city centre took us past toxic factories, squatter slums and roadside humpies selling hubcaps. The lake itself, while prettily set against the backdrop of a volcano, was heavily polluted and the shore littered with plastic, cans and the carcasses of bloated fish. San Salvador simply convinced us of what Santa Ana and La Libertad already had suggested – we had to get out of El Salvador as quickly as possible. But before we headed back into Honduras, there was one thing I wanted to do – visit the tiny craft town of Ilobasco, 54 kilometres east of San Salvador.

Ilobasco is not a flash town. If you can imagine a town of 48,000 people where every citizen took a course in ceramics at the local community college and then set up a shop in their living room, then you've got a pretty good idea of what Ilobasco is like. And like the graduates of community colleges the world over, the good folk of Ilabasco seemed to specialise in producing badly glazed ceramic dogs and nativity scenes. What sets Ilabasco apart from other craft villages that seem to pop up anywhere within driving distance of a major urban centre is the dramatic tale of its sorpresas, surprises.

Typically, sorpresas are tiny ceramic scenes and figures hidden under egg-shaped shells. The shells are about the size of a walnut and can be designed as apples, oranges – anything round. They are lifted off a base to reveal a 'surprise', usually a scene of village life. Somewhere along the line, however, an entrepreneurial potter came up with the idea of replacing the typical village scene with a naked couple indulging in a bit of horizontal folk dancing. These were called pícara (sinful) sorpresas and they sold like hotcakes. Naturally, the local priest was not amused and after marshalling the reactionary and prudish forces in the village succeeded in driving the pícara off the shelves and under the counter. I wanted to see if you could still buy them.

The GND did not share my fascination with the sorpresas and the whole battle in ceramic between the forces of good and evil, and decided to sit on a bench under a tree with our packs while I went looking. My first stop was the local Artesana school, where young villagers were trained in the skills of making ceramic dogs and vases, as well as sorpresas. I was pointed towards the sorpresa teacher, a matronly women in her fifties, who proceeded to show me a selection of typical sorpresas that revealed nothing more sordid than a man and his donkey. I asked if she had any 'pícaras' and she reacted like I was a schoolboy asking a newsagent where the copies of *Penthouse* were kept.

'Pornografica!' she spat. 'No!'

I found little joy in the craft shops that lined the main

streets, either. Most pretended that they didn't know what I was talking about, others winked suggestively before shrugging their shoulders.

In one shop, a young guy called Wallis, who could speak English, moaned about the loss of the pícara trade. 'They used to be everywhere,' he said. 'And people would come especially to Ilobasco to buy them. But no more!'

I asked if he knew if anybody still made them or if they were available 'under-the-counter'. Finding a pícara had become something of a personal crusade to me.

'My boss would know, but he is having lunch,' he said sadly. 'I'm sorry.'

The priest had done an excellent job running the evil pícara makers out of town and now, in craft shops of Ilobasco, I was known as some pervy gringo with a fascination with X-rated pottery. I returned to the GND, disheartened and disappointed, beaten by El Salvador again. She was eating an ice cream – a chocolate-covered treat called a Fiesta that she'd become quite partial to – and chatting in English with a Christian woman who was taking her children to school. Noticing my disappointment, the woman asked if there was any way she could help me. Just as I was trying to get out of that one, Wallis rode up on a bicycle and motioned for me to jump on. 'My boss told me who makes the pícara!' he said, excitedly.

I shrugged my shoulders and gave my best lop-sided smile to the Christian lady. I'd let the GND explain.

The pícara maker, a women called Maria, lived in a small whitewashed house on the outskirts of town. Her workshop and furnace were out the back of the house and

Wallis explained to her in Spanish why a gringo was so intent on meeting her. (I would have liked a translation of that actually – I wasn't altogether sure why myself.) She showed me her furnace and the table she made things on, and then, on Wallis's prompting, she quickly and dextrously made a tiny clay couple going at it hammer and tongs. A little embarrassed, I asked Maria how many other people make pícaras in Ilobasco.

'Me, Catarina, Angeline, Natalia and Juanita,' she said, counting them off on her hand. 'Cinco!'

'Five!' I repeat. 'And all señoritas!'

She laughed. 'Si!'

I asked if I could buy one and Maria showed me a shelf with a dozen or so pícaras, all with different covers and all with different sorpresas underneath. I chose a chaste bride with a couple in what can be best described as a 'honeymoon' position underneath her skirt. Maria waved goodbye from her door, bemused, as Wallis gave me a ride back into town. Keen to celebrate my purchase, I asked him if he would join the GND and me for a beer.

'Thank you,' he said politely, 'But I must go back to work.'

And now, the business of buying a pícara and defying the Catholic church done, it was time for us to move on too. The next day was the GND's birthday and I'd got it into my head that she should spend it in Honduras.

CHAPTER EIGHTEEN

Honduras (again)

Annoying habit >>> Rule breaking
Culprit >>> Peter

I'd like to think that one day the GND will look back fondly on her 31st birthday. She got to spend the night before it in San Miguel in a hotel painted an extraordinary shade of pink. She awoke on her birthday to enjoy the kind of breakfast that only the third largest city in El Salvador and transport hub for the eastern part of the country can provide – a plate of beans and rice. And instead of trundling down the more straightforward route to Honduras along the Interamericana to the border at El Amatillo, she got to traverse the more obscure northern route through the FMLN guerrilla stronghold of Perquín and cross the border that was the scene of the infamous Football Wars of 1969.

As early as 1957 the Hondurans had expressed their annoyance at the number of El Salvadoreans illegally entering their country through this tiny forgotten border. In 1969, however, that annoyance developed into a full-scale war, triggered by a disputed decision in a third-round qualifying match for the World Cup between the two countries. The war lasted 13 days and 2000 people were killed before a cease-fire was arranged by the Organisation of American States. A peace treaty wasn't signed, however, until 1980, and as late as early 1997 there had been skirmishes in the area.

To historians, the root cause of the war was not the football match but rather the social tension caused by workers migrating from overcrowded El Salvador to Honduras. But for soccer fanatics, it will always be regarded as proof positive of the importance of the world game – 'Football is so passionately followed in Latin America', read the soccer books, 'a war was fought over it.' Having said that, those same books forget to tell you the important stuff: What was the decision that caused the ruckus? Who was the ref? And, most importantly, who won the football match?

The border was only three kilometres from Perquín, another place etched heavily into El Salvador's military history. This dusty town high in dry mountains had been the headquarters of the FLMN guerrillas during the civil war. The surrounding district, Morazán, had seen some of the ferocious fighting and suffered the heaviest bombing from US-sponsored troops in Honduras. Our bus journey up through the barren hills was like a lesson in leftist military history. The bus stopped at Ciudad Segundo Montes, a cooperative named after one of six Jesuit priests killed in 1989, and we ate at a restaurant called La Guacamaya Subversiva. Then, only ten kilometres before Perquín, we passed the wrought-iron art sculpture of three lonely figures that marks the turnoff to El Mozote, the site of one of the worst massacres in Latin American history. In 1981, in retaliation for guerrilla successes in the north and east, government troops massacred over 900 villagers here – men, women and children.

Elsewhere, the district was dotted with cooperative farms set up by ex-FLMN combatants and funded by left-leaning aid agencies from around the world. Each agency was keen to advertise their involvement and the road was cluttered with billboards. It was like a road in the US, except instead of signs advertising an all-you-can-eat buffet at Barnacle Bill's, these signs told you that this particular irrigation project was brought to you by the Swiss Red Cross and that a farm assistance scheme was sponsored by the Canadian government.

We arrived in Perquín just after lunch and decided that it looked like it could have done with a little international aid itself. It was a tiny village with low houses and a few shops that sold beans from hessian sacks. Strangely, the town seemed to be centred on a rundown basketball court, not the Museo de la Revolución, which was up a dirt road on a hill overlooking Perquín.

The museum was built on the site of the guerrilla headquarters to commemorate and chronicle the FLMN's armed struggle during the civil war. I asked the woman selling tickets if she knew anything about the Football War, but she just shrugged her shoulders and gave me a brochure in English. 'Not fútbol,' she said. 'Agrarian reform!'

The museum was housed in a simple building with adobe walls and a tin roof. One room featured solidarity posters from around the world. In another, there were examples of the weapons used – AK 47s, M-16s, mortar launchers and a tiny Casio FX8208 computer that the FLMN used to calculate arms captured, prisoners and other details. (Strangely, this was the only section of the museum you weren't allowed to take photos in.) Outside, the museum grounds featured the remains of US planes and helicopters shot down during the conflict, including the ejection seat of a Dragonfly A-37, the abandoned studios of Radio Venceremos and a crater left by a 500-pound bomb.

The most sobering display was the collection of pictures drawn by children during the war. They were bright and colourful and looked exactly like the pictures stuck on fridges by proud parents around the world. Except that instead of Mum and Dad outside in the sun beside a tree, these pictures featured stick people with their heads cut off or blood spurting from wounds. Others showed stick soldiers with guns shooting animals and children.

A podgy man standing beside me shook his head and sighed. 'It was terrible, the war,' he said. His name was Roberto and he had migrated to the US at the start of the civil war. He was visiting with his family. 'My children were born in the USA,' he said. 'I wanted them to see their country, but also to realise how lucky they are.'

I asked him if he remembered the Football War of 1969. His face lit up. 'I was eleven,' he beamed. 'But it was very exciting. It was the second round for the qualifiers for the 1970 World Cup in Mexico. Honduras beat us one–nil in Tegu, but in the return match at San Salvador we won three–nil. A play-off had to be staged in Mexico to see who would go through.'

His kids, brought up on baseball and basketball, were bored and couldn't understand their father's passion for football. 'It was a torrid game,' he reminisced, 'and in the second half the referee sent off two players. We won three–two and the war started.'

I asked him who the referee was.

'I can't remember,' he said, 'Some guy from Europe. All I remember is that it was a very proud day for us.'

That proud moment didn't last long. The El Salvador team didn't make it past the first round in the 1970 World Cup. In fact, they didn't score a goal and were walloped by the Mexicans, Belgians and Russians. You've got to ask yourself, was such a fate worth fighting over?

The bus for Honduras left at 2 pm, and after a false start that saw the driver replace a flat tyre with one just as tattered and slick, it began its climb up the pine-clad mountains towards the border. It seemed the border was in a constant state of flux, currently placed only three kilometres from Perquín, but always being pushed and tested by settlers, encouraged by the government of El Salvador to move there. The hills were covered in communities of log huts, freshly built but with nothing else around them. Children played in the dirt tracks between them. Men, with nothing to do and nowhere to work, stood in doorways. It was like structural pissing, a way the El Salvadoreans marked their territory, and judging by the number of half-finished houses, the Football War wasn't over by a long shot.

Beyond these villages, the bus laboured up steep hills, sharp rocks popping ominously against the tyres. It was slow going but offered beautiful vistas across the hills. Soon we came upon a collection of white demountable buildings with a Hondutel satellite dish that served as the Honduras border post. The driver stopped and indicated for me and the GND to get off.

Inside one of the demountables, two immigration officials were lazily reading a newspaper, a revolver sitting on the desk. They looked up when we entered. 'Where are you going?' one of them asked, surprised.

'Tegucigalpa,' I answered.

He turned to his friend and laughed. 'Why are you going there?' he chuckled. 'Haven't you heard the news? Mitch has destroyed everything. There are no houses, no bridges, no nothing!'

The GND looked alarmed, which I think was the reaction he was after.

He started copying our details from our passports onto a form. 'Where will you stay?' he asked. 'The Hotel Granada, perhaps?'

I nodded. Our guidebook had said it was the best deal in town.

The immigration guy turned to his friend and laughed again and I began to suspect that the Hotel Granada may have been washed away. He stamped our passports and handed them back with a smile. 'Enjoy your stay in Tegucigalpa!' he smirked.

As soon as we left the room they burst into raucous laughter.

'Why did they laugh?' asked the GND. 'Do you think Tegucigalpa is really that bad?'

'No!' I said unconvincingly. 'They were just pulling our legs!' Deep down, however, I wasn't so sure.

The Honduran side of the border immediately looked more established. The houses were older, the roads better and the countryside cultivated. It was a pretty spot of blue skies and rolling green fields and reminded me a little of the Swiss Alps, although that may have been because some of the cows wore bells. The bus stopped at a small village where all the passengers got off and lounged on the grass while the bus driver ate a meal in a shack nearby. The GND and I lay on the grass, watching the clouds skitter past. It was a nice moment – quiet, peaceful, soothing. A small child, wearing a Pope John II T-shirt came up and offered us some boiled sweets.

'What a birthday I'm having!' said the GND, lying on her back, watching the sky. 'I've spent it in two countries!'

I was glad she felt that way. I had been beginning to worry that it might not have been turning out quite as she had expected. Besides, it looked as though we would only get as far as Marcala that day.

Marcala is the heart of one of the finest coffee-growing regions in Honduras, and home to the Comarca coffee cooperative, whose factory marks the beginning of the town and fills the air with the smell of freshly roasted coffee. We arrived just on dusk, and as we had spent most of the GND's birthday travelling, I was determined to make it up to her. We would stay in a nice hotel – one with clean sheets, an attached bathroom with hot and cold running water – and eat at the best restaurant in town.

The Hotel Medina fitted the bill and, more to the point, was willing to accept us as guests. Unfortunately, the best restaurant in town, El Mirador, had been booked for a wedding reception. The second-best restaurant, the Riviera Linda, was holding a wake. The only other place recommended in our guidebook, Geminis, had been turned into a disco. Two Honduran guys propping up the bar at Geminis suggested we try the Fuk Lim Chinese Restaurant on the other side of the park.

The Fuk Lim was a bare, scruffy place, with grubby blue walls and a faded poster of the Great Wall stuck up above the counter. The laminated tables were chipped and the chairs wonky. It was run by a Chinese guy with a bowl haircut and a gruff manner, who spoke to the kitchen staff in Spanish with a Chinese accent, and to us in English with a weird Spanish-Chinese hybrid accent. After perusing the menu, handwritten on a tattered piece of A4 paper, the GND ordered sweet and sour chicken.

'No chicken, only pork!' the owner snapped.

The GND asked for steamed rice.

'No rice, only salad!' he barked.

The GND was shocked. This was a Chinese restaurant. How could there not be rice?

'Take too long cook!'

Only a year before, the GND's previous boyfriend had taken her to the Waterfront Restaurant in Sydney for her birthday. There, looking over the Opera House and one of the most beautiful harbours in the world, she tucked into a huge plate of lobster, prawns, Balmain bugs and oysters, quaffing champagne and chardonnay. Now, a year later, she was pushing what may or may not have been sweet and sour pork around her plate while looking at water stains on the wall and drinking cheap, albeit cold, Honduran beer. When I asked her if she was happy, she smiled weakly.

Just as she had pushed away her salad – nothing more than a plate of bean sprouts – we were joined by two guys we had spoken to at Geminis. Nothing was happening at the disco so they decided to check out the Fuk Lim. One was short and round, and spoke in short, sharp bursts. He looked like James Belushi, and on finding out it was the GND's birthday, took her hand and kissed it, declaring that she was 'banda' (beautiful). The other was taller and older, and looked a lot like the actor James Coburn. Both seemed determined that the GND should celebrate her birthday in style. And in the Fuk Lim Chinese Restaurant in Marcala, Honduras, style meant cold beers, and lots of them.

I don't remember much more of that evening. Judging from the number of bottles on the table in the photos taken that night, we had quite a bit to drink. But for every drink we had, our new friends had three. We all staggered out of the restaurant just after midnight a little worse for wear. We stumbled back to our room – the bus to Tegucigalpa was leaving at the ungodly hour of five am. James Belushi and James Coburn set out for the disco again.

When we woke the next morning it was raining and a fine mist had settled on the town. It was the kind of weather for sleeping in, and it took some convincing to get the GND out of a bed that was perhaps the most comfortable we had slept in on our journey so far. But we had a bus to Tegucigalpa to catch, and we found it down by the town park, the engine ticking over in the pre-dawn chill. I had lured the GND from bed by telling her that we would spend most of the journey sleeping, perhaps even all of it, with the driver gently shaking us from our slumber to tell us we had arrived. Of course, I hadn't realised that James Coburn was driving the bus and James Belushi was his offsider.

Quite frankly, they looked like shit. Their clothes were dishevelled, their eyes were bloodshot, and if a match had been lit anywhere near their breath the whole bus would have gone up. The GND supposed that they had come straight from the disco, but by the look of them I suspected that they had managed a couple of hours sleep in a gutter along the way. The GND and I took our seats alarmed – we'd seen how much they'd had to drink – but the rest of the passengers sat around chatting, unaware that their lives were in danger.

James Coburn drove the bus like he was trying to get the four-hour trip to the capital over as quickly as possible. He rattled around the misty mountains at a great pace, slowing briefly to pass through a small village, but only because the roads were crowded with donkeys and pick-ups in town for the Sunday market. As soon as the village was cleared and we were into the mountains again, he put his foot flat to the floor.

To take my mind off our certain demise – I had foolishly taken a window seat and saw how close we came to plunging into ravines – I read the ten rules for riding the bus. They were a remnant from the bus's previous incarnation as a US school bus and were clearly posted over James Coburn's head. I checked off each one I was breaking.

1. Observe the same conduct as in the classroom. (How could I be bored and disinterested when my life was at stake?)
2. Be courteous and do not use profane language. (I had broken that one the first time we nearly plunged over a ravine. Luckily this wasn't a Catholic school bus because I had blasphemed as well.)
3. Do not eat or drink in bus. (I obeyed this one. I was too distracted to even think of eating.)
4. Keep the bus clean. (No one else was, so why should I?)
5. Cooperate with the driver. (Did that mean not reporting him to the appropriate authorities?)
6. Do not smoke. (Not a problem for me, maybe more of one for the GND.)
7. Do not be destructive. (Didn't have to. Our driver seemed hell bent on that.)
8. Stay in your seat. (A bit hard when your driver insists on taking corners on two wheels.)
9. Keep head, hands and feet inside the bus. (Impossible in the inevitable crash.)
10. The bus driver is authorised to assign seats. (. . . and plunge over ravines . . . and take your life.)

Tegucigalpa is the capital of Honduras, a city of 800,000 people that stands in a basin at between 950 and 1100 metres above sea level. It came into existence as a mining camp in 1578 and is surrounded on three sides by high rugged peaks riddled with old silver mines. Unlike most Central American capitals, it was well off the major fault lines and had not fallen victim to any major earthquakes or any other natural disaster for that matter. The topography that had served it well in the past, however, betrayed the city in the face of the heavy rains that came with Hurricane Mitch. The mountains surrounding Tegucigalpa acted like a natural funnel, directing the floodwaters towards the city with ruthless efficiency. Only in Tegucigalpa, there was no hole at the bottom for the water to drain out.

Our bus terminated in Comayagüela, a poorer district in the south of the city and the one worst affected by the flooding. Whole street blocks were deserted, the buildings still standing empty and looted without any doors or windows, ugly brown stains just below the ceilings marking the high-water mark. Down by Río Choluteca, the river that runs through the centre of the city and the cause of most of the destruction, teams of American marines were clearing rubble with bulldozers or busily rebuilding Molina Bridge. The bridge linked Tegucigalpa and Comayagüla, and was one of the city's busiest thoroughfares. Of the six bridges over the Río Choluteca, five had been washed away by the floods, leaving one bridge to carry all the town's traffic. There was a brown gash clearly visible on a mountainside in the west of the city, caused by a mud slide that had thundered through a poorer district. The houses it had collected on the way through lay in a pile of rubble at the bottom.

We waved over a taxi and caught it through the worst of the destruction to Plaza Morazán in the heart of Tegucigalpa's central business district. Only 400 metres from the river, this area was high enough, it seemed, to avoid the worst of the damage. Here life continued as normal – a McDonald's doling out Big Macs, a cinema showing the latest movies from Hollywood and offices where people in business clothes went about their business.

'It looked like the whole city had been destroyed on CNN,' said the GND. 'Up here it's like nothing has happened.'

Despite what the immigration officials at the border implied, the Hotel Granada had escaped unscathed too. It was a large hotel that had the feel of a YMCA and was full of American Peace Corp workers. They were not in town to help with the reconstruction, but rather to watch the XXXIII Superbowl between the Denver Broncos and the Atlanta Falcons. Most, it seemed, lived and worked in villages too small or too poor to have satellite TV. They had planned their journey to the capital for the big match months in advance and weren't about to let a little thing like the worst hurricane in history get in their way.

I can't say that I'm a great fan of American Football. It's one of those sports, like cricket, I guess, that you have to be born with. For one thing, how can a 60-minute game end up taking two or three hours to play? And for God's sake, what is it with all the padding? I just can't take seriously these guys who say how tough it is when they have the equivalent of a queen-sized mattress around them.

Of course, I didn't express these views to the gang of Peace Corp workers who had gathered around the TV in the hotel's cafeteria. I didn't have the benefit of the said padding and figured it would be wiser to sit quietly and see if I could pick up some scraps of information that would make the game a little less mystifying. Not having anything better to do, the GND joined me. By the fourteenth minute I was none the wiser, and was secretly relieved when the broadcast was interrupted by a special message from the Honduran President Carlos Flores Facussé, just as Denver's Jason Elam lined up to take a field goal. The Peace Corp workers, however, were furious.

'Not again!' one yelled in a growl not becoming of the Peace Corp. 'Why does this prick always do this?'

One guy, a younger version of Gomez from 'The Addams Family', shook his head. He'd served in the military and still had the bearing of an enlisted man.

'Since the hurricane he hasn't shut up,' he said. 'The guy thinks it's his chance to strut on the world stage.'

Considering that the president had just jammed every satellite channel into the country to broadcast his message, I thought it was going to be something of national import. Instead it turned out to be nothing more than a PR exercise on how 'presidential' President Flores was. We saw him visiting areas devastated by the hurricane and helping to deliver relief. We saw him open a bridge and then, a few months later, visit what little was left of it after the floods. There was even footage of the president meeting President Clinton.

The Clinton footage sparked a debate among the Peace Corp workers about the whole Lewinsky affair. Gomez was particularly strident in his views. 'Clinton should have said, "Hell yeah, I screwed her. I'm the Goddamn President of the Yew-nited States of America. I can screw whoever I want!"' Then spotting the GND he added, 'Excuse me, Ma'am.'

Gomez was more upset about the lying than the sexual indiscretion. Clinton was the commander-in-chief of the armed forces after all. 'You get kicked out of the military for that sort of thing,' he said.

Eventually there were no more bridges to view or victims to mourn and the broadcast of the Superbowl returned. Denver had a 31–6 lead and the game was as good as over.

'Fucking great!' said Gomez. 'Just in time to see who got MVP!'

John Elway was named MVP, having passed for 336 yards and for scoring a touchdown, which we'd missed. The only Peace Corp worker who didn't seem too upset by the interruption was a chap from San Diego. He was good-looking in a David Cassidy kind of way and fancied himself as a bit of a ladies' man. He had spent most of the Superbowl and the president's message chatting to a blonde Dutch girl. When she got up and left, he turned his attentions to the GND. 'Is this the first time you guys have travelled together?' he said softly, hoping I wouldn't hear.

The GND nodded her head.

'Any problems?'

The GND shrugged and asked him why he'd asked.

'No reason,' he said, noticing that I was listening. 'It's just that you guys didn't talk to each other much during the game.'

The incident concerned me. It wasn't that I thought the GND would leave me and run off with a Peace Corp Worker from San Diego – I was carrying her hairdryer, after all. It was just that guys like that are very good at sensing problems in relationships and moving in for the kill. I thought things were okay with the GND at the moment. I'd taken her to the Fuk Lim for her birthday, for Christ's sake. But maybe I was wrong.

After checking our e-mails – most were from family and friends warning us not to go to Tegucigalpa – we packed our bags and headed to the bus station to catch a bus to the border with Nicaragua. Our taxi took us back down to the river, along roads still slick with mud and between leaning telegraph poles with debris tangled in the wire. Here Tegucigalpa was abuzz with workmen building new drains and bulldozers clearing away rubble. As we sat in traffic we spotted smaller, more poignant reminders of the tragedy that had struck the city – a doll, a photo album, a single shoe, a computer keyboard all stuck in mud that was drying and cracking.

Elsewhere, there were examples of the indomitable spirit of Tegucigalpa's residents. A film crew filmed children playing in the rubble. People came down to the river to look at the rubble, to 'ooh' and 'aahh' as humans are prone to do, but most were going about their lives as normal.

'Look at those people crossing the bridge,' the GND said. 'They're not even looking at the destruction anymore.'

They had already become blasé about the devastation wrought by Mitch.

Our plan was to enter Nicaragua, via Danlí and El Paraíso, at Las Manos. According to our guidebook the journey to the border would take three hours. By my calculations we could probably be in León, the old colonial capital of Nicaragua, by nightfall.

Our journey didn't start auspiciously. The next bus to the border wasn't leaving for an hour. And when it did finally leave, I misheard the conductor, and thinking our fare was 15 lempiras gave him a 20-lempira note. The fare turned out to be 30 lempira, 15 lempira each, so I took back the 20-lempira note and gave him a 50. The conductor walked off with my money thinking that the 20 lempira I'd taken back was the change.

The GND wanted me to let the issue lie.

'It's only $2.50,' she said. 'And besides, you don't speak Spanish well enough to explain.'

She was right, of course, but I wasn't going to let my Spanish lessons in Quetzaltenango go to waste. I tried to explain what had happened in Spanish, and, after that failed, I tried to re-enact the scene. This was complicated by the fact that I didn't have a 50-lempira note and had to ask the conductor to imagine that a 100-lempira note was in fact a 50-lempira note. Luckily another passenger figured out what I was trying to say and explained. When the conductor reluctantly handed back a 20-lempira note, everyone else around laughed. I thought they were laughing at me, the stupid gringo. He seemed to think they were laughing at him.

At Danlí, an attractive town in the heart of a sugar cane and tobacco district, most of the passengers got off, including the guy who had helped sort out the change problem. He seemed perplexed that we were staying on the bus. 'Frontera?' he asked, with a knitted brow.

'Si, frontera,' I said. That was our ultimate aim, the frontera (border) with Nicaragua. He shrugged his shoulders and waved goodbye.

'Are you sure this is the right bus?' asked the GND, alarmed.

I wasn't, so I went up to the conductor to make sure. In broken Spanish, I listed all the places that I hoped the bus would go through – El Paraíso, Las Manos, the frontera, Nicaragua. I pulled out my guidebook and pointed to Las Manos right on the border with Nicaragua. He nodded his head vigorously and said, 'Si', and gave me the kind of look that said, of course that's where we are going, you stupid gringo.

The bus set off down a sealed road with only a handful of passengers. Within five kilometres the road was unsealed, and shortly after that we were bouncing along a bumpy track, fording streams and passing washed-out bridges. This was a vast land of swamps and farmlands, with very few settlements and no electricity. The only sign of civilisation was the occasional cowboy riding on his horse.

Although my guidebook clearly stated that the road to El Paraíso was sealed and that the 18 kilometres would take no longer than 30 minutes, it was not until an hour and a half later that I finally admitted to myself that we were heading in the wrong direction.

'I thought this was only supposed to take 30 minutes,' said the GND.

'We've probably had to take a different route because of hurricane damage,' I argued. It is amazing how you can justify anything when you're afraid of the consequences of a particular answer.

'Well, this way isn't better,' she said pointing at a washed-out bridge. 'Go and ask again.'

I went up to the front of the bus and asked the conductor again. This time the driver overheard what I was saying. 'Las Manos?!' he asked with alarm. When I nodded he let loose with a stream of Spanish at the conductor that was fast, heated and pointed. The conductor looked duly chastised, but not enough to stop him shooting me a filthy look. The bus driver said something to me in a tone that suggested I should sit down and he'd sort it out.

I was furious and told the GND that the conductor was obviously a moron. I know I wasn't speaking his language, but anyone with a modicum of intelligence would have figured out what I was trying to say. Especially when I showed them a map.

'Maybe he's illiterate,' said the GND. 'In which case showing him a map wouldn't have meant a thing.'

She was probably right. What she didn't understand was that letting loose with a torrent of abuse, well out of earshot, of course, helps calm the nerves.

'Listen,' I said. 'Even if he is illiterate, even if my pronunciation is rooted, surely it should have struck him as weird, two gringos heading off into the backblocks of Honduras. Surely he could have figured that one out!'

Ten minutes later the bus driver waved down a bus heading back towards Danlí, and put us on it. He even paid for our fare (hopefully out of the conductor's wage). I thanked him and resisted the urge to give his offsider the finger. He must have also told the other driver of our plight because when we finally arrived back in Danlí he made quite a show of putting us on the right bus to El Paraíso. The condescending way he ushered us to our seat made me feel like we were on an outing from a sheltered workshop.

As our guidebook had said, it only took half an hour to get from Danlí to El Paraíso, past cigar factories and coffee plantations and farms. Earlier in the day that would have given us plenty of time to get to Las Manos and the border. But when we arrived in El Paraíso, still 12 kilometres from the border, the sun was setting on a long and frustrating day. We wouldn't be getting to León after all. In fact, we wouldn't even be getting into Nicaragua.

CHAPTER NINETEEN

Nicaragua

Annoying habit >>> Quick to accuse
Culprit >>> Peter

We turned up at the Nicaraguan border without a visa and,
after the hassle of getting there, prepared to pay handsomely
should we need one. As it was the immigration guy on
duty issued us a visa on the spot and only charged us $7
to boot. The only complication was that he insisted that it
was all paid in one-dollar bills.

'You are lucky you are not German,' said a young
Nicaraguan woman crossing with us. 'The government here
still think they are Nazis. Even the money changers won't
deal with them.'

The girl's name was Maria. She was confident and well

dressed and spoke perfect English, albeit with an American accent. She had perfected the accent studying international trade at university in Louisiana, a course her father hoped would help with the family business. Her family owned most of the coffee plantations around Ocotal, and, since the demise of the Sandinista, her father was expanding the business.

'My dad wants to start exporting directly,' she said. 'That's where the big money is.'

The area around Ocotal had been among those worst hit by Hurricane Mitch in Nicaragua. The main bridge leading out of town had been washed away, leaving the town cut off and isolated from the rest of the world for a month. Maria was home from university for the holidays at the time. 'Luckily my mother loves food,' she laughed. 'She had enough in her pantry to get us through.'

I asked her how the coffee crops had fared.

'They're up high,' she said. 'So the flooding didn't affect them. A few landslides, but that's it. Actually, with all the damage in Honduras it could be a good year for us. Coffee prices will be high.'

Maria was no stranger to natural disasters. She had been born during the 1972 earthquake and had seen her country survive earthquakes, fighting and flooding before. She had just visited friends in Tegucigalpa and was concerned by how Honduras was coping. 'We're used to starting over again,' she said, as we passed another washed out bridge. 'But the Hondurans. The Hondurans are not coping well at all.'

The road to Ocotal wound its way through the mountains,

passing coffee and banana plantations. Our progress was slowed by a gang of bulldozers clearing the road of landslides. When the bus came upon a washed-out bridge too damaged to cross, it turned off the road and drove along a bumpy temporary road through the riverbed.

'Thank God Mitch was the last storm of the season,' said Maria. 'These roads will wash away after the next rain.'

The bus only went as far as Ocotal, a quaint town of whitewashed buildings. Maria led us to another bus, and spoke with the driver to make sure he knew that we wanted to go to León, not Managua, and to drop us off at the appropriate crossroads to change buses. We thanked her as she got into the Mercedes, complete with chauffeur, which her father had sent to pick her up.

'No problem,' she said. 'One day I might need help in your country.'

She was probably one of the few Nicaraguans who could afford to get to Australia.

Our journey was unremarkable except for the fact that for the first time since Mexico we were assigned a seat number and, more surprisingly, people respected them. The bridge leading out of town had been patched up, if only temporarily, and supported a constant stream of cars, buses and trucks heading further into Nicaragua. The bus travelled from the highlands to the hot dusty plains, passing dusty towns where every boy under twelve seemed to be playing baseball on dusty pitches. As per Maria's instructions, it dropped us off at a crossroads just outside of San Isidro, where, after only a short time, another bus turned up and took us the rest of the way to León.

In the short time it took us to walk from the bus station to our hotel, it became apparent that León was the rocking chair capital of Central America. As we walked past the low colonial houses we looked in the front rooms to see people sitting in wooden rocking chairs, rocking backwards and forwards. They sat in groups, rocking as they watched television, read newspapers or simply gossiped. Sometimes there were just clusters of empty rocking chairs around a silent television.

León is regarded as the intellectual capital of Nicaragua, but the day we arrived it was simply dusty, hot and neglected. Transport around the city had not progressed beyond carts pulled by cattle and it appeared as though no one had bothered to paint a building or sweep a street since the Spanish left in 1858. In the middle of the day, when the scorching heat drove the people of León indoors and back to their rocking chairs, it was like a ghost town. The only signs of its intellectual leanings were the leftist murals that covered some of the walls.

We wanted to see the city's cathedral, the largest in Central America, so after getting a room and showering, we stepped out into the dry, crackling heat. Legend has it that the city fathers sent more modest plans to Spain for approval, fearing that the plans they intended to use would be knocked back for being too extravagant. Started in 1747, the cathedral took over 100 years to build. It is a massive pile of stone, and that day, the neglect, the peeling paint, made it seem even larger.

The interior of León cathedral had just been painted, that yellow-cream colour favoured by inner-city landlords because it is light and bright and goes pretty much with anything. As far as we could see, this was the extent of the restorations sponsored by the Spanish in 1990. After checking out the tomb of Rubén Darío, the country's most famous poet and a man regarded as the 'Prince of Spanish-American literature', we wandered through the cathedral admiring the huge paintings of the stations of the cross by Antonio Sarria. The paintings are regarded by many as masterpieces of colonial art and they were huge, dark and quite stunning.

'Is that what I think it is?' asked the GND, peering at a yellow splotch on the third station.

It was a drip of paint. And on closer inspection, there was not just one, but many. Worse, there were splotches on every painting. On one painting, the eighth station of the cross, there was a pale smudge where a painter must have noticed that he'd dripped paint and tried to wipe it off. Incredibly, the painters hadn't bothered to cover the artworks when they were painting the walls and the ceiling. Perhaps they thought protecting priceless pieces of art would take too long. Maybe they'd cut it fine on the tender. Probably, they had another job to go to. Bloody tradesmen! They're the same the world over.

We spent the rest of the afternoon visiting the monuments to León's past importance. We visited the house where Rubén Darío was born, which is now a museum celebrating the poet's life and work. We dropped in on the Mothers Gallery of Heroes and Martyrs, a collection of 300 photos of revolutionaries who lost their lives fighting the Somoza regime. And we admired the huge mural in Jérez Park that told the story of Nicaragua's struggle against Somoza and the triumph of the revolution. But at no time did we get a sense of the city's current inclinations. León had been the only city that voted for the Sandinistas in the 1990 and 1996 elections, and our guidebook had said León was the radical and intellectual centre of the country. As far as I could see, however, being radical and intellectual in León amounted to nothing more than sitting in a rocking chair all day.

'Perhaps they're more politically active when it's cooler,' said the GND, hinting, not too subtly, that she was hot and had had enough.

■   ■   ■

That night we gave the city one last chance to prove its intellectual cred and visited the Cafetín Rincon Azul, a place popular with university students. Sadly, it reflected the trend we'd noticed throughout Central America, where the new intellectualism consisted of aping 'Beverly Hills 90210'. The students all wore jeans and T-shirts and had mobile phones. The walls were covered in graffiti, but instead of political slogans, they reflected baser concerns. 'Thank you for being with me when I really needed you,' said one. 'You're the best I ever had.' Another stated, weirdly, 'Orgasm Existential in León.' The lone Australian contribution was a roughly drawn map of Australia with the deep slogan 'Aussie Rules!' We had a beer, American of course, and left disappointed.

On the way back to our hotel we passed Poets' Park. I'm not exactly sure if that was its proper name. The GND had named it that when we had passed earlier because in the centre was a full-sized statue of Rubén Darío, surrounded by the busts of lesser known Nicaraguan poets and intellectuals. Now, in the cool of the evening, a small crowd had gathered, many of them bringing their rocking chairs with them, to listen to serious-looking poets read out their work under the watchful gaze of Mr R Darío.

The poets all had the same look – a tortured, hunched-shouldered, artistic kind of vibe – and approached the microphone that had been set up with dread and hesitation. Most read from clipboards, as if they were still working on the pieces, and had a propensity to mumble. Although we couldn't understand what they were reading – although I did pick up trabadjor (worker) a few times – they were obviously passionate about their work and were well received by the audience. After finishing, each poet stared at the ground while the MC thanked them. After he gave them a clenched-fist sign of solidarity, they would scurry off into the dark.

The GND and I sat on the kerb opposite and watched. It was a lovely evening – balmy but breezy – and there was a real communal feel. People laughed and chatted. Kids, freshly washed and in their best clothes, ran around the legs of the adults, or sat fidgeting whenever a poet got up to read their work. When the last of the poets finished, the audience packed up their chairs, gathered their children and wandered home, stopping occasionally to chat to friends.

The GND and I wandered back to the hotel arm in arm. I was happy. I had been worried that the spirit of the revolution, the respect for literature that the Nicaraguans had fought for, had been lost. That night, under the watchful gaze of Rubén Darío, my faith had been restored.

■   ■   ◨

Our bus to Managua the next day was decorated with tiny ceramic animals. They were the kind of things that kids collect or you'd win at a fair – cats, dogs, horses and deer. They all sat on a shelf above the driver, neatly arranged along species lines, and they managed, to my amazement, to stay there for the entire journey. The driver was obviously a bit of an old softy, because he had similarly soppy tastes in music. The journey started with 'All That I Need'. We travelled along the alley of the volcanoes listening to 'To Sir With Love'. Finally, when we arrived in Managua, Foreigner, and I guess the driver too, wanted to know what love is.

Managua is situated on the southern shores of Lake Managua and was declared the capital of Nicaragua in 1858. It only got the job because of the incessant squabbling between the intellectuals in León and the wealthy folk in Granada, the conservative city to the south. Being about halfway between the two, Managua was suggested as the compromise capital. It has not had a good time of things. In 1931, Managua was destroyed by an earthquake, and five years later a fire swept through what remained. The city was completely rebuilt and enjoyed a period of prosperity until another earthquake levelled it in 1972. After geologists found the entire downtown area riddled with fault lines, the decision was made not to rebuild the city centre. Instead, the city fragmented, decentralised if you will, into a variety of market, commercial and residential districts.

Can I say right now that I hate cities like Managua? The bus station is always in the area furthest from cheap hotels and all the banks and post offices are in an area furthest from both. Worse, in Managua, we stayed in a hotel that wasn't really close to anything, and was full of fresh-faced American college students in town to do a bit of volunteer work.

'Whoah dude!' one yelled, late at night. 'We're in Nicaragua!'

Nicaragua, it seems, had become summer camp for Americans with a conscience.

'Monica,' one yelled. 'Whatta ya doin?'

'Unpacking,' replied Monica.

'Come and unpack in here!'

Not content with waking every one in the hotel with the sharp, painful pitch of their voices, they turned a cassette player on. It was a tape of some tortured American female singer doing a version of 'Tangled Up In Blue'. To make matters worse, they started singing along.

The GND was furious. 'Don't they know there are other guests?' she hissed.

To be honest I don't think they did. Americans rarely do. For some reason they don't comprehend anything beyond a two-foot radius around themselves. It's not that it's malicious, they just don't realise that there is anything else outside their limited realm of existence. I'm sure when the Romans ruled the earth they were the same. Everyone was speaking Latin, all the important stuff was happening in Rome, and all the highest-paid gladiators were appearing in Roman stadiums. Who cares what's happening in outer

Galacia? My point was proved when I went out to the bathroom and they spotted me. It suddenly dawned on them that there were other guests and they immediately turned the music down.

There was nothing to keep us in Managua – well apart from the new mall with a McDonald's, a Pizza Hut and a five-theatre cineplex with high-backed chairs and a THX sound system. But you'll understand, even an airconditioned cinema experience loses its allure when all you can see in English is *You've Got Mail*. We'd tried our hand at sightseeing, visiting the old downtown, only to find goats grazing in what once had been the city's major cathedral. It was an eerie ghost town where the wind whipped off Lake Managua, tossing litter around an amphitheatre built especially for the pope's visit and abandoned shortly after. When I fell into an open drain hole, covered only by a rusty piece of tin, we decided it was time to move on to Granada.

Granada is Nicaragua's oldest Spanish city. Standing at the foot of Mombacho Volcano, on the north-western shore of Lake Nicaragua, it is a quaint town of low, Spanish-style houses, white adobe walls and quiet, cool inner courtyards. Access to the Caribbean Sea via the lake and the San Juan River made the city a major trade centre and a favourite target for French and English pirates, who took the same route to come and pillage. They sacked the city three times between the time it was founded in 1524 and 1685. In fact, trashing Granada proved to be a favourite pastime. When American filibuster William Walker was driven from the town in 1856 after being briefly in control, he burned the city to the ground, his troops leaving a placard that read 'Here was Granada'.

Granada was rebuilt, and despite a few skirmishes between the Sandinistas and pro-Somoza forces, the city has been able to retain much of its colonial character. The area around the Cathedral and Parque Colón was particularly charming, a little piece of Castille in Central America, complete with horses and carts. If nothing else, Granada was proof that it is the conservatives who have all the money. While it didn't have the massive cathedral that León had, or the rich cultural heritage afforded to León by Rubén Darío and his mates, the city did have enough money to give some of its finest buildings a lick of paint. It gave the place a refined charm and meant that the few tourists who came to Nicaragua, spent most of their time here.

One of those tourists was Rebecca, a 24-year-old New Zealander who had the demeanour of a sprightly old rambler. She was obscenely optimistic and liked to 'muck in', and within minutes of meeting us had arranged for us to visit the Masaya Volcano National Park with her.

The area around Masaya Volcano was declared a national park in 1975, the first in Nicaragua. A bus heading back to Managua dropped us off at the park entrance, and from there Rebecca convinced a Nicaraguan family visiting the park for a picnic to give us a lift to the crater. We sat in the back of a pick-up with granny and the kids, smiling inanely, as you do, as it bounced along a potholed road through scrubby vegetation and up a gentle slope, surrounded either side by black lava flows. Five minutes later, we pulled into a carpark that overlooked the crater.

'This is the kind of volcano I like,' said the GND with a smug smile. 'One you can drive right up to.'

To the right of the carpark, a wooden cross marked the highest point of the volcano and a viewing platform that was reached by a crude set of stairs. Father Francisco de Bobadilla planted a cross in the same spot in the sixteenth century to exorcise the 'Boca del Infierno'. According to legend, in pre-Columbian times children and young virgins were thrown into the crater to appease the gods. There was something about the Masaya Volcano that encouraged craziness. In 1538, a Spanish adventurer called Blas de Castillo descended into the crater looking for gold and returned empty-handed and a little singed. And only 90 years ago two German engineers, Schomberg and Scharfenberg, drilled into the cone hoping to produce sulphuric acid. They accidentally drilled into a 400-metre-wide lava tube, sparking off explosions and landslides, and barely escaping with their lives.

From the viewing platform it was possible to look straight into the mouth of the volcano. It was the first volcano I had been able to see into and it was creepy. As the sulphuric fumes danced around, shaped by the wind, it was possible to spot fissures and gaps through which the volcano hissed.

'It's like looking at the entrance to hell,' said the GND with a shudder.

That was probably why the native Indians had chosen this point to throw virgins into the volcano as a sacrifice to appease the gods and why Somoza chose to dispose of his political enemies here in a similar manner as well. The mouth of a volcano is the gateway to the underworld and to die here was to go straight to hell. The mother of a Canadian family, in Nicaragua for holidays from an assignment in Panama City, knew that too. She told her open-mouthed kids that it was where naughty children were thrown as well.

We stayed a few days in Granada, wandering the cobbled streets and eating in restaurants set in pretty courtyards. For all its colonial charm and beauty, Granada seemed to lack a soul. We never stumbled upon Poet's Night, nor did we see families gossiping on street corners. Instead we spotted a woman selling glue to homeless kids in the Central Plaza, moving among them, dribbling a small portion into plastic bags that they blew up and then inhaled. I think it was then that the GND decided that it was time to move on.

Our immediate destination was Ometepe, an island in Lake Nicaragua that our guidebook described as 'an ecotouristic jewel'. It is the largest island in the world – set in a freshwater lake, that is – and was dominated by two volcanoes, one at each end, and could be reached by a ferry that left Granada twice a week. From Ometepe, eventually we would catch another ferry to San Carlos, where we could cross into Costa Rica.

The ferry was not a large boat, it was more like a barge actually, so we were forced to cram in among Ometepians returning home after buying enough supplies in Granada to survive a nuclear winter.

One guy, dressed like a Homey, was returning after seven years in America and sought me out to speak English. He had a wife and two sons on the island, and he had sent them $100 a month while he was away. 'I don't like my own country,' he said. 'The people are too poor.'

Lake Nicaragua is the tenth largest freshwater lake in the world, 177 kilometres long and an average of 58 kilometres across, so, not surprisingly, it took most of the day for us to cross it. I spent much of the time moving our packs, trying to avoid a growing puddle of water, or trying to spot freshwater sharks. They were unique to Lake Nicaragua, trapped when a Pacific bay was cut off from the ocean by the uplifting of the earth's crust to form the lake, and they adapted as the water slowly turned from salt to freshwater.

As dusk approached, the twin volcanoes of Ometepe came into view, brooding in the twilight sky. I checked to see if our packs were still dry and noticed a girl looking at my camera bag in a suspicious manner. I kept everything in this bag – my money, my passport – and had rather foolishly left it unattended. Spooked, I checked to see if everything was there. To my alarm, my passport was missing.

'That girl stole my passport!' I said to the GND.

'Are you sure you didn't put it in another bag?' asked the GND, sensibly. 'Perhaps you left it somewhere?'

'She has it!' I exclaimed. 'I saw her looking in my bag. And she *looks* like she'd steal a passport!' (Of course, I was desperately clutching at straws. If someone had asked me at the time I probably would have said Mother Theresa looked like she would steal a passport too.)

I tried to ask the girl in broken Spanish if she had my passport but she simply gave me a blank look. I was convinced it was a clever ruse, extinguishing any look of guilt to throw me off her trail. The GND said she probably didn't understand what the hell I was saying. I tracked down my Homey friend and got him to ask her in Spanish, and he got the same blank look as well.

Now if you're from one of the more important countries in the world, losing your passport is not a big deal. You simply front up to your embassy in the country you lost it and get a new one. But as an Australian, I have to cope with the fact that Australian embassies are few and far between, especially in Central America. If I had to get a new passport I would either have to go to Mexico or Venezuela to find an Australian embassy. I would have to return to Managua and visit immigration to get special permission to leave Nicaragua without a passport. And then visit the Mexican or Venezuelan embassy to get permission to enter without a passport. The time and money involved would probably mean the end of our trip. The very thought of it made me sick to my stomach.

The Homey and I went to the captain of the boat to explain what had happened, and he radioed ahead for the police. I began to imagine the scene at the docks – the police waiting, the girl being dragged off, the brutal interrogation – and got a sinking feeling in my stomach. What if I had left my passport somewhere? But where? The hotel we had stayed in Granada hadn't insisted on seeing our passports on checking in. The only time I would have taken my passport out would have been to change money. I had been to the bank in Granada. Had I left it there? I couldn't say for sure that I hadn't left my passport at the bank. But nor could I say for certain that I had.

The port authority radioed the captain back and told him that the police had gone home early and wouldn't be able to get back before the ferry was due to continue on to San Carlos. I went back to the girl and got the Homey to ask her if she had seen anyone else near my bag. She shrugged her shoulders again. Through the Homey, I offered the girl $100 if she gave it back. It was my last shot.

'She says she hasn't got it, man' said my Homey translator. I could tell from the look on her face that she wished she did. So did my Homey.

From the port we hitched a ride on the back of a truck into Altagracia, a small neat town that was the largest settlement on the island. Our original plan had been to head for Santo Domingo Beach, a point midway between the two volcanoes and a place recommended by other travellers. But now that I'd lost my passport I would have to go back to Granada, and the bank, to make certain that I hadn't left it there. It was getting dark, so we took a room at the Hospedaje Castillo for the night.

The hospedaje was simple and clean, and named after its owner, Señor Ramón Castillo. Señor Castillo was reputed to be very knowledgable about Ometepe, so I asked him if he could help me with my problem.

'I could ring the bank tomorrow and check if you'd like,' he said.

That seemed to be the sensible approach. Señor Castillo would call the bank. If my passport was there I would set out for Granada to get it back. If it wasn't, the GND and I would spend a bit of time on Ometepe before heading back to Managua to begin the long drawn out process of getting a new one. I asked Señor Castillo how I could get back to Granada if I didn't want to wait.

'You will have to catch the 4.30 am bus to Moyogalpa,' he said. 'It is the only one that will get you there in time for the morning boat to the mainland.'

The GND saw that as settling the matter.

'So you'll get him to call tomorrow,' she said.

But I shook my head. I needed to find out if my passport was at the bank as soon as possible. If that meant getting up an hour before dawn, so be it.

■   ■   ■

The bus to Moyogalpa left in the dark from beside the park where an enterprising guy had set up a stall selling boiled corn. On the window beside him, the driver of the bus had that picture of a baby wearing a leather jacket and sunglasses. The poster was very popular in the eighties – the kid looked like a sort of miniature Fonzie – and I've often wondered what happened to the little fella. I suspect that he didn't get much money from the poster and any cash he did get had been spent by his parents well before he was legally entitled to it. I imagine he's probably grown up as a drug addict or an alcoholic, and is, at this moment, propping up a bar somewhere saying, 'I used to be that Fonzie kid, I used to be somebody.' Of course, he could also be an extremely up-tight lawyer who reads travel literature in his spare time . . .

By dawn the bus had reached Moyogalpa, just as trucks from around the island were arriving with bananas to be loaded onto boats, and as the sun fetchingly lit the east face of Concepción Volcano, the ferry left for the mainland. A small bus met the boat there, taking passengers to Rivas where a bus heading to Granada left within minutes of our arrival. By 9 am, the bus was approaching Granada. It had all gone so smoothly that I began to worry whether I'd left my passport there at all. And the closer I got to the city, the less confident I became. By the time I had walked up Calle Atravezada and entered the bank, I was convinced that my passport wasn't there.

What little confidence I had left disappeared as I anxiously stood in the queue in the bank. I tried to catch the eye of the teller who had served me, hoping for some kind of acknowledgment, a smile perhaps, but when she looked up she didn't even recognise me. I was served by a different teller, a woman of a similar age, who listened to my plea in broken Spanish and then shrugged her shoulders. On my insistence, she asked the teller who had originally served me if she had seen my passport. She shrugged her shoulders too.

I was devastated. Just as I turned to leave, my shoulders slumped, they both burst into laughter. I looked up to see the first teller waving my passport. They had obviously planned this little routine for a while and were happy they had been able to pull it off so successfully. When I told them that I had got all the way to Ometepe before I realised that I had lost it they laughed even harder.

When I finally got back to Ometepe, right on sunset, the GND and her new friends, a pack of English and American backpackers, had a good laugh too.

We had arranged to meet at Villa Paraíso, a hotel on

Santo Domingo Beach recommended to us by a Canadian couple in León. It was a wonderfully rustic place with lovely gardens overlooking the lake and a beach. Here the lake was as wild as an ocean, the wind whipping up the waves and making them crash on the shore. We ate at the restaurant there, looking out over the lake, a brisk breeze chilling the evening air. It was a wonderful moment: I had my passport back and the fish I had for dinner was too big for the plate, its head and tail flapping over the side.

'It was really good having a day to myself,' said the GND, as she tucked into a similar sized fish. 'I hadn't realised how much you were getting on my nerves.'

So much so, it seems, that she refused to come along with the group of backpackers she had befriended – Peter, an American guy taking a break from college, an English chap called Jon who had just finished university, Rebecca the Kiwi, and a French-Irish couple – to climb Madera Volcano. At 1340 metres, it was the lower of the two volcanoes. It had been long dormant, its slopes covered in jungle, its lower reaches rich farmland. In its cone was a lake. 'You go along,' she said. 'It'll do us good to spend some time apart. And besides, I'd only hold you up.'

I was getting used to the GND's aversion to climbing volcanoes by now. Earlier in the trip it had upset me – I saw it almost as an 'un-traveller' thing to do. But now I accepted that she just didn't see the sense in doing it. It would have been nice to share with her the bizarre thrill I got from it. But let's face it, there are successful marriages out there where the wife has never fully comprehended her husband's obsession with fishing or he her dedication to patchwork quilting. After three months travelling together the GND and I were beginning to understand the real key to successful long-term relationships – your own time and space, and lots of it.

The path to the summit began at Hacienda Magdelana, a farm just up a hill from Balgüe, a small village at the foot of the volcano. The hacienda was one of the oldest farms on the island, with a large wooden farmhouse, cattle pens, and an inordinate number of cowboys riding horses. It was also a popular spot for left-leaning tourists and American archaeologists studying the petroglyphs – ancient rock carvings – that were dotted around these parts of the island. The hacienda made much of being a cooperative farm and all visitors were directed to a big notice pinned on the wall. 'Dear visitor,' it read. 'Since 1985 Hacienda Magdalena has belonged to a cooperative consisting of 29 families that have their own parcels of land. They produce organic coffee, plantains, milk, honey, corn, beans and rice. They are self-sufficient.'

The notice was careful to underline the emotive words that would strike the right cord with earnest young folk.

'It hasn't always been this way,' it continued. 'As in much of Nicaragua, the land used to belong to an absentee landlord and run by a manager who lived upstairs on the hacienda. Here the manager could open any of four doors and look down on the progress of workers, workers who did not have any rights, no access to schools or health care.'

I wondered why the manager was so insistent on making us read this. Then came the sting. Since the 1990 elections many of the changes by the Sandinista era have been reversed. Many have had to sell land or take out loans. We welcome you to share our experience and welcome any donations of money, equipment and labour.'

We did our bit by hiring one of the lads to lead us up the mountain. At first the walk was an easy stroll through farmland and then coffee bushes, but after we passed our first petrogylph, a rock with a few prehistoric scratches on it, it grew considerably steeper and wetter. The coffee plantation gave way to secondary forest and then to lush jungle. Near the top we were clambering through fallen trees, ferns, moss and cloud forest. The highest point was marked by a sign in German, and from here we were forced to clamber down a series of rocky ledges to the crater lake below.

It was a beautiful spot. The lake was shrouded in mist and dotted with reeds, and was surrounded by the steep walls of the crater, covered in the jungle. I was annoyed that I had to share it with a group of smelly backpackers and not the GND.

I returned to the hotel determined to chastise the GND for not coming along. Suspecting that I might do this – it was an issue that raised its head every time there was a volcano to climb – the GND had arranged for us to go horse riding the next day.

'It'll be fun,' she enthused.

This was an alarming turn of events. I'm not a naturally gifted horseman, despite growing up on a small farm across the road from the local pony club. In fact, I should be on an instructional video on how not to ride a horse. That was my sister Vanessa's domain. She loved horses and had been riding them since she was eight. The only time I got on the back of one of her horses, a lively grey called Prince, it took off down the paddock as if possessed. I abandoned the reins and threw my arms around his neck, determined not to fall off. Luckily, when he came to a fence he decided to stop rather than jump it. I got off shaking and swearing never to get on the back of a horse ever again.

Of course, the GND wouldn't have a bar of it. Horse riding was an exciting and romantic thing to do. The plan was to canter along the road to a spot full of petroglyphs and then we'd ride back along the beach, like in one of those old cigarette commercials. I realised with alarm that there wouldn't be any fences.

Our guide the next day must have sensed my ineptitude because he gave me the oldest and most decrepit horse he had. It plodded along, dutifully following its friskier stable mates, its spirit beaten out of it by a long life on the farm. But even at that geriatric pace I was bouncing up and down on its back like a pogo stick.

For most of the ride this was not a problem. We ambled along bush tracks at a rate that would not endanger my long-term ability to father children. We had a look at the petrogylphs, conveniently poking out of a clump of bushes beside a track, and then plodded through a farm to a spot where the locals were using a petroglyph as a washing stone, the carved grooves particularly useful at getting out those difficult stains. Soon, however, we were down on the beach, the part of the ride the GND had been looking forward too and I had been dreading.

As soon as we hit the sand the horses took off. It was if they had been jabbed with a hot poker and soon they were kicking up a spectacular shower of sand and water, scattering birds that had been innocently standing around on the beach. The GND immediately fell into the rhythm of the horse and was galloping along so smoothly and masterfully she looked like she was doing it in slow motion. I bounced up and down on the horse like a pneumatic drill, my stuttered cries for help sounding like they were being spelled out letter by letter. A group of small boys stopped throwing rocks to watch me ride by, wincing every time my groin slammed into the saddle. They seemed to realise, as I did, that my child-producing days were over.

I limped back to Villa Paraíso and found the GND flushed and euphoric. 'That was fantastic!' she shrilled, ignoring my crab-like gait. 'Easily the best thing we've done on this trip. Can we do it again tomorrow?'

Luckily for my battered testicles, there was a ferry heading south to Costa Rica the next day.

CHAPTER TWENTY

Costa Rica

Annoying habit >>> Intolerance
Culprit >>> Peter

We arrived in Fortuna, a small town in the northern highlands of Costa Rica, to find it overrun by American DINKS dressed in freshly pressed chambray shirts and designer cargo pants on two-week eco-tours. They wandered the neat and clean streets with fresh haircuts and earnest expressions, or drove by in shiny new Japanese four-wheel-drives they had hired for the duration of their stay. At five o'clock there was a flurry of activity as other eco-tourists arrived back in new Japanese vans from guided tours to the waterfalls and hot springs of the nearby Arenal Volcano National Park.

The GND was nearly bowled over by a woman in a panic because she had forgotten to tip the tour guide. 'Where is he? Where is he?' the woman called out, looking around wildly. 'Oh my God, I can't believe I forgot to tip the driver!'

American eco-tourists love Costa Rica. It is probably the safest country in Central America – the armed forces were abolished after the 1948 civil war and the country has avoided the dictators, the despots and the insurgencies that have been a fact of life for their neighbours. And the Costa Ricans were quick to realise the benefits of jumping on the conservation bandwagon. Twenty-seven per cent of the country is protected – 11 per cent of that in the national park system – so there is ample opportunity for your North American urban professional to see a monkey or a sloth or a toucan in its natural environment. Offer security and a pristine rainforest and it seems affluent, conscientious tourists will beat a path to your door. And, if you're lucky, they'll bowl over the more undesirable grubby backpacker in the process.

The upshot of it all is that Costa Rica is much more expensive than its less alluring neighbours. From the moment we arrived in Costa Rica, after a beautiful river journey from San Marcos, we were shelling out the equivalent of a day's budget in Nicaragua for an ice cream and a packet of crisps. Transport was also horrifically pricey, and we paid three times the price for a Coca-Cola that we'd paid in Nicaragua. By my trusty Coca-Cola pricing index (patent and dot com pending) that meant that we could expect to pay three times the price for everything.

Unfortunately, the GND and I were travelling with Australian dollars. The Aussie dollar is a currency that you can leave on a park bench in most countries and come back a week later to find it still there. The cost of Costa Rica meant that the GND and I would have to economise. And economising meant sharing a room with the other backpackers we had crossed into Costa Rica with – Rebecca the Kiwi, Peter the American, and Jon the English boy.

Sharing a room is never the preferred option when you're travelling as a couple. It's like you're saying 'Okay, the romance is dead, I don't want to shag you anymore, so let's get on with saving money.' I was loathe to do it, but if we wanted to continue on to Panama, Jamaica and Cuba, the state of our finances meant that we had to do it. We still had a couple of months to go and our bank accounts were already looking a little bare. I only wish that we'd at least been able to get a double bed, but the room had five single beds, all bolted to the floor, making it impossible to even push two beds together. Worse, the next day was St Valentine's Day. The GND had agreed to sharing a room, but I could tell from the look on her face that it was under extreme sufferance.

Fortuna was celebrating a fiesta that weekend, so the town was full of farmers, cowboys and dancing horses from the surrounding districts. We joined them that night as they gathered in a muddy field on the outskirts of town, next to a small wooden stadium where a rodeo was held, and among the rides and games of the carnival that had come to town for the weekend. It was raining constantly, so the crowds sought shelter in the huge marquees selling food, laughing at the cowboys and their horses as they slipped in the mud. We were in Costa Rica, so there was a portable Pizza Hut van and a portable KFC stall as well.

The highlight of the evening was our visit to the mechanical bull tent. Realising the inherent entertainment value of gringos making complete idiots of themselves, the spruiker ushered us to the front of the queue. Within seconds I was on the back of the 'bull', milliseconds later I was face down on the red mats.

Pretending he felt sorry for me, but in reality just playing to the crowd, the spruiker gave me another go. 'Lean back,' he said, helpfully.

I fell off more quickly than the first time.

The GND was next and impressed the locals with her innovative riding style that involved slamming her chin on the bull's head and then holding on for dear life. Much to the crowd's delight, the operator spun the bull around slowly, giving everyone the opportunity to admire the position the GND had got herself into. Her graceful dismount – landing flat on her bum – also drew appreciative applause.

The rain never let up so we spent most of the evening dashing from one tent to another, drinking beer in the beer tent, playing tabletop soccer in the tabletop soccer tent, and eating Chinese food in the Chinese food tent. Rebecca bought some fairy floss and ate it with vodka chasers.

She certainly made an impression on an American guy who had latched onto us. He had a beard, so we had imaginatively called him 'Beardy'. 'Why don't you come back to my room and drink rum?' he said sidling up to her. 'Naked!'

Alarmed, Rebecca, suggested we go to the fiesta disco. It was held in a huge hall and was packed with cowboys, still wearing white hats, dancing to bad Latin music. Realising that I wouldn't be able to cut it on the dance floor – I'd pulled all my salsa muscles when I fell off the mechanical bull – I begged off and went back to the hotel room.

The GND stayed on and it was after midnight – so officially St Valentine's Day – when she finally staggered in. She lurched over to my bed and hissed in my ear, waking me from my slumber. 'I can't believe someone I'm so close to can be so far away,' she slurred. Angry that I'd been asleep when she came in, the GND snapped. 'Look at you, asleep!' she hissed. 'It's over! I've had it!'

Then she collapsed into her bed, fully dressed, her clothes still damp from the rain. Within seconds she was snoring loudly. Obviously sharing a room with scruffy backpackers had upset her more than I had realised.

We spent St Valentine's Day, the most romantic day of the year, listening to our Walkmans or reading in our cramped room, the air thick with moisture from the wet clothes of five backpackers hanging around the room. The GND denied saying anything when she came in the night before, arguing that if she had, she was drunk and hence didn't mean what she'd said.

'Actually,' I argued, 'what you say when you're drunk is probably closer to what you are really thinking. I reckon alcohol's like a truth serum.'

'Rubbish,' she said. 'I can't even remember what I said, so how could I mean it?'

I was unconvinced. I began to suspect that all the tension and all the little fights had begun to create resentment and that the GND was just biding her time, waiting for the right moment to leave.

I certainly wasn't given many opportunities to win her back with romantic rambles through virgin rainforest. It rained so constantly in Fortuna that we hardly got out of the room. Arenal Volcano was constantly under cloud, and our visit to the Río Fortuna waterfall only ensured that our last pieces of dry clothing were drenched. The track down to the waterfall was litter-free and had a handrail all the way. A sign said, 'People with heart problems should not go beyond this point'. The only thing that was spontaneous was the Costa Rican couple who asked me to take a photo of them together in the pool. What I thought would be arm in arm turned out to be a full-blown pash.

'Why aren't we like that anymore?' asked the GND, with a sigh.

I wanted to tell her that it was hard to be romantic when we were financially bereft and sharing with a gaggle of backpackers. But instead I sensitively pointed out that when she sat on a rock her damp jeans left a wet patch in the shape of a map of Australia.

On our last night in Fortuna the rains stopped so our roommates decided to visit the hot springs, ten kilometres north of the town. The springs are a popular tourist spot and the main ones at Balneario Tabacón have bars, restaurants and a carpark full of coaches from the capital,

San José. We visited the cheaper hot springs across the road where the changing rooms had all the ambience of the ones at council swimming pools. The setting of the springs, however, was stunning. They sat at the foot of Volcano Arenal, heated by the magma, and in the cool night air were shrouded in an eerie mist.

It was a beautiful night. We sat in the springs, hot water up to our bellies, drinking beer we'd bought from the convenience store back in Fortuna. The bottom of the pool was lined with pebbles, and when Jon, the English boy, went for a swim to the far end of the pool we decided it was a good idea to throw them at him. It was fun throwing them, skilfully pinning him into a far corner without actually hitting him.

At first Jon ignored the rocks, hoping that we would eventually lose interest and go back to our beers. But his silence only seemed to spur us on. He tried to throw rocks back, but really, the numbers were against him.

In the end he appealed to our sense of fair play. 'Now come on chaps,' he said, in a proper English accent. 'Someone is going to have an eye out.' That someone was obviously him.

It dawned on me that these kinds of hijinks are often a precursor to some dreadful catastrophe – the drunken revellers unaware that a psychotic murderer or mutant monster is sneaking up behind them. I mean, we were sitting in hot springs, heated by a live volcano that still had lava dribbling down the side of it. If disaster movie conventions were anything to go by, this would be the first place any signs of a forthcoming eruption would appear.

Movies like *Dante's Peak* always feature fish being cooked in lakes or an unfortunate couple floating face first in a hot springs they were using as a late night jacuzzi, their underwear boiled right off.

At that moment, the fog cleared momentarily, exposing the red, glowing volcano behind us. The thought of staying in the pool, lovely as it was, suddenly lost its appeal. I made my excuses and got out. Soon the others followed, and we hitched a ride in the back of a pick-up truck to Fortuna.

※   ※   ※

The next day we headed for Montezuma, a beach town on the Pacific coast on the Nicoya Peninsula. Why there was a town in Costa Rica named after an Aztec ruler was beyond me – as far as I could figure, the Aztecs never got this far south. But I'm sad to say that it was the name that compelled me to choose Montezuma from all the other beachside villages on the peninsula.

Jon the Pom and Rebecca the Kiwi were coming to Montezuma with us (Peter the American was heading to the capital, San José, to meet a friend). As our bus pulled away, a pack of middle-aged Americans rode past on hired mountain bikes, led by a guide, also an American. They were all wearing orange safety vests.

Our journey took us through the Cordillera de Tilarán, a region of lush rainforest and pretty farmland. We crossed an old iron bridge, hundreds of metres above the Río Renãs Blancas, that snaked its way down from emerald-green mountains to form a series of foaming white shoals.

'This is the most beautiful country I have ever seen,' said the GND. It was hard to disagree. It was as if it had been designed this way by an eco-tourism travel agency.

The road, however, was shit. It was a series of huge gaping potholes, deep enough to expose the rich red volcanic soil that the roads had been built on. The potholes, it seems, had been there longer than anyone could remember, and alternative routes around them had been formed. The bus driver drove on the verges and even crossed to the other side of the road, all without slowing down.

It was obvious from the deeply formed tracks that this was how it had always been done, and I wondered if there was some sort of protocol for driving on it. Did the person on the undamaged side of the road have right of way? And how long did this right last as a pothole on one side of the road was invariably followed by one on the opposite side? By the time we got to San Ramón I had figured it out. Our bus had not given way once, so I suspect that it was the biggest vehicle that had right of way. In that way, Costa Rica was no different to its less-developed neighbours.

We changed buses at San Ramón and now our journey took us down the mountains to the dry plains and Puntarenas. Puntarenas was a ramshackle harbour town that smelled like an oversized can of catfood had been opened and left in the sun, and if we hadn't had to go there to catch the ferry across the Gulf of Nicoya, we wouldn't have. It was a town of crumbling concrete buildings, exhaust fumes and Chinese restaurants, perched on the end of a sandy peninsula and never more than four blocks wide. Our guidebook said it was popular with holidaying

Costa Ricans who were willing to overlook the oily, polluted beaches and the fact that there was absolutely nothing to do there.

The backdrop to our ferry ride across the Gulf of Nicoya to Paquera was suitably dramatic – folds of mountains, low clouds, and a rusting car ferry, beached on a sandbank in the harbour. With nothing much to do we started a ferry sweepstakes, guessing how long it would take to get to Paquera. The prize was a beer from each of the losers. I was the most optimistic, saying we'd do it in one hour, 29 minutes. The GND said one hour, 43, Rebecca one hour, 40, and Jon one hour, 48. My chances of winning were scuppered when the ferry rounded the point and stopped for ten minutes, and then, halfway across the bay, got stuck on a sandbank. I argued that the clock should be stopped for such hold-ups, but it fell on deaf ears.

The ferry finally arrived at Paquera one hour and 50 minutes later, and Jon was grudgingly announced the winner. A fleet of coaches waited to whisk passengers away to all points of the peninsula. The bus to Montezuma was coated in dust, giving a pretty good indication of the roads it followed along the east coast of the peninsula.

We passed through tiny towns and villages of box houses with neat gardens splashed with the red and yellow of tropical flowers. It was slow and peaceful here, our bus one of the few vehicles to pass through, as well as the occasional four-wheel-drive full of surfies.

After Pochote, however, the quaint villages gave way to massive tourist developments like the Los Dolphins Golf and Country Club and the Playa Tambor Resort. They looked like beach-side developments the world over – rows of identical houses and cabañas in mustard, mauve and blue, surrounded by security walls with entrance gates watched over by uniformed guards. They offered a hermetically sealed experience, with a private airstrip only a kilometre away to make sure that any dealings with the local people were kept to an absolute minimum.

The road to the airstrip was lined with billboards advertising the villas that were available within the complex. 'Let our sun shine on you,' said one, as if venturing beyond the perimeter would mean plunging into darkness. Another promised 'your dream home in paradise'. We gawked at it all with the same wonder as the locals on the bus. For us four smelly backpackers, it was totally beyond the realm of experience too. Within half an hour the bus was winding its way down a steep mountain track and into Montezuma.

On first appearance, Montezuma appeared to be a collection of vegetarian restaurants and craft shops selling beads, bracelets and hash pipes, and populated by tanned, fit American college students. Like the eco-tourists of Fortuna, they had a uniform, but one designed by the Pepsi Max stylist. The guys all wore boardshorts, that's all, the girls scanty bikinis with optional sarongs wrapped around their waists. A Celtic tattoo, circular, seemed mandatory for both sexes, although the girls wore it on their left shoulder blades, the guys on their biceps. Goatees and sculptured side burns were essential for the guys, optional for the girls. A tan, it seemed, was de riguer.

Having said that, it was a pretty spot, and we were able to find a room right on the beach that we could afford to take on our own. It had hammocks hanging between palm trees and a restaurant with tables in the sand. The GND thought it was perfect. She was near the sea again and all thoughts of leaving me had seemed to have gone by the by.

The GND and I spent a few days at Montezuma, taking long walks along the beach south. Here the perfect figures, ripped abs and Celtic tatts thinned and we could find a stretch of sand pretty much to ourselves. We visited the waterfall, a pleasant spot, spoiled only by a guy with a goatee wearing a fisherman's hat doing somersaults. It was lovely and relaxing and, most importantly, affordable.

'This is more like I imagined our trip would be,' said the GND, swinging in a hammock outside our room one night.

I was glad to hear that. 'So you won't be leaving me then?' I replied.

The GND smiled. It seemed that she was beginning to accept my idiosyncrasies after all. And, at times like these, when the light from a full moon refracted off a platinum sea, I could see the appeal of her sand-and-sun approach to holidays.

■   ■   ■

Like so many traveller hangouts, Montezuma had a restaurant that showed movies each night. But in keeping with the get-away-from-it-all, retire-at-30, wired generation, it was more hi-tech than the battered video players and televisions you see in Asia. Here the owner of the restaurant had a DVD player, a projector and a special screen that came down from the ceiling. The picture was crisp and the sound was awesome, but, unfortunately, the guy's choice in movies was dreadful. On the first night we had been forced to suffer through *Six Days, Seven Nights*, a very bad attempt at a screwball comedy with Harrison Ford (too old) and Anne Heche (bats for the other team).

On our last night in Montezuma, on returning to our bungalows after watching *The Spanish Prisoner*, we found an American guy in his late thirties lining up pieces of bamboo on the porch outside our room. He had cut them to different lengths and was arranging them like a chunky xylophone. I had seen this guy a couple of times. He had a piano accordion as well, and would spend some of the day and most of the night wandering up and down the beach playing it. When he spotted us he gathered up the pieces of bamboo and handed them to us.

'I'm making an instrument and I'm trying to tune it,' he said. 'Hit these pieces with a stick as I play.'

It was not exactly our cup of tea – I'm not sure if it would be anyone's – but our efforts to excuse ourselves fell on deaf ears.

'Don't be stupid,' he said as he began to play his accordion. 'It'll be fun!'

It was a ridiculous scene. Him playing some unrecognisable tune on his accordion, us tapping on pieces of bamboo.

'Make it go tush, bang boong,' he yelled over his accordion. 'Let them talk to each other. Leave space for conversation.'

Now it was getting all too patchouli for me. I put my

pieces of bamboo down and got up to leave. He stopped playing his accordion and put on his most earnest expression. 'I don't mean to be rude,' he said, knowing full well that was what he meant to be. 'But I don't understand why you can't want to do this. You should *love* doing this, man!'

I said I couldn't understand why anyone would want to do it. The noise we were making was dreadful.

'Man, I want to understand,' he continued. 'Are you afraid of making a fool of yourself?'

I told him that I made a fool of myself every day but I was tired and wanted to go to bed. He shook his head, amazed. 'I can't understand how you can't like music, man!'

I love music. But the noise we were making wasn't music. It was a caterwaul and, worse, one simply serving his need to be the centre of attention. I got up and went to our room, afraid that if I stayed long enough he might actually convince me that I was enjoying the racket. The GND followed. When we got back to the room we both burst into laughter.

'Quick, give me the Walkman,' she giggled. 'I don't want that noise to be the last thing in my mind before I go to sleep.'

CHAPTER TWENTY-ONE

Costa Rica, too

Annoying habit >>> Pool sharking
Culprit >>> GND

Santa Elena is a laid-back town shrouded by a perpetual mist, sitting as it does at 1600 metres in the mountain chain of Cordillera de Tilerán. Surrounded by cloud forests, where moss hangs from trees like a veil, Santa Elena sprang up originally to service the dairy farms and cheese-making enterprises of the North American Quakers who moved here in 1951. Now it services a different bunch of intruders, the eco-tourists, who come to visit the area's nature reserves, primarily the Monteverde Cloud Forest reserve.

With them has come the room touts. Anyone who has wandered along the Lonely Planet trail knows the drill. You turn up at a place popular with backpackers and you are immediately besieged by the local equivalent of a used-car salesman trying to entice you to a particular establishment, an establishment, they conveniently forget to tell you, that rewards them with a handsome commission for your business. We had re-traced our steps from Montezuma back to Puntarenas and caught a bus directly to Santa Elena from there. On arrival in Santa Elena the bus was surrounded by people banging on the windows, waving photocopied pieces of paper at us and imploring us to stay with a ferocity that suggested that the commissions on offer in Santa Elena were very generous indeed.

Having said that, these touts were amateurs compared to the guys at Siam Reap in Cambodia. There, they were in cahoots with the travel agencies in Phnom Phen, who sell the tickets for the boat from the capital across the lake to Angkor Wat. The touts find out in advance the names of those on board so that when you arrive at the wharf Siam Reap you find a pack of screaming touts waving cardboard signs with passengers' names on them, just like the ones you see when you get off a plane. I've never been met by someone carrying one of those signs, and have always been envious of the people who are. So when I saw a little chap jumping up and down with a sign with my name on it, I very nearly accepted his gracious offer of a room for $4. Then another tout came along and offered me a similar room for only $1 a night, so I went off with him.

Still, it was interesting to watch the different tactics used by the touts of Santa Elena. Jon the English boy had joined us on our trek to the mountains and was immediately latched onto by a local boy who listed the attractions of his particular establishment while playing music from the ghettoblaster on his shoulder. A little old lady had taken the GND aside and was telling her about her clean comfortable rooms, taking the tack that she found that girls 'appreciate the nicer things'. I was approached by a French guy who sidled up beside me, disarming me by starting his spiel with an apology.

'Please forgive me for approaching you like this,' he began. 'It is not pleasant, I know. But it is how we have to do business around here.'

I was flattered that he had picked me as a weary, cynical world traveller – obviously his plan – and waved the GND and Jon over. We followed the French man 50 metres down the hill to the wooden building that was his guesthouse. Chances are it would have been the first place we would have checked once we had shaken the touts.

The Frenchman offered us a selection of rooms. If the GND and I got our own room, we would have to make do with a poky room with bunks. But if we shared with Jon we could afford a nicer room in a lodge up the back. It was clean and spacious, with a huge attached bathroom.

I looked at the GND, not sure if she wanted to share again.

She took one look at the huge bath and bidet and was convinced. 'I can have a bubble bath,' she enthused.

Some things, it seems, are more important than shoring up a relationship.

The Frenchman had quite a set up. His guesthouse had

its own Internet connection plus a communal kitchen where the budget conscious – that is, us – could prepare their own meals. It was in the kitchen that we discovered another sub-breed of traveller, just as earnest as the others we had encountered in Fortuna and Montezuma, but driven by a need to tramp through rain forest rather than catch a wave or go whitewater rafting. Our time in Costa Rica had been quite the anthropological journey, following the holidaying habits of touring Americans. Here, with maps laid out on a table, slurping on packet noodles they had just added boiling water to, they discussed the best walks to do, debating the merits of the Santa Elena private cloud forest or the more popular Monteverde National Park reserve.

These travellers seemed to alarm the GND more than the others we had come across. 'They all look so healthy,' she said. 'I hope you don't expect me to go on any of these walks!'

Well, yes I did. It was kind of the whole reason we had come to Santa Elena and Monteverde – to walk in the cloud forest, to be at one with nature, to work up a bit of a sweat, rather than just lie around on a beach.

'I thought we could go somewhere and just look at the cloud forest from a platform or something,' she said. 'Can't we do that?'

In the end, I compromised. I told the GND we would choose a cloud forest that would suit her temperament. After all, there seemed to be a cloud forest available for every taste and for every level of fitness available in the Santa Elena-Monteverde district.

Personally, I found the fact that you could choose a

cloud forest – like choosing a new sofa from the IKEA catalogue – quite bizarre. It was very Costa Rica though. Landowners have discovered that it is more lucrative to fence off a couple of hectares of forest and charge eco-tourists over the odds to walk through it than to get the once-off windfall of letting in some Japanese lumber merchants. Each reserve touts their wares – cloudier cloud forests, more animals, better paths – and offer varying grades of difficulty. There was even a children's rainforest that had been set up with donations from school children in America. I told the GND that you weren't allowed in if you were over ten or couldn't stand underneath the outstretched arm of a sign of a cartoon three-toed sloth. She believed me, God bless her.

After checking all the brochures, the GND decided on the Santa Elena Reserve. It wasn't the cheapest, but it had a variety of trails of varying difficulty and length and it worked out better value than its more famous rival, Monteverde Reserve, on a cost per kilometre ratio. We caught the early morning van there, paid our entrance fee and got a poorly photocopied trail map and animal and bird recogniser and set off down the muddy track and into the forest.

It was very beautiful – as well as very green and very wet and spookily shrouded in fog. The track was clearly marked and wound its way picturesquely through old-growth forest and over tiny streams that had to be forded across fallen trees. It was fun for the first half hour – we spotted a group of howler monkeys playing in the trees – but soon the novelty of walking in the damp forest lost its appeal. I'm of the opinion that when you've seen one clump of green trees you've seen them all. The only real excitement came when we discovered puma prints in the mud – our animal guide had illustrations of paw prints as well – but this was spoiled when we caught up with some Canadians who admitted they had made the tracks with their fingers because they were bored.

'I bet you wished you'd thought of doing that,' said the GND, a little too insightfully for mine.

On the way back to Santa Elena, we stopped at the Skywalk. Touted as the 'Walk of a Lifetime', the Skywalk was in effect just a series of suspension bridges over the top of a private reserve of rainforest. The brochure rather grandly promised 'a vision of the forest from a different perspective' and 'the excitement of looking to one side and seeing the tops of the trees and at the same time feeling the sensation of walking among the clouds.' It came in two sizes – the $8 regular Skywalk or the $25 deluxe Skywalk that included a flying-fox ride over the rainforest canopy. We took the cheaper option and spent an hour walking over suspension bridges, resisting the urge to sway the bridge from side to side or spit on the fragile ecosystem below.

Back at the guesthouse, a new batch of eco-tourists had arrived. One, a young American guy, was chatting to the French guy's sister who ran the place while her brother was out chasing business. He looked like a guy out of a Diet Coke ad and walked around with his shirt off, exposing abs you could wash clothes on. He had the kind of body that makes the likes of Jon or me change clothes in the dark and immediately lowers the IQ of seemingly intelligent women.

The French woman gazed dumbly at him as he spoke with the sort of weak smile cartoon characters get when they've been hit on the head with an anvil. 'Oh yesterday, I had the most amaaazzing day!' he said. ' I like, found a gym, and did so many chin-ups I can't shave! It was *awesome*!'

The French woman silently mouthed 'awesome' back. But I don't think it was a workout at the gym that she had in mind.

Having tramped through our mandatory piece of cloud forest – and endured more than our fair share of pseudo-trampers – Jon, the GND and I caught the 7 am bus for San José, the Costa Rican capital, the next morning.

I was in an upbeat mood and clambered on the bus, another recycled American school bus, humming, 'Do you know the way to San José?' I knew the song was about the San José in California, but figured that maybe that was where our bus had spent its previous life so deemed it appropriate. Our bus driver that morning no doubt wished he was in California. His mother was catching the bus and sat up the front in her Sunday best – including the sort of hat only the queen seems to wear – looking over her half specs, disapprovingly, at everything he did. She criticised the way he changed gears, derided his approach to sharp corners and, on one particular bend, got up and straightened his tie and brushed dandruff from his shoulders. The driver kept looking into his rearview mirror with a tired, exasperated look, wondering if anyone else had noticed this humiliating scene.

It would have been funny except for the fact that we were driving on one of the steepest and most treacherous roads in Costa Rica. Worse, the driver's mother insisted that he look at her when she spoke to him. At first, he'd turn around completely to face her, turning his attention back to the road as he approached a hairpin bend, just in time to reel the bus in and prevent it from plunging over a ravine. After nearly missing a curve and ploughing into an ancient, moss-covered tree, he took to looking at her in the rearview mirror.

When she wasn't haranguing her son, the mother would tut at people who did not move to the back of the bus quickly enough or scold those that did not have the correct change. After chastising them, she would turn her attention back to her son and take him to task for not saying something to the passengers himself. I was surprised that we arrived in San José at all. I was sure the driver would decide to end it all by taking his mother, the bus and its passengers with him over a cliff.

Despite a pretty setting in a valley surrounded by farmland, San José was another grubby third-world capital. The fixation with cleanliness and order apparent in the eco-tourist centres of Fortuna and Santa Elena was sadly missing here. Litter was piled on the streets, traffic moved slowly, spewing fumes into the air, and homeless people shuffled about in torn clothes. It was another town with too many people and not enough for them to do.

We took a room at the Gran Hotel Imperial, a dark grubby place opposite the markets in a part of town where rubbish was piled shoulder high and rats scurried underfoot when you walked out of the security grill that acted as a door. It was squalid in the grand tradition of American doss houses, with small cell-like rooms off long, dark corridors. The beds were tiny camp beds with linen that made you itch just looking at it. The toilets and showers were in blocks at the end of the corridors, and it wasn't unusual to see guests peering cautiously into the bowls of each toilet before deciding on which one to use. But at only $5 a person per night, it is the closest thing San José had to an absolute bargain.

Of course, at that sort of price, the place was going to attract a certain type of clientele. Clientele like the legendary Esty Katz. Esty, an Israeli, had stayed at the Gran Hotel Imperial between 29 and 30 December. In that time she had allegedly defecated in her room, vomited in her bed, and stole two pillowcases and two blankets (presumably clean ones). I know this because the management had plastered her crimes, as well as her passport number and a general description of her, on the glass of the reception section. I wondered why they did this. Were they hoping to shame her? The GND remarked that it would just give other guests ideas.

Most of the guests, however, lingered in the reception area, under the sign that warned that there was a good chance of being robbed at night in the streets north of the hotel. They had been chased there from their rooms by the odour or the ardour of the bed bugs and sat about reading books or swapping information. They were all on their way somewhere else, to the more pristine parts of Costa Rica, more in keeping with the eco-tourist brochures. The Gran Hotel Imperial was just a necessary evil while they changed money, secured visas or organised a plane ticket home.

We didn't stay long in San José either, just long enough for Jon to buy a Best of the Bee Gees tape at the sparkling new shopping mall on Avenida Central and for me to get into an altercation with an Internet cafe owner who tried to insist that the GND and I pay for two terminals, despite the fact that we were only checking one Hotmail address. We tried to visit the Museum of Criminology, which our guidebook said displayed an entire human torso, but a guard at the Supreme Court of Justice, used to such inquiries, smiled and said it was closed. We had wandered back to the pedestrian mall in the city centre intending to check out the National Theatre, supposedly San José's most impressive public building, but ended up eating a Whopper at Burger King instead. I think it was then that we decided to head to the Caribbean again.

We left San José from a shiny new terminal in a sleek yellow coach with a banana tree motif and travelled along a smooth highway through green hills and farmland. We were heading for Cahuita, a village on the Caribbean coast, a journey that would take us alongside the Barva Volcano through the spectacular Braulio Carrillo National Park, where trees grew right down into ravines so thick we could see the canopy descending over 2850 metres to the lowlands on the other side. After hitting the Caribbean coast at Puerto Limón, our coach turned right and travelled along a thin road, neat farms or jungle on one side, the sparkling Caribbean on the other. The GND's mood brightened noticeably. In her mind's eye she was already back in her little swing dress, working on her tan.

Cahuita was a laid-back little town, just off the 'main' highway. To reach the town 'centre' our coach was forced to manoeuvre down tiny lanes lined by brightly coloured wooden houses with hedges made out of the kind of ornamental plants that would cost a fortune down at the local nursery. We were dumped outside a convenience store at the beginning of the long dusty road that constituted the main drag. A black girl road by on a bicycle and smiled. The Caribbean, framed by palm trees, was just across the road.

On our way through the 'town' Jon had noticed a blackboard hanging on one of the hedges advertising a bungalow for $15 a night. If we shared it, he argued, we would only have to shell out $5 a night each – a bargain price for Costa Rica.

I hesitated, remembering how upset the GND had been the first time we shared a room in Fortuna, but she surprised me by agreeing. 'We can afford to get something nicer if we share,' she said.

Secretly, I think she appreciated the way having Jon around had helped things between us. He broke the tension. We were fighting less. And he was someone with new stories and new antics. It had got to the stage long ago that the GND was finishing off my stories and me hers.

The bungalow was an inspired decision. It was set among hedges and palm trees just across from the water and had its own kitchen and bathroom. We set up the Walkman and speakers, whacked on Jon's Bee Gees tape and settled in.

'This certainly beats working in an office,' sighed the GND, looking out from the veranda towards the ocean.

Our life quickly settled into a routine in Cahuita. Each morning we'd breakfast at a clapboard bakery opposite a tiny cove. The owner had set up a wooden table and chairs across the road overlooking the beach, and strung up a hammock between some palm trees. It was an idyllic place to start the day, swinging in a hammock, eating Caribbean pastry while the sea lapped up on white sands. The only sour note was the erratic availability of freshly squeezed juice. On our first day we couldn't get an orange juice – 'The crops are finished, man' – but the next day we could. But I guess that was part of its charm.

The best part of Cahuita, however, was its beach. Located at the southern end of the long dirt road, it was part of the Cahuita National Park, a long stretch of white sand backed by thick jungle. It was like something out of a castaway fantasy – a totally untouched beach without a condo or architect-designed beach house in sight. It struck me that this was the way all beaches were before greedy developers came along, and the way beaches should be.

The GND was delighted. 'This is so beautiful,' she purred. 'Thank you for bringing me here.'

'My pleasure,' I answered only half jokingly. Despite the fights, the disagreements and the hardships of our trip so far, it had been.

As part of a National Park, it should have cost us $6 each time we visited the beach. There was even a wooden ranger's hut at the entrance, at the other side of a wooden bridge crossing a creek that ran down to the sea, and a ranger on duty to hand out brochures and field inquiries. But in an act of civil disobedience, the townsfolk of Cahuita had decided not to impose the fee. In doing so, they figured they could entice visitors to the park to use their entrance, rather than the main entrance further along the highway, and ensure that they purchased all their ice-cold soft drinks, ice creams and sunblock from the tiny businesses of Cahuita. In the few days we spent there, it didn't seem to be a very effective policy. More often than not we got the beach pretty much to ourselves, the only chatter coming from the monkeys in the jungle at our backs.

On our last night in Cahuita we ate at Miss Edith's, a popular restaurant run by a West Indian woman with braids by the name, funnily enough, of Miss Edith. As a West Indian, she spoke English, but when we tried to order our meal, she wasn't sure that we could. 'What?' she said, screwing up her nose. 'What the hell are you saying?'

We repeated our order, this time more slowly.

She still couldn't understand us. 'Where are you people from?' she asked. 'England or something?'

In the end we made our orders in really over-the-top American accents and she got them first time. It was worth it. The fresh fish baked in coconut cream was delicious.

Jon, the GND and I walked back towards our bungalow, the moonlight streaming through the palm trees, the air thick with the smell of hibiscus. We called into Picolos, a bar owned by the same guy who owned the bungalow, a Spanish guy from Madrid called Pedro, for a night cap. Pedro had read about Cahuita in Spain and had come directly there three years before and hadn't left since. He bemoaned that Cahuita was losing business to Puerto Viejo, a town further down the coast. 'It is a party town,' he said, almost wistfully.

Cahuita certainly wasn't. Pedro's bar was deserted except for a local drunk called Rafael. The only distraction offered, apart from a satellite TV playing American sports, was a pool table. Pedro and Rafael started a game, playing the kind of shots that tear felt. The GND challenged the guys to a game. First Rafael played, but he was having problems making contact between cue and ball. He made quite a show of chalking the cue between shots, but all this resulted in was a series of blue chalk swipes on the felt. When he fell backwards after one particularly energetic shot that he missed altogether, Pedro stepped in to take over, and even managed to sink a few balls, albeit the GND's.

But the GND was in her element. She loved playing pool. She had been taught to play when she was young by her father, quite a pool player himself and a friend of the great Walter Lindrum. I, on the other hand, am quite dreadful. I find that I am 'in the zone' for approximately ten minutes after my second beer, a magical period of time when I am mysteriously able to pot balls, most of them mine. This invariably encourages me to have a third drink, after which my 'skills' deteriorate rapidly.

Having already had two beers at Miss Edith's and my third here watching Pedro and Rafael, my moment had well and truly passed. I excused myself and retired to the bungalow, leaving Jon and the GND to wipe the floor with our new drunken friends.

They staggered in about an hour later. The GND was a

little tipsy and annoyed that I hadn't stayed to watch her beat Pedro, Rafael and Jon. 'You never want to have any fun!' she slurred.

I whispered back hoarsely that at least I knew my limits to which the GND countered, again in a hoarse whisper, that I was a wowser. This 'discussion' continued for ten minutes, never getting above a harsh whisper in deference to Jon pretending to be asleep only a metre or two away.

I felt sorry for Jon. It couldn't have been too much fun for him, rooming with a bickering couple. I suspected that it would be like when children hear their parents fighting in another room. Except that instead of worrying about which parent to go with after the divorce, Jon would have to worry about the cost of getting a room all by himself.

Not that Jon was that mercenary. I suspected he also had a bit of a crush on the GND. I had no proof of that, of course. Only that I had spent a month or so travelling with an English couple in Turkey in similar circumstances and I had a crush on the girl. They figured I was hanging around because I was lonely, and when we reached Ölüdeniz on the Mediterranean coast, they tried to line me up with a pretty English film student we'd met one night at the Buzz Bar. Unfortunately, I got stinking drunk and started dancing on the table, effectively stymieing their match-making efforts. Regardless, I decided that it was time we did the same for Jon, maybe not with an English film student, but with a suitably vivacious, friendly fellow traveller. And if Pedro was to be believed, the place to do that was Puerto Viejo, the party town.

Puerto Viejo was an 18-kilometre bus drive along the

coast, the last stretch alongside a black sand beach with a shipwrecked barge rusting just off shore. Although our guidebook insisted that it was more 'tranquil' than Cahuita, I found it to be bigger and more rundown, and overrun with gringos. In the time it took us to step off the bus we saw more westerners than we had seen in three days in Cahuita. Rooms were more expensive and harder to find, too, forcing us to grab the first vacant room we came across. For $25 we got a cramped room with bunks and a single bed, and a shower that didn't work down a hall.

Eager to get out of our tiny, airless cell, we dumped our bags and headed for the beach. Although we had towels and sun hats and all the other accoutrements of a day in the sand, we were stopped by an aging American on a bicycle. He was so tanned that his skin was like leather, and he was bald, except for a few long wisps of grey hair at the back.

'You kids looking for a casa?' he asked.

We told him we already had one.

'Damn!' he said. 'I hate it when that happens. Do you want some marijuana?'

We knocked him back on that one too, but only after he had pointed the way to the beach.

'If your casa don't work out, come see me,' he called after us. 'My name's Dave. You'll find me at the Bambu Bar.'

The beach at Puerto Viejo was a major disappointment. It wasn't as pretty as Cahuita, and where the beach there had been deserted, this one was full of vacationing American college students surfing, juggling and playing frisbee. While the crowd didn't make for a relaxing bit of sunworshipping, it did auger well for my plan of finding Jon a companion.

After the sun had set, we showered and got ready for a big night in Puerto Viejo. Jon put on his Bee Gees tape for inspiration. His favourite song was 'Stayin' Alive' and he played it loud to get himself pumped up. When he started singing something about being a woman's man we decided it was probably best to let him get ready alone.

Our evening began at the local bottle shop, buying a bottle of Nicaraguan Black Label Rum, a cheeky drop with a smooth palate and a bargain at only $3, plus a two-litre bottle of coke and a bag of ice. We picked a spot on the beach where a group of other travellers had lit a bonfire. It was in front of Johnny's Bar, appropriately enough, and close enough to be able to listen to their music. After lying on our backs watching the stars for an hour or so, we ran out of rum and made our way around the bay to the Bambu Bar. It was a reggae night and the bar was packed with tanned surfies in long shorts and girls in short skirts and tight tops. The GND and Jon disappeared onto the dance floor, and I sat on a log outside near the beach chatting to a guy from California.

When Jon and the GND returned, I told the GND that Jon wouldn't meet anyone while she was around. To spite me, the GND started a flirtatious conversation with the Californian.

'So what side is California on?' she asked.

He answered, to his credit, without looking astonished. Then he started talking about surfing in Baja.

'And where is that?' asked the GND.

I sat on the log fuming. It upset me that she was asking such stupid questions. I didn't want people to think she was a dumb blonde – she wasn't – and I told her so.

'It's all part of the game,' she said. 'Guys like to think they are sharing their knowledge with you. You're all so easily manipulated.'

For some reason, that answer angered me more. I remembered the first time I met the GND and how she had asked me all kinds of questions and how I answered them. At the time I felt intelligent, witty and knowledgeable. Now I felt stupid.

Jon, however, was impressed by the GND's tactics, and used them when he approached a pretty Argentinian girl he'd had his eye on. Unfortunately, she wasn't as easily impressed as the Californian and when Jon asked her where Argentina was, she turned to her friend and muttered, 'Stupido!' When we left him, just after midnight, he was well oiled and saying 'Are ya dancin'? Are ya askin'?' to no one in particular. It was a line, apparently, from the British television show, 'The Liverbirds', but, unfortunately, the humour was lost on the Buenos Aires beauty, as was the irony of the tacky Guatemala souvenir T-shirt he was wearing. Jon staggered back into the room at 2 am, alone and too smashed to notice that the wooden slats under his pillow had fallen out. He slept with his head a good few inches lower than the rest of his body.

We spent the next day on the beach, nursing our throbbing heads. All the people we'd seen at the Bambu were there too, looking as bleary-eyed and shattered as we were. The Californian was half-heartedly scoping the waves.

Dave the Casa Man was wandering from one person to another trying to interest them in a room or dope. And the Argentinean girl, looking very fetching in an orange bikini, lay on a towel working on her tan. You could almost hear the moans when someone turned over or got up too quickly.

Just after lunch, we were approached by an American student doing market research for the Costa Rican tourist board. He was tanned with bleached dreads, and wore only boardshorts and a shark's tooth necklace. He had a wooden clipboard and asked us if we would mind doing a tourist questionnaire.

The first few questions were simple enough. Questions like 'Where are you from?', 'How did you hear about Puerto Viejo?' and 'How much are you spending each day?' We could answer them without having to think too hard. Then he asked us if we knew what eco-tourism meant.

Jon, the GND and I sat in silence, our heads throbbing, trying to figure out the answer to that one. Finally, after what seemed an infinitely long silence, Jon cleared his throat and turned to the GND and I.

'I don't know about you chaps,' he said. 'But I think this means that it's time for us to go to Panama.'

I couldn't have agreed more.

CHAPTER TWENTY-TWO

Panama

Annoying habit >>> Overzealous haggling
Culprit >>> Peter

We arrived at the border with Panama at Sixaola after a long, slow bus ride through endless banana plantations. We'd lost sight of the Caribbean now – it lay somewhere over the other side of the broad leaf canopy – and the air was still and thick with humidity. The border was marked by a dirty brown river and crossed by negotiating an old iron Meccano-style bridge, barely wide enough for the empty semitrailers lining up along it to get back into Panama.

It was more an obstacle course than a border crossing. We were forced to shuffle along the narrow gap between the trucks and the side of the bridge, clinging to the rigging of the trucks like Spiderman so that the weight of our packs didn't send us tumbling into the shallow river below. To make matters worse, many of the planks were rotting or had fallen away, and while makeshift measures had been taken to patch the bridge for trucks to cross, there were still holes big enough for a pedestrian to fall through. The only thing missing was a pack of crocodiles circling in the water below, waiting for their next feed.

'This is worse than climbing a volcano,' said the GND. 'I feel like Indiana Jones.'

Once we had successfully navigated the bridge, however, the immigration procedures on the Panamanian side were cursory. A black guy stepped out of the customs and immigration office, and after a quick glance at our passports told us we were 'free to proceed'. So we did, on an air-conditioned minibus from the border town of Guabito through prime banana growing territory – 20 million boxes of bananas exported annually to Europe alone – to Almirante.

Almirante was a dilapidated fishing town so rundown that even the sparkling Caribbean Sea, which it overlooked, could not distract from the town's ugliness. Worse, getting from Almirante to Bocas del Toro, a small town on Colón Island and our ultimate destination that day, was more difficult than we had imagined. Our guidebook said there were regular ferries to the island, and that when they weren't running, there were private companies that ran faster, slightly more expensive boat services. Unfortunately, our minibus was met by a gaggle of scruffy lads with nothing better to do than tell us that the docks were too far away to walk to and that we'd have to clamber into the back of their mate's pick-up truck and have him take us there.

I was immediately suspicious of these guys. For one thing, they spoke English too well. Secondly, they insisted a little too forcefully that we get in the back of the pick-up. I suspected it was a scam, a ploy to get us to pay over the odds for a ride to the docks. Sensing my hesitation, the ringleader of the touts, a tall guy in a shiny tracksuit with a wispy moustache, said that he would pay for the pick-up truck. After making it quite clear that we weren't going to pay, Jon, the GND and I jumped in. The pick-up set off, and after a quick left and then a right, we were down at the docks. It had taken 30 seconds. It would have taken a minute to walk.

There were three different companies offering water taxi services to Bocas del Toro. Each of them used the same kind of boat, an aluminium speedboat that could fit about ten people, with a canopy to keep off the sun. Each charged the same price – $3 – and each claimed they were leaving first. The company the tout was pushing us towards, however, was still waiting for its boat to return from an early journey to Bocas del Toro. The tout assured us it would arrive soon and leave immediately. I didn't believe him, so I reluctantly paid him for the lift and suggested to Jon and the GND that we choose one of the two boats already waiting.

Choosing a boat for the twenty-minute ride to Bocas del Toro was like picking a queue at the supermarket. If you got it right, you zoomed straight through. But if you got it wrong you'd be waiting forever. Here though, we had no cultural clues to pick up on. Back home, I knew that a line of sad, single males went faster at a supermarket than a mum loaded up with two screaming kids and a week's worth of Pampers. I could pick the kind of people who pay by EFTPOS and forget their PIN number. But what was it that made one of two seemingly identical speedboats leave first? If we waited and chose the boat that filled up first, we could miss out altogether. If we jumped in a boat, hoping others would follow, we could get stranded when the other company lowered its price to entice passengers.

In the end, I took it on trust. A lady selling tickets for one company said that their boat was leaving now and I believed her. Any doubts I may have had vanished when we clambered into the boat and the touts who had brought us to the dock reacted with alarm and dismay.

'Don't go with them,' one warned. 'They don't even go to Bocas. They are trying to trick you!'

'They are only new,' another warned. 'Our company has been going for eight years!'

The ringleader tout was even more dramatic. 'Don't go with them. They'll keeel you!'

It was then that I realised that I'd made the right decision. If my travels have taught me anything it's that the more desperate the touts become, the closer they are to losing their commission. I was right. The boat was full now so the driver started the engine. I think the GND was secretly impressed.

Bocas del Toro is the capital of the Bocas del Toro province and lies in the heart of the Bocas del Toro Archipelago, a collection of pristine islands and cayes off the north-west coast of Panama. It is home to Panama's first national marine park, the Bastimentos National Park, renowned for its abundant coral reefs and many species of Caribbean wildlife, and was once the region's major banana producer. With the revival of Panama's mainland plantations those days have passed and the region now relies heavily on fishing and tourism for income.

The town of Bocas del Toro certainly didn't feel like a capital, provincial or otherwise. It was a sleepy little community, centred on a single road that ran along the waterfront. It was populated by English-speaking black people of West Indian descent, a heritage that was reflected in the clapboard houses and general stores and the somnolent lifestyle. We got a room at Las Brisas, an old wooden hotel beside the bay, with a covered back porch that sat directly over the water. We shared a room with Jon again, partly to save money, but mainly because that was the way we did things now.

'It would be rude not to share,' the GND pointed out. 'Jon'd think we didn't like him any more!'

The next day we organised a day trip around the archipelago with one of the boatmen who hung around the back porch of the Las Brisas, called Livingston. Livingston was a very big, very black man with beady red eyes and a propensity for saying 'fuck' at least five times in every sentence. He looked a little like Idi Amin, if Idi Amin had spent all of his time drinking instead of oppressing his people. Livingston claimed he didn't drink, but his sluggish demeanour and bleary eyes suggested otherwise.

'Perhaps he is taking his alcohol intravenously these days,' quipped Jon.

Livingston had agreed to take us on what he liked to call an 'eco-treat'. For the princely sum of $8 each, he would chauffeur us around the archipelago in his brightly painted wooden boat for the day. The highlights would include snorkelling off coral reefs, lunching at a waterfront restaurant and visiting Magic Island, a nature reserve and home to rare red tree frogs and three-toed sloths.

After a few attempts at starting the outboard engine – the strain of pulling the rope very nearly triggering a massive coronary – the tiny two-stroke came to life and Livingston manoeuvred his boat out through the harbour and made towards Carenero Island and Bastimentos Island and the national marine park there. We passed by tiny mangrove islands and men fishing from canoes and, after a while, stopped at a point between two islands. Livingston cut the engine, threw out an anchor and handed us snorkels, masks and flippers. We had an hour, he said. He wasn't coming with us. He had a bit of sleep to catch up with.

After the disappointments of our snorkelling trips in Honduras and Belize, where the coral reefs had been stripped bare by Hurricane Mitch, the GND and I were blown away by the reef here. The ocean floor was covered with coral of all kinds of shapes, colours and sizes, and among it darted colourful fish. The coral was alive and vibrant and because there was so much of it there were fish everywhere, all insanely bright. It was like diving into an extremely well-stocked aquarium. Livingston had brought along a fish identification book and in the hour we spent there I swear we saw most of them.

After lunch – delicious grilled fish in a restaurant on stilts in the water in the middle of nowhere – we continued to Magic Island, an old banana plantation that had been turned into a nature reserve. Livingston led us along a muddy path across to a beautiful deserted beach on the other side. While we swam in the turquoise sea or sat on the sugar-white sand, he picked a shady spot under a tree and slept. Later, feeling as though he should actually do something, he took us on an 'eco-tour' of the island which consisted of poking sloths sleeping in trees with a stick to make them move and harassing endangered red frogs so they'd leap onto a more photogenic log. After the overly PC atmosphere in Costa Rica, Livingston's 'eco-hostile' approach was a refreshing change.

We finished the day snorkelling off Hospital Point, which had once been a hospital for the banana workers but had since been turned into a magnificent private residence. We returned to Las Brisas just in time to see the Spice Girls movie, dubbed into Spanish. The best part was the station announcer before it started. He listed the Spice girls in a normal voice – Baby, Scary, Sporty, Posh – before putting on his best raunchy voice ' y Gerry!' No prizes for guessing Panama's favourite Spice Girl!

We spent the rest of our time in Bocas del Toro eating in waterside restaurants, drinking in harbourside bars or wandering along the dirt road that circumnavigated Colón Island. It was a lovely walk that took us past tiny villages or the remains of a plane – maybe a drug-running plane –

and saw us stumbling upon tiny coves that looked like something out of a holiday brochure. It was relaxing and laid-back and it was tempting to stay longer. The trouble was, we had to be in Jamaica for the cricket in just over a week.

From Bocas del Toro we made our way back to the mainland and on to Boquete, a town of wooden houses nestled beside the Río Caldera in a valley surrounded by mountains. With its gardens, bright flowers, twin-spired church and temperate climate it was easy to imagine that you were somewhere in the Alps, not in Central America. Only the nearby coffee plantations and the farmers wearing white cowboy hats hinted otherwise.

We stayed in a guesthouse close to the pretty town centre. It had just been opened, and the Panamanian guy who ran it was still putting the finishing touches to the front. He greeted us enthusiastically, a paintbrush in one hand. His name was Pancho, and he proudly showed us the rooms, the bathrooms and the kitchen, and explained his plans for an outdoor barbecue area. He was infatuated by the whole idea of running his own guesthouse and offered to drive us out to nearby hot springs, rock carvings and other places of interest. When Jon and I told him we were thinking of climbing Barú Volcano, he said he would drive us to the start of the trail at 5 am the next morning.

I don't know why Jon and I wanted to climb Barú Volcano. It wasn't active. It didn't have a steaming crater. And from what we'd heard the top was covered with antennae anyway. Worse, it was an 18-kilometre walk up a steep, rough road to the top. But a kind of competitive thing had developed between us, and once the climb had been suggested – I can't remember by whom – there was no backing down. The GND didn't mind, in fact she encouraged it. With Jon and me off proving our manhood, she'd have a rare day to herself.

It was still dark when Pancho dropped us off at the park gates. He lingered a few minutes, illuminating the steep potholed road for us with his headlights. I think he thought he was helping us, but in all honesty I wish he hadn't. It only highlighted how steep it was. We set off, bounding up the broken, potholed road, foolishly expending energy. I was determined to keep up with Jon – I wasn't going to be shown up by my younger rival – but before long my lively gait became a sluggish crawl.

I have heard since that the climb to the top of Barú Volcano is a beautiful one. One book I read about it describes 'tall cloud forest, thick with hanging creepers, lichen and bromeliads'. The steep cuttings, it said, were 'carpeted with a glorious array of ferns and colourful flowers'. If a climber were alert, he could spot wild turkeys, bee-sized hummingbirds and squirrels. But that day I was hunched over so badly that all I saw was one foot moving in front of the other, and maybe a few ants crawling past me in the dirt. To be honest, I tried not to look up too often – I found I was discouraged by how little ground I was covering. The only joy I got was noticing that Jon was struggling too.

Having said that, when I reached the top, just ahead of Jon, I was overwhelmed by a real sense of achievement. If I hadn't been so buggered I may have whooped with joy, and maybe even taunted Jon for letting an older man beat him. Instead, I sat at the base of the white cross that marked the highest point, catching my breath and appreciating the magnificent view. Because we had left early, the clouds hadn't moved in for the day and we could see clear across Panama to both the Pacific Ocean and the Caribbean Sea. Besides, I didn't want to gloat. We still had to walk all the way back. And the way I was feeling, I might have needed Jon to carry me.

As it was, we ended up getting a lift back to town in the back of a pick-up full of onions. As we bounced down the mountain, an onion wedged uncomfortably between my buttocks, I decided that peering into the craters of volcanoes, alive or otherwise, had lost its appeal. I vowed silently to myself that Barú Volcano would be the last volcano I would climb. Of course, the GND had sensibly realised this after her very first volcano and had left me to climb them alone. But then she is a lot quicker than me.

It was Jon's birthday the next day, so instead of heading straight to Panama City, as had been our plan, we decided to spend it at Playa Las Lajas, a deserted stretch of black sand on Panama's Pacific coast. Our guidebook intimated that it was a popular spot with local Panamanians, but when we arrived the place was empty and the few shacks along it looked like they had been abandoned years ago. The only place to sleep was an old American school bus, up on blocks, that had all the seats taken out and a couple of beds thrown in. It was 'owned' by a guy who was squatting in a shack nearby. If we were hungry, his wife could cook us beans and rice. And if we were thirsty, he could sell us a couple of warm beers.

But, apart from a flock of pelicans that flew overhead and a couple of stray dogs frolicking in the waves, we had a 20 kilometre stretch of beach to ourselves. The GND lay on the beach, tanning – she'd read in a brochure on Panama beaches we'd picked up in Bocas del Toro that 'it only takes a couple of hours to get a nice suntan in Panama, that wonderfully bronzed look that sun lovers adore'. Jon and I went for a swim, but soon got bored. Still a little miffed that I had beaten him to the top of Barú Volcano, Jon challenged me to a quick round of Beach Olympics, a series of beach-related activities like running, jumping and coconut tossing that we had devised in Costa Rica to amuse ourselves.

'Did you see that?' I'd say to the GND, hunched over and dragging in deep breaths after beating Jon in a beach sprint. 'I beat him by a good couple of yards.'

The GND would look up momentarily from her book and say, 'That's nice dear.'

◎　　　◎　　　◎

That night we sat on the empty beach playing Jon's Bee Gees tape on my Walkman. (Out of deference to him because it was his birthday, Jon got to choose what we were listening to.) The sky was a patchwork quilt of stars, and the high-pitched falsettos of Robin, Barry and Maurice coming through the tiny speakers struggled to be heard over the sound of the crashing waves.

We sat drinking from a bottle of rum we'd bought off

the squatter-landlord – I suspect it was from his own private collection – and, as usual, hard liquor had its wicked way with me and I retired to the bus early, leaving the GND and Jon sitting on the beach. I guess it should have been me and the GND sitting romantically on the beach, staring at the stars. Lord knows, it would probably be the last time we'd find a beach as deserted as this one. But the way my stomach was churning and my head was spinning, I knew that it wouldn't have remained romantic for too long anyway.

Still, I was upset when the GND came back and told me she had stripped to her underwear and gone swimming with Jon. I mean, I liked Jon. And he was enough of a proper English gentlemen to ensure nothing untoward would have happened. Even so, I thought it was a bit out of order that the GND had gone swimming so scantily clad with him.

'It's no different to wearing a bikini,' she said. 'You're very bitter. You must have been hurt badly in the past.'

It wasn't the bloody past I was worried about. I just felt that drunken midnight swims in one's underwear was the sort of thing she should be doing with me. For the moment, it appeared that Jon had devised and won a new Beach Olympics event: near-naked midnight swimming with another guy's girlfriend.

Early the next morning we caught a taxi back to the highway, and a bus on to Panama City. Our bus approached the city over the Bridge of the Americas, an iron-arch bridge not dissimilar to the Sydney Harbour Bridge, which spanned the Pacific entrance to the Panama Canal. From here Panama City looked like an amalgam of a lot of different cities. The high-rises that rose in the distance could have been American. The canal administration buildings to the left in Balboa were pure British colonial and wide, palm-lined streets gave the area a distinctly Gallic flair. Down around the bus station the city was as grubby and rundown as the worst parts of India. San Felipe, the old part of town where the state of our finances dictated we stay, looked as though it hadn't been touched since the Spanish left.

I was excited about visiting Panama City. For me it's a city that reeks of international intrigue and treachery, a place of corrupt dictators and money-laundering banks and, of course, the site of one of the greatest engineering feats of the twentieth century – the Panama Canal. Panama City has long been one of the world's most important geopolitical battlefields.

As soon as the world's major powers discovered that this was where the Isthmus of Panama was at its narrowest, and hence that this was the narrowest point between the Atlantic and Pacific Oceans, it could never be any other way. During the Spanish conquests, Panama City was the start of the El Camino Real, the King's Highway, a track used to transport gold and other treasures from Peru to the Caribbean side, where galleons waited to take the spoils of the New World back to Spain.

In the 1800s Colombia, which controlled Panama at the time, signed a treaty that permitted the USA to build a railway across the isthmus and gave them the right to protect the line with military force. During the Great

Californian Gold Rush it was quicker for a prospector from New York to catch a boat down to the Atlantic side of the isthmus, get a train across the 50-kilometre isthmus to Panama City, and then a boat up to the gold fields of California than cross America by land.

It was the idea of a great canal joining the two oceans, however, that captured the imagination of mankind. In 1524, King Charles V of Spain ordered a survey to see if it could be done. In 1878, the Colombian government awarded a contract to build a canal to the French, still basking in their success after building the Suez Canal. When that ended in financial ruin, the Americans stepped in. In order to get the deal they wanted, they supported Panama's declaration of independence, stationing a couple of battleships off the coast at either end to discourage the Colombian military from doing anything about it. After ten years, at the cost of millions of dollars and many thousands of lives, the canal was completed. In return the USA received 'sovereign rights in perpetuity over the Canal Zone' – quite a dividend, considering how important trade between Asia and the rest of the world was set to become.

Of course, it didn't – or couldn't – end there. The canal, and the absolute control the USA had over it, was a constant source of friction with the Panamanian government, and in 1979 the treaty was redrawn and a timetable for the complete handover of the canal to Panama agreed upon. When we arrived, the transition was about to be completed and a new row was developing. The Panamanians were negotiating to sell the ports at either end to a Hong Kong company called Hutchinson Whampoa. For the growing

Asian economies, the canal has become indispensable.

As far as the world is concerned, Panama is the Panama Canal. I've got to admit, before I arrived in the country, that's all I thought there was to the place – a canal, a port at either end, a couple of locks and a bit of jungle each side. Of course, I also knew that it was a country that once had a president with acne so bad his constituents called him Pineapple Head (not to his face, of course). And after close to a week in its northern backblocks, I now knew that it had a bloody big volcano and a burgeoning eco-tourist scene. But I wouldn't be able to leave the country without seeing the canal up close and personal.

Our attempt to see the canal was a little like the French attempt to build it. Our hearts were in the right place, but in the end time and money ran out. I wanted to travel along it, from one end to the other, and see the Gaillard Cut, Gatún Lake and the massive locks at Miraflores and Pedro Miguel. A few travel agents in Panama City offered tours on largish cruise ships, but they were expensive and the next scheduled departure was not for another month. Our only other option was to get work as linehandlers on one of the smaller yachts heading through the canal.

Every boat that goes through the canal needs a designated number of linehandlers on deck before they are allowed to pass through the locks. Linehandlers catch the ropes needed to hold the boats securely in place while they are in the locks. This was not a problem with the huge cargo ships – they had more than enough crew to be able to drag a couple of blokes out of bed and have them stand on deck for a while. But for the owners of smaller sailing vessels, often a retired couple realising a life-long dream of sailing around the world, that meant paying people to come along for the two-day passage through the canal.

We'd heard that the best place to find a linehandling job was at the Balboa Yacht Club, out near the stately canal administration buildings. This was where the yachties waited while they applied for the appropriate permissions to pass through the canal from the Pacific to the Caribbean side. The old wooden clubhouse was one of the world yachting scene's favourite resting spots and a symbol of the Zonian way of life, and one of Panama City's favourite bars and restaurants. We caught a taxi out there and found that the club had burned to the ground.

As we stood looking at the charred remains, the plastic crime-scene tape still strung up between charred pylons, we were approached by a black guy with a grisly grey beard. His name was Harper and he wore the kind of hat the skipper wore in 'Gilligan's Island'. We asked him if he knew of any yachts going through.

'Don't know any more,' he said. 'The captains used to come into the bar. Now they just wait out in the harbour until it's time to go through.'

I asked what had happened to the yacht club. He told us that no one knew for sure. The police were still investigating how the fire had started and were looking at the insurance records. The fact that the club had been pleading with the Panama Canal Commission for permission to build a new club had caused some raised eyebrows. 'Ashes to ashes,' said Harper, diplomatically. 'Everything has to go sometime.'

I don't think he thought much of us as potential linehandlers. He looked Jon and I over and sniffed. 'You better keep dat boat away from those edges,' he warned, 'Or that captain he be cursing you!'

We asked him where we should go. He suggested we try the Cristóbal Yacht Club at Colón, on the other end of the canal.

'You be careful of thieves there though,' he cautioned. 'They hide in bushes waiting for you. Take your shoes before you know it!'

The taxi driver we waved over to take us back to town tried to charge us twice the amount it had cost us to get out to Bilboa. I figured that he had mistaken us for Canal Commission staff – although how, I wasn't sure, as we were dressed in grubby shorts and T-shirts – and I insisted that he turn on the meter and charge us the normal fare. When he refused, I motioned for Jon and the GND to get out. As I clambered out, I called him a ladrón, the Spanish word for thief. While I was well pleased with myself – the Spanish lessons had come in handy after all – the driver, a small, grey-haired fellow, wasn't. He drove after us, stopped the taxi and got out brandishing a knife.

I had never had a knife pulled on me before and I was surprised how calm I felt. Instead of apologising profusely, I taunted the guy, telling him that if he thought he was scaring me, he was wrong. The GND begged me to walk away, but I refused to let this guy think he was intimidating me. I hadn't done anything wrong. He had tried to rip us off and I had let him know exactly what I thought of him. In the end it was a stand off. He was waving his knife

50 metres away. I was acting as if I couldn't give a toss. I think it was my arrogant demeanour that really upset him. He probably thought I was American and was treating him this way because I thought I was better than him.

In the end, the taxi driver yabbered something in Spanish at me which I'm sure wasn't very flattering to my mother and drove off.

'What was that all about?' asked the GND. 'You were prepared to get stabbed over $2?'

I nearly said it wasn't the money, it was the principle of the matter. But I didn't.

■   ■   ■

Early the next morning we caught a bus to Colón, the city on the other side of the isthmus and home to the Cristóbal Yacht Club. We paid an extra 50 cents for the express service, thinking it would get us to Colón quicker, but instead we got tatty velour seats and airconditioning that was Arctic cold. Unfortunately, the television worked and we were subjected to *Wrongfully Accused*, a send up of *The Fugutive*, starring Leslie Nielson. We arrived in Colón just as it reached its unfunny conclusion.

Colón was a notorious shithole while the canal was being built. It was home to the West Indian labourers brought to Panama to do the digging and was a hovel of pestilence and disease. If you see any photos of the living quarters from the time, you see sad dark faces with lifeless eyes staring out from shacks. A visiting New York reporter described the town as 'unspeakably loathsome'. Marie Gorgas, the wife of Dr Gorgas, the guy who eradicated

Yellow Fever from the isthmus, described it as 'unspeakably dirty' and 'swarming with naked children, ugly, dilapidated and terribly depressing'. In the years since the canal was finished, it hasn't got any better.

Harper's dire warning about thieves had spooked Jon and the GND, so we caught a taxi from Colón bus station to the Cristóbal Yacht Club, just on the edge of town, out near the container terminal. A few discreet inquiries at the bar revealed that there was a French couple looking for linehandlers, and the office manager radioed their boat to tell them that we were here. Ten minutes later, a middle-aged French woman, tanned and leathery, turned up out of breath and excited. She had rowed a dinghy to shore.

'I must call the port authority,' she said, not bothering to ask if we were the ones who wanted to be linehandlers. 'We have to take a Panamanian too. Please wait here.'

So wait we did. When she rang at nine, they told her to call back at 11. When she rang at 11, they told her to call back at one. At one they told here to call back at four. This was the latest possible time they could start a passage through the canal. We passed the time drawing caricatures of each other on the polyurethane cups we were drinking from and writing lists – favourite meals, favourite albums, two people we'd most like to meet, male and female. Jon, always the nice boy, said he'd like to meet Jesus Christ and his mum. I went for the more secular Alby Mangels and Liz Hurley. The GND nominated Bertrand Russell and caused a ruckus by saying that she wanted to meet Elton John as her 'female'.

At five, the French woman returned and told us that

there weren't enough yachts to form a group to go through that day and that the canal authority wouldn't be allowing yachts through again until Thursday. The GND and I were flying out for Jamaica for the cricket on Thursday so it didn't look like we'd be sailing through the canal after all. Worse, we'd missed the last bus and would have to spend the night in Colón.

Our hotel was in the middle of the ghettos, across the road from the derelict shells of houses where a teenage boy, dressed like a gang member from South Central, was stalking through the wrecks of houses with a slingshot. I think that this may have freaked Jon out more than he let on. He had trouble getting to sleep that night, claiming that the telephone in the hotel lobby sounded like the one on 'The Rockford Files'.

On the way back to Panama City we visited the Miraflores Locks. Ships transiting through Miraflores to the Pacific are lowered the last two steps to sea level. The gates here are the heaviest and largest – they weigh 745 tons each – to deal with the extreme variations in the Pacific tides. When they were built these locks were at the cutting edge of early twentieth century technology and even today they inspire awe. We watched a series of huge cargo boats lifted up and down like plastic boats in a bathtub.

This happens 24 hours a day, seven days a week. Stretching as far as we could see either end of the locks was a line of cargo boats waiting to come through. If you looked back towards the Pacific Ocean and the Bridge of the Americas, you could see them lining up to come in, like planes lining up as they approach a runway.

Presidential elections were only a couple of months away and the future of the canal was an important policy issue. While we were at the locks a candidate was filming a commercial. He had his jacket off in a 'man-of-action' pose and talked to the camera as one of the large cargo ships made its way through the lock, thumping his clenched fist into his other hand. Two workers, wearing orange hard hats and reflector sunglasses, leaned against the rail watching and laughing. Eventually, one of the film crew came over and asked them to move out of the way.

I asked them who the candidate was. 'Alberto Ballarino,' they said. 'He has no chance!'

(I kept an eye out for the results of the Panamanian presidential elections later that year. And you know what? They were right.)

■   ■   ■

It was our last night in Panama City. The cricket was starting in Jamaica on the following Saturday and the GND and I had a flight to catch. Jon was heading south into South America, although he had made noises about coming along with us. He'd been reading my guidebook on Jamaica and was quite taken with the idea of checking out the notorious dancehall queens, the scantily clad girls at Jamaican nightclubs who specialised in dancing in a very sexual manner.

We spent our last night at Bennigans, an Irish Bar that overlooked the Bay of Panama. The only concession to being Irish were the shamrocks on the menus and coasters and the Guinness on tap. Our waiter was called Jesus, and between pouring drinks he practised bottle-twirling manoeuvres like Bryan Brown and Tom Cruise in *Cocktail*. He was still learning, so the bottles were empty and there was a rubber mat on the floor beneath him. We disappointed him by simply ordering beers.

The televisions were all tuned to ESPN which was showing a female fitness pageant, Miss Fitness America. If you ever wonder why the world has such a bizarre view on America, it's because of programs like these. The Miss Fitness America pageant was basically a bunch of women with smiles fixed on their faces while they went through a strenuous series of aerobic routines that would have even the fittest of us grimacing in pain. It didn't take long for Jon and I to figure out what the judges were looking for – an ability males are born with – and soon we were competing with each other, trying to correctly guess the winner. It was our last bit of competitive camaraderie, and I'm pleased to report that not only did I pick the winner, Tanya Merryman, but also her score of 54.9.

■   ■   ■

It was sad to see Jon go. Not only was I losing a damn fine Beach Olympics rival, but I was saying goodbye to a new friend as well. In all honesty, he was probably the reason the GND and I were still together.

Clearly the GND was sorry to see Jon go too. When he finally said goodbye she threw her arms around him and sobbed uncontrollably.

'I say, take a photo of the Dancehall Queens for me, will you?' said Jon, turning to me as he wiped back a tear.

I promised I would.

CHAPTER TWENTY-THREE

Sabina Park

(Jamaica)

Annoying habit >>> A lack of appreciation for the
fine game of cricket
Culprit >>> GND

Norman Manley International Airport in Kingston was
crawling with Australian males. They were all dressed in
boardshorts and T-shirts and were wearing those Oakley
sunglasses that Warnie likes. They huddled in packs, waiting
beside the luggage carousel or over by the tourist information
desk, where they tried to line up accommodation.

'We were the ones who broke the pool in Trinidad,' one
guy said to the girl behind the counter, who looked bemused.
'It flooded the outfield and stopped Lara from getting a
four!' The guy acted as though he had played an instrumental

part in the Australian victory in the First Test there. But the West Indies had been bowled out for only 51 in the second innings, so it had been no real feat.

It was bizarre to see so many of our compatriots. We could count on one hand the number of Australians we had met on our journey so far – and those we did meet were there for a particular purpose, like the medical students in Honduras. Yet that day in Jamaica, nearly everyone arriving at the airport was Australian.

'It's like hanging around the SCG before a day–nighter,' I said to the GND. As the GND was not a cricket fan, she had no idea what I was talking about.

The GND wasn't the only Australian woman at the airport that day. There was the occasional female cricket fan hanging out in the packs, wearing shorts and Oakleys too. But most of the other Aussie chicks were wives or girlfriends who had been dragged along on the promise that after the cricket was over, they would get quality romantic time on a Caribbean beach.

Standing in the immigration queue that day, it struck me that the West Indies was one of the few places in the cricketing world you could do that. It was certainly the only place you could crack the old gag: '"Took my girlfriend to see the cricket the other day." "Jamaica?" "No, she went of her own accord!"' Let's face it. You'd never get away with dragging your girl along to a tour of the subcontinent: 'Hey honey, after the test at Eden Gardens in Calcutta, we can spend some quality time in the black hole!'

In the West Indies, however, every Test location in the Cable & Wireless Test series had an exotic ring to it –

Trinidad, Jamaica, Barbados, Antigua, Guyana. What self-respecting sun worshipper would knock that back? Sure, your bloke is going to spend five days in each place watching cricket, but how else are you going to get him to take you to the Caribbean? A jaunt to the Caribbean from Australia is a long and complicated affair that involves changing planes at least 20 times and necessitates a second and possibly third mortgage on the house. Certainly, it was with the promise of Caribbean beaches that I had been able to talk the GND into coming along, not just to see the cricket, but to Central America altogether.

The immigration officer knew that too. He simply stamped us in and said, 'Enjoy the cricket.' I was disappointed he didn't say, 'Welcome to Jamaica. Have a nice day!'

The airport is on a spit that forms a natural barrier between the Caribbean and Kingston Harbour. The harbour is the seventh largest in the world, and the most important in the West Indies. It ensured Kingston was the trade capital of the region, and was a happy hunting ground for English buccaneers during the sixteenth century.

We caught a bus from the airport to Downtown Kingston, a grubby spot of crumbling buildings and street hawkers. Right on the harbour, this had once been the heart of the city, a place buzzing with the energy of the sugar and slave trade, but an earthquake flattened the area in 1907 and the banks and other commercial enterprises had moved north towards the Blue Mountains, to New Kingston. Downtown never recovered and that day it reminded me of the poorer parts of India – squalid, desperate, hopeless – but a hell of a lot more laid-back.

We had decided to stay at the Artland Guest House. Our guidebook described it as basic, but it was the only place in Kingston that we could even remotely afford. It was up near Half Way Tree, another bus ride away. But when a passing local called me a 'white motherfucker' for no apparent reason (well, apart from the fact that I was conspicuously white) I decided it would be prudent if we caught a taxi.

As we clambered in the taxi, I had the distinct feeling that I'd left something behind. You know how you get used to a particular weight on your shoulder when you're travelling – from a day pack or camera bag – and when it's not there you feel kind of naked? I checked everything off – my backpack was in the boot, my camera bag was on my lap, my wallet was in my pocket. Then it dawned on me. It was Jon that I was missing. In Costa Rica and Panama I was always checking to see that we hadn't left him behind.

The taxi made its way north through Jones Town and Trench Town, home to a huge underclass of the poor and unemployed. Here Kingston was as rundown as the worst parts of Asia, but where the rows of slums in Bangkok or India are occasionally broken by a pretty temple, perhaps, in Kingston there was nothing. It had once been a popular residential area, central and well laid out, but with the exodus of the rich to more upmarket suburbs in the north and the influx of the rural poor, drawn to the bright lights of the capital, it had been transformed into a no-go zone of crowded tenements, cardboard shacks and shocking poverty. It was the domain of yardies – organised criminals – and a hotbed of drugs, guns and prostitution.

Noticing our alarm, the taxi driver turned the conversation to cricket. 'We will beat you this time,' he said with a confidence unbecoming of a supporter of a team that had just been walloped by 312 runs.

'I hope so,' I replied. 'I'd like to see five days of cricket.' Like most Jamaicans, the taxi driver had strong views on Brian Lara's captaincy. Cricket in the West Indies is fractured down national lines. Lara was from Trinidad, and not much liked outside his home island. Our taxi driver called him a poodle, slang for homosexual, and said that Jamaica's favourite son, Courtney Walsh, should be captain, despite his less-than-spectacular record in the role. According to the taxi driver, although Lara was one of the best batsmen in the world, he was not standing up for his side when they needed him. To prove his point, the taxi driver related a story he'd heard on the radio that morning. 'Apparently, when Lara arrived yesterday, the customs official asked, 'Tell me, Mr Lara, what is your business in Jamaica?'' He slapped his thighs as if it was the funniest thing he'd ever heard.

Personally I felt sorry for Lara. In Australia, it's difficult enough keeping all the different states happy when choosing a national team, especially the Queenslanders. Imagine the complications captaining a side made of various – and very different – countries.

Although situated close to the more upmarket suburbs of Kingston, the Artland Guest House was in an area that can be best described as 'alarming'. It sat in a compound behind thick concrete walls topped by barbed wire, and after our taxi driver beeped his horn, a security guard came to the gate and unlocked it. For $25 a night we got a small room with an overhead fan and an attached bathroom. The shower was cold water only, but it was hot so it didn't matter.

Although the test was being played at Sabina Park, on the other side of Kingston, the Artland Guest House was full of Aussies. They sat in the restaurant-bar, underneath a sign saying 'No Ganja Smoking', drinking Red Stripe beer and watching television, flicking through the channels and yelping with delight when they came upon the porn channel.

The bar was run by a slovenly girl with braids, who sat slumped, either dozing or flicking through the channels on the television with a remote. Her favourite channel was the one that showed amateur footage of street parties held in Kingston. The stars were the dancehall queens, most of whom seemed to sport blonde beehives, thigh-high boots and negligible clothing. They were more scantily clad and their dance styles more explicit than I had imagined. It was like televised lap-dancing. The barmaid, plump and plain, obviously hoped that one day she could be a dancehall queen.

She certainly had a rather arbitrary approach to the prices she charged. Although the prices of drinks were clearly posted behind the bar – a bottle of the local Red Stripe beer listed at $J60 – she would charge anywhere between $J70 and $J90. When questioned, she said the prices had changed. Aussies, being Aussies, asked her why the sign hadn't been changed and when she answered that she wasn't authorised to change it, they said they weren't authorised to pay the higher price.

This kind of price gouging was rampant in Kingston. A street-side soft-drink hawker charged me three times more for a Coke than the Jamaican he served before me. When I questioned him he said it was because I could afford it. At the local general store, the shopkeeper 'forgot' to give me my change when I bought a packet of washing powder. Everyone, it seemed, was adding their little bit extra on.

Even the security guard at the Artland Guest House got in on the act. On our first night we asked him if there was anywhere cheap to eat nearby. He said it was too dangerous for us to go out on the street and offered to go and buy chicken and rice for us. I asked him how much it would cost and he said, 'A hundred.' When he spotted $J150 in my hand he snatched it and said, 'That will do.'

The next day we caught a crowded bus towards New Kingston and the banks to change money. It was neater and cleaner here and the buildings higher and better maintained. From under the armpit of a rasta I spotted Shane Warne and Steve Waugh walking down the street. I pointed them out to the GND, excited.

'They look like those blokes we saw at the airport yesterday,' she said, unimpressed at seeing some of the best cricketers in the world. 'Warnie looks like he could do with losing a bit of weight.'

They turned into a Pizza Hut restaurant and we lost sight of them.

I couldn't understand why the GND wasn't as excited about going to the cricket here as I was. Ever since I stayed up late as a child to watch my first live broadcast of a Test match from the West Indies I'd always wanted to go there to see one. It wasn't necessarily for the cricket. Back then the likes of Michael Holding, Andy Roberts, and Joel Garner were ripping through our top order with consummate ease. It was what was happening off the field that captured my imagination – the steel drums, the drinking, the dancing and the carousing. Hell, even the guy swinging from the grandstand seemed exotic.

I guess that's why I didn't sleep too well the night before the start of the First Test. And why the GND and I were among the first people lining up outside Sabina Park to get in.

I had been able to swing a press pass for both the GND and me – don't ask how, I'd have to kill you if I told you – so we were able to get into The Mound, the all-you-can-drink party section of the ground, for free.

From the moment a pretty Red Stripe girl wrapped a coloured hospital bracelet around my wrist I knew that watching a Test match in the West Indies would be different to any other cricket match I had ever been to. For one thing, there's a beach under the scoreboard. Yep, a beach, a real one with real sand shipped in especially from Negril Beach. What's more, there are deck chairs with huge umbrellas big enough to keep the sun off the largest of beer bellies. And a pool. Not a big pool, just a rubber inflatable thing. But big enough, all the same, to fit a couple of big boofy Australian blokes and half a dozen Red Stripe girls.

The Red Stripe girls were like The Mound's very own

flight attendants. They were pretty girls, probably models most of the time, and for the duration of the Test they donned tiny Red Stripe bikinis and tight denim shorts (inexplicably with the buttons left undone) and lolled about in the pool or rubbed suntan lotion on patrons' backs and bellies. Sometimes they hung around the entrance to The Mound putting on the colour-coded bracelets that showed you had paid your entrance fee. Other times they wandered through the crowd handing out the complimentary KFC lunch vouchers.

The Mound also came with its very own 'on-board' entertainment. Just to the left of the scoreboard there was a stage and a DJ. During the course of the day, during the breaks and often between overs, musicians, rappers and dancing girls would do their thing. In the West Indies they realised that it takes more to entertain the fans than play ads from sponsors on a huge electronic scoreboard.

The best part of The Mound, however, was that once you paid to get in – or waved your Press Pass – you could drink as much beer, spirits and soft drinks as you could put away. When you finished one beer – or Gin & Ting, the GND's drink of choice in Jamaica – you simply walked back to the bar and got another one. No one counted and no one cared.

The Mound was the brainchild of West Indies cricket official Chris Dehring. The idea came to him at a test match in Antigua. Music and drinking had always been a part of the cricket there and he noticed that the visiting supporters really enjoyed it. He simply moved it onto a more professional level.

As part of the deal in securing the press passes, I had to catch up with Chris during the lunch break on the first day. He told me they had tested the all-inclusive concept during the Jamaican Test against Australia in 1995. The Red Stripe brewery happily supplied the beer, but they hadn't counted on the Aussie capacity for putting a few away. 'Red Stripe had provided beer for other big Jamaican events like Carnival and Sunsplash and based supplies for the whole Test on that,' he said. 'The Aussies had drunk the place dry by two o'clock on the first day.' A few hurried phone calls to warehouses throughout Kingston, however, saved the day. This time, Chris assured me, Red Stripe was prepared. Especially for the Test, they'd set aside more beer than was drunk during a whole month in Kingston.

The GND was particularly taken with the music. Between each over, during drinks and in the time it takes a new batsman to come onto the ground, one of Kingston's best DJs pumped out the latest in Jamaican ragga and dancehall. And during the lunch break, a live musical act was featured. 'This is better than the game,' she said, sashaying among a sea of very happy Jamaican males. 'They should cut back on the cricket and have more dancing!'

Chris Dehring had been quick to point out that The Mound had been a breaking ground for Jamaican musicians. Shaggy previewed his world-wide hit 'Bombastic' here in 1995. And this year one of Jamaica's best-known rappers, Zebra, provided the lunchtime entertainment.

I've got to admit, even the West Indies theme song was annoyingly catchy. It claimed that cricket between Australia and the West Indies was 'bad boys' business!' and throughout the rest of the song proclaimed, 'It's our time, it's our team, it's our game!' Although it bordered on being treasonous, the tune was so infectious – and got played so many times – that I couldn't help but sing along.

The real success of the music at The Mound, however, could be seen in the number of Australian blokes up and dancing. These were the same guys who would normally spend an evening in a nightclub cradling a beer, refusing their girlfriend's entreaties to get up on the dancefloor. Yet here in the Caribbean, a few Red Stripes under their belts, they were up prancing about like they were Shabba Ranks. Unfortunately, this also had the effect of proving something that I have long suspected. The Aussie male can't dance. And draping a boxing kangaroo flag over your shoulder doesn't help.

Realising that it takes more than unlimited beer, an international-class reggae act and a game of cricket to keep your average Aussie punter entertained, Chris Dehring had also devised a number of other activities. At tea, beer-drinking contests were held as well as dirty dancing and Bob Marley sing-along competitions. (I'm pleased to report that your author came a very commendable third in the tightly contested hairy-chest competition.)

The thing that amazed me most about The Mound, however, was the behaviour of the Aussie tourists. Considering that once you got inside it was an open bar, they were surprisingly well behaved. When a West Indian supporter mocked the Aussie chant of 'Aussie, Aussie, Aussie, Oi, Oi, Oi', by turning it into an orangutan mating call, the semi-sober lads took it in good spirits. And when one lad yelled 'Show us your tits' at the Red Stripe girls, he was roundly chastised by his mates and doused in Red Stripe from a Red Stripe yard glass. The only discordant note came when the ground staff confiscated the Australian contingent's Aussie Rules football in an attempt to get the crowd off the ground so that the covers could be laid. The lads surrounded the guy and abused the hell out of him.

The poor guy obviously hadn't realised just how important the impromptu game of footy at the end of each day's play had become to these Victorians. Stumps were barely pulled before every Victorian male, no matter how many Red Stripes he'd sunk, was on the ground carrying on like he was Wayne Carey. As a New South Welshman untouched by the hysterical fervour induced by aerial ping-pong, it always amazes me how seriously Victorians take these kinds of kick-arounds. They all acted like there was a talent scout for Geelong in the stands and that they were undiscovered superstars.

The other great thing about cricket in the West Indies is that the players are a lot more accessible. One guy from Sale in Victoria had bumped into Justin Langer at the bar at the Hilton and had spent a good hour or so chatting to the Aussie number three. Apparently Langer had told him that once they got rid of Lara they'd clean up the rest of the Windies in no time. He was right, of course. It's just that it took them the good part of a day and a bit to get Lara out.

After the end of play on the second day the GND and I decided to go to the Hilton and check out the players' digs and maybe have a chat with some of the players ourselves. The locals were in a better frame of mind – your team batting through the day without losing a wicket tends to have that effect – so we were able to jump into the back of a passing pick-up and get dropped off right out the front of the Hilton.

Thankfully, the Aussie guests actually staying at the hotel weren't dressed any better than we were and we were able to walk by in our shorts and complimentary Red Stripe Mound T-shirt without raising an eyebrow. Nor were we stopped from jumping in the pool while McGrath and Gillespie did laps under the watchful eye of the team physio. Two Aussie girls in bikinis were in the pool as well, and they exclaimed in fake surprise, 'I didn't know you guys were staying here!' when Jason and Glenn swam by. (Either that or they were talking to me.) Regardless, a quick chat with the boys revealed that they were of the same mind as Langer. Once they got rid of Lara things would be easy. The fact that he'd already scored 212 runs, largely at their expense, wasn't mentioned.

Perhaps the biggest difference about watching the cricket in the West Indies was their attitude towards ground invasions. In Sydney or Melbourne the grounds are ringed by hired security guards with enough hardware to fight a small war. And if you should get by them, there's also the trifling matter of a $5000 fine. They have guards at Sabina Park too, but they only have truncheons and politely step out of the way when an invasion begins. When Lara was on 199 and every Aussie in The Mound was forming lines on the beach under the scoreboard to invade, the Jamaican security guards moved to another part of the ground. But when someone fell or was trampled under foot, they were the first there to help them up and safely see them back over the fence to receive first aid.

I'll admit, it must have been freaky for the players on the field. At the sight of a couple of hundred drunken Aussies invading the field after he scored his double century, Brian Lara scampered off to the dressing room to hide. (The fact that one of the Aussie supporters was naked might also have had something to do with it.)

Stuart McGill wasn't particularly impressed, however. He turned to the crowd and yelled, 'Get off the field you bastards, we're trying to play cricket.' He didn't understand that at that moment the cricket didn't matter. And nor would the commentators, sitting up in their boxes condemning the supporters for running onto the pitch. How could they? They hadn't been to The Mound, listening to Zebra, taken part in the hairy-chest competition, drinking more Red Stripe than they should and having sunscreen rubbed into their belly by girls who made Elle MacPherson look rather plain. And until they did they'd never understand that on a hot March day in Kingston there are sometimes more important things than cricket.

In the end I was thankful for the distractions The Mound offered. Out in the middle Australia wasn't doing too well. Courtesy of Lara's knock of 213, they were battling to even set the Windies a second-innings target. By the morning of the fourth day, the Windies had the game in the bag. By now The Mound was fairly empty – despite a reduced cover price – and elsewhere in the ground, boys in grey school uniforms who had been allowed to come along to watch the final sessions made up most of the crowd. The GND and I sat in the stand, getting as many free Red Stripes and Gin & Tings in while we could and tucking into the complimentary KFC that they had started serving at 10.30 am.

Just before play started we were joined by a local guy in a suit and tie. His name was Winston and he looked like the West Indian cricketer Viv Richards. Winston was a public servant and had taken time off work – signed what he had to sign – to come to the cricket. I asked him if he was worried about getting sacked.

'I told my manager he can dismiss me, but I am going to the cricket,' he said. 'But it is fine. We will spend tomorrow talking about the cricket.'

He was excited about seeing the West Indies win. He had been here when Australia won the corresponding test in the previous tour, paving the way for a historic series win.

'May 5, Monday afternoon,' he said gravely. 'I will never forget that day. It was the Australians who were dancing to that song.'

Winston was one of those fans who never felt completely comfortable until the game was over and his team had won. In that way he was a lot like a supporter of the St George rugby league team. Even though the West Indies had the game well and truly under control, he was still anxious about them losing. He was especially concerned by the fact that Ian Healy (he pronounced Healy's first name 'Iron') the Australian wicketkeeper, was still batting. 'We fear Iron Healy,' he said. 'You can't catch him. You can't bowl him. You can't get him lbw. You have to run him out!'

Once Iron Healy was gone, run out for 10, as it happened, Winston breathed easy and spent the rest of the time explaining the finer points of the game to the GND. To her credit, she had tried to understand the concept of silly mid-on and leg before wicket, but more often than not was distracted by the appearance of a new rapper on stage or the offer of more KFC or Gin & Tings.

To be fair, this lack of appreciation for the gentleman's game wasn't limited to the GND. We had met a couple from Melbourne, Sally and Corker, who were staying at Artlands as well and were going to all the Tests. In Trinidad, Sally had met Michael Slater in the Pelican Bar. Slater had opened the batting for Australia and scored 106. Not knowing him from a bar of soap, Sally just thought he was another fan, and she asked where he had sat that day. 'In the middle,' he'd answered tersely.

Despite Winston's fears, the Australians could only set the West Indies a second-innings total of 17 runs and the match was all over by lunchtime. After being flogged in Trinidad, the West Indies had levelled the series with an emphatic ten-wicket victory.

With the Test over and our source of free food and drink gone, the GND and I decided to head back to the Hilton for a swim. The Australian team were already there, trying to forget their woes with a few quiet cold ones at the pool-side bar. Only one player was swimming – Matthew Elliott, the opening batsman.

From what I could gather, Matthew Elliott was a fitness

freak. Every evening, whether he had batted or not, he came down to the pool and swam laps. He didn't just swim them. He pounded them out. And before starting and after finishing, he would go through a series of complex stretching exercises, one of which involved him hooking his heel over the lip of the drainage that went around the pool and touching his outstretched toes.

Inspired by watching Matthew pound up and down the pool, the GND had got it into her head that she should be doing laps too. By the second lap she was tiring, and without goggles was veering dangerously across the pool towards Elliott, who was in the middle of his stretching exercises. I could see what was happening. I was sitting at one of the pool-side tables, sensibly enjoying a cold beer. I jumped up, yelling at the GND to stop. It was like one of those bad movies: everything was in slow motion, my voice a slowed-down 'Nooooo!'

The GND didn't hear me, but Elliott did. He looked up and on spotting the GND closing in on him, tried to hop out of her way, his heel still hooked over the lip. But no matter where he hopped the GND followed. It was as if she was a heat-seeking missile targeted on the poor man's groin.

It is a testament to the character of Matthew Elliott that he apologised to the GND. It is also instructive to note that he was dropped after that Test and his career has struggled ever since.

CHAPTER TWENTY-FOUR

Negril
(Jamaica)

Annoying habit >>> Cheap-Charlieism
Culprit >>> Peter

You don't need to spend too long in Kingston to realise just how important music is to your everyday Jamaican. There are posters on every wall and telegraph pole advertising bands and dances. There are makeshift stalls on every corner, with huge speakers, selling bootleg copies of tapes. Even the city buses sacrifice a couple of seats for speakers to play music. It seems you can't go anywhere in the city without hearing reggae or dancehall booming out at levels guaranteed to cause industrial deafness. Nor could you walk the streets without passively inhaling enough ganja to bring on an attack of the munchies.

That Jamaicans measure their self-worth in terms of music is demonstrated by the almost religious reverence still felt for Bob Marley. Despite the rise of dancehall as a music genre and its trademark sexually explicit and boastful lyrics, Marley's more politically focused lyrics continue to strike a chord across the social strata. He is widely tipped to become Jamaica's next National Hero, an honour normally bestowed on politicians. Basically, Bob is the only Jamaican that no one ever says a bad word about.

Of course, it helps that Bob was held in equally high regard everywhere else in the world and that each year thousands of reggae fans come to Jamaica to pay homage to their hero. And, reverentially or otherwise, the Jamaicans have long figured that there is a lot of money to be made from the memory of Marley. Stories abound of tourists blithely walking into Trench Town to take photos of Bob Marley's childhood haunts only to lose their camera and anything else they may have been carrying. A more legitimate money-making venture is the Bob Marley Museum up on Hope Road.

The museum is in a building that was Marley's home from 1975 until he died of cancer in 1981. Every visitor to Kingston goes there – the word on The Mound was that Steve Waugh had visited it the day before the test started. Our guidebook described it as 'a gentle monument to Jamaica's greatest musical legend', but without wanting to sound too harsh, it seemed to me to be a very neat way to extract $35 from silly, starry-eyed tourists like the GND and me.

'It wouldn't cost that much to get into Disneyland!' said the GND indignantly.

And you didn't get much for your money either. A sign at the gate said that no cameras or taping equipment were allowed and made it quite clear that 'idlers' weren't welcome at all. I wondered if that meant we would be thrown off the tour if we didn't ask a lot of questions.

As we waited for our guide, we discovered that the museum was also home to every itinerant rasta in town. They milled around, greeting each other with elaborate handshakes, saying, 'Respect, mon,' and handing around a joint. One rasta was atop a wall adding his bit to the mural depicting Bob Marley's life. He had the beanie and the dreds, the whole rasta works, and I thought it might make a good photo. I got a few shots off before the guy noticed me and demanded the equivalent of $20 for the privilege. I pretended I didn't 'overstand' what he was saying. In the end, an older rasta entered the fray to translate, no doubt hoping to pick up a commission for helping to clear up the misunderstanding. 'It is nothing, it means nothing,' he said. 'Give him the money and I will give you a blessing.'

Just as I was about to give him a blessing, a dark girl approached the GND and me and asked us to join a group of other tourists, many of whom we'd spotted at The Mound. 'I Natalie,' she said, 'and I be your guide.'

Our tour began, as you would expect, in the asphalt carpark. Apparently this was where Bob enjoyed many an impromptu game of football. Next, we stopped at a rather bad statue of Bob playing a guitar while kicking a soccer ball, before heading around to the back of the two-story house where the tour 'inside' the museum would start.

Natalie stopped and pointed to a beehive up on the roof,

under an eave. 'The bees settled there soon after Bob moved in,' she said. 'This is significant because in Ethiopia bees mean king and in Jamaica they mean wealth.'

Seeing that we were struggling to understand the significance, she continued.

'Bob became the king of reggae and very wealthy,' she scolded.

We all went 'Ohhhh!' and felt suitably chastised.

Natalie took us into the house and showed us the bullet holes in the wall from the 1976 assassination attempt. Marley had become embroiled in the violence of Jamaican politics by agreeing to play at the Smile Jamaica Concert organised by Prime Minister Michael Manley and, well, some yardies came around and paid the King of Reggae a visit. 'They came in and sprayed their deadly bullets,' said Natalie.

'I didn't think anyone got killed,' I piped up.

'They weren't,' replied Natalie.

'Then how were the bullets deadly?'

The GND jabbed me in the ribs.

'I didn't want her to think I was an idler!' I hissed.

Natalie ignored me and took us further into the house.

Every single thing in the house had a significant meaning. We stopped at the bottom of the pine staircase and Natalie told us that it was an essential part of Bob's daily fitness regime. 'Each morning he would spring up and down them,' she said breathlessly. 'Often taking three steps at a time!'

The 'press room', looked like a teenage girl's room that had been plastered with posters of and articles about their favourite band. Except instead of The Backstreet Boys or Westlife it was all about Bob. The clippings included the front cover of the now defunct Australian music newspaper, *Juke*. It seemed incongruous, standing in Kingston, Jamaica, looking at a poster advertising features on underwhelming Australian bands like Skyhooks, Ol'55 and Sherbet and screaming 'Norman Gunston: Eight months to live!' But I got over it.

We made our way to Bob's bedroom - 'a simple room because he was a simple man' – and on to his kitchen where he prepared 'healthy meals of fresh fruit and vegetables' and 'used honey instead of sugar'. Natalie told us to take special note that all the kitchen appliances were either beige or brown. 'Brown and beige was Bob's second favourite colour combination,' Natalie said. 'After red, green and yellow, of course.'

Hmmmmm.

After watching a video in the old Tuff Gong studios, we were herded towards the Bob Marley shopping complex. It included souvenir shops selling overpriced keyrings, postcards, reggae coloured caps, clothes and, alarmingly, footballs. There was also a restaurant selling Bob's favourite meals, and an ice cream parlour selling Bob's favourite flavours.

'I wonder if they use honey in the ice cream,' said the GND.

We left the museum without buying anything. Alarmed, another old rasta chased after us, and after inflicting a five-minute handshake on us both, tried to sell us aloe vera – 'great for your skin'. When we refused that, he offered his services as a protector – 'raggamuffin security' he called it. When we refused that, he gave up any pretence and tried begging for some small change.

'We can barely afford to eat in this country,' I said. 'We have no money!'

It was true. Since the cricket had ended, and we weren't frequenting The Mound anymore, we had been forced to buy food and drink. And after Central America, everything was horrendously expensive. With a plate of rice and beans setting us back $5 a serve, we could barely support ourselves, let alone a bunch of indolent rastas.

Our dire financial circumstances was also affecting our Jamaican itinerary. We had had grand plans to wander through Jamaica, going up to the Blue Mountains, to Ocho Rios and the north coast. And before visiting the Bob Marley Museum I had even toyed with the idea of visiting the Bob Marley Mausoleum up at St Ann's Bay. But if we wanted to get to Cuba, which we did, we'd have to spend as little time in Jamaica as possible.

The trouble was, the GND didn't want to leave without seeing a bit of sea and sand. 'We can't come all this way without going to a beach,' she argued. 'What am I going to say? That I went to Jamaica just for the cricket?'

I very nearly pointed out that, in many pubs around the world, that would afford her instant-legend status. But in the end I compromised and agreed that we would stop at the beach resort of Negril on our way to Montego Bay to catch our flight to Havana.

Negril is a former fishing village set on an incredibly beautiful beach. The water is unnaturally blue and the town has an international reputation as a party centre. The main beach at Long Bay is lined with all-inclusive resorts like Hedonism II, Risky Business and Margueritaville that entice European and American holidaymakers with the promise of sand, sun and the opportunity to indulge themselves or 'someone else'. Anyone who has seen 'Paradise Island', a tacky 'fly-on-the-wall' program filmed at Hedonism II, knows that at Negril anything, and I mean anything, goes. It's a reputation the place has had for centuries. Cap'n Calico Jack Rackham, the most notorious buccaneer to terrorise Jamaican waters, often moored here to celebrate recent plunders with a bit of heavy-duty rum drinking.

It was also spring break when the GND and I arrived in Negril. Spring break is a mid-semester holiday institution for American college students that sees them flocking to places like Florida, Cancun in Mexico and, increasingly, to Negril, to drink themselves into a stupor and flash their breasts. The local paper, *The Gleaner*, boasted that over 8000 'breakers' had descended on Negril this year, a 50 per cent increase on the previous year. MTV was in town to shoot a show called 'The Grind'. Ziggy Marley was playing a concert on the cliffs. The resorts were offering all-you-can-drink deals and wet T-shirt competitions for the less inhibited.

The spring breakers roamed the beach in packs – either all boys or all girls – still awkward and white and apart. Thankfully, most had come on special, pre-booked spring break packages to one of the resorts, so we were able to find a relatively cheap room right by the beach on Long

Bay next to the Norman Manley Sea Park. The accommodation was from another time, a collection of old
weatherboard cottages on a large block of land. Soon, no
doubt, the cottages will be bulldozed for a resort like
Hedonism VII, but for the time being the little old Jamaican
lady who ran the place was renting out rooms for a piddling
$20 a night.

It really was a fantastic bargain. There was nothing
between us and the beach and obscenely blue water except
for a few ornamental plants and a rasta and his boat.

The GND was ecstatic. She changed into her bikini and
ran down to the water immediately. I wasn't so sure. To
be honest, the rasta worried me. The rastas of Negril are
notorious the world over and are often referred to as
rastitutes. They are invariably well-built young men, and
many make quite a living servicing the 'needs' of visiting
foreign women. To be honest, it was because of the
'rastitutes' that I'd been worried about coming to Jamaica
in the first place. I'd seen the Lonely Planet show on the
country and watched alarmed as women complained that
Jamaican men hit on them all the time, even if they were
obviously with a husband or boyfriend. These guys figured
that every white woman had a sexual fantasy that included
a buffed rasta rolling about naked. Trouble is, most of the
time they were probably right.

The rasta in front of our cottage certainly fancied himself
as a bit of an Adonis. Each day he would sit in his boat,
which was brightly painted and had an outboard motor
and a roof, trying to drum up business – either a full-day
snorkelling tour, or if business was slow, a quick trip around

to the cliffs of the West End. Each day I'd lie on the beach and watch him.

Soon a pattern emerged in his sales techniques. Whenever a group of girls passed, he would flirt with them, do a somersault into the water, show off. If they refused to take his offer of a snorkel trip to Booby Cay, he would smile and would try to arrange to meet them at some bar later in the evening. 'You've never known love until you've known a rasta!' he would yell after them. The girls always wandered off giggling.

If a group of guys passed, his attitude changed completely. He would become aggressive, surly even. 'Are you ignoring me?' he'd say. 'I'm a human being. When I speak to you I expect to be answered! Respect, mon!'

The guys, usually a bunch of gormless college kids, would panic. Was this guy going to attack them? 'Hey man, we're sorry,' they'd say. 'How much is it?' The rasta would tell them a ridiculously expensive price and they'd get in, too scared to do anything else.

This went on every day that we stayed in Negril. And every day, this guy would use his downtrodden and oppressed state to seduce or intimidate young American spring breakers into using his boat.

He never approached us. He probably heard our Australian accents and figured he would be wasting his time. He didn't know how right he was. Earlier in the day I'd gone to the ATM at the National Commercial Bank and got the dreaded 'Insufficient Funds' message. My bank account was now officially empty. We were living off the last of our travellers' cheques and cash. It was the moment

I'd been dreading, the moment I'd been warning the GND about every time she tucked into a huge meal and then asked for another serve. She'd said we'd deal with it when it happened. Well, it was happening and she wasn't dealing with it. She seemed to think that if we scrimped and saved we could get by on $3 a day.

My solution was for her to ring her father and ask him to lend us some money. I'd done my sums – I had a few cheques coming in and would be able to pay him when we got home. It was just a cash-flow problem, and I figured he could help us out. (I couldn't call my parents – they had just gone through a messy divorce so it would have been a little insensitive to ask them for 'emergency funding'.)

'You don't understand,' the GND said. 'I've borrowed money from him before, but I've never paid him back. Can't we just make do?'

I knew what she was going through. No one likes asking parents for money. No matter how good your intentions are, or theirs, for that matter, there's always the feeling that you've let them down.

Unfortunately, there was no way around it. We'd been 'making do' since we'd arrived in Negril and we couldn't do it for much longer. While most of the spring breakers were living it up in Margueritaville, eating the equivalent of their own weight in seafood and drinking more rum than a fleet of buccaneers, we were down at the local supermarket buying dodgy processed meats and day-old loaves of bread. It had got to the stage that we were visiting different supermarkets for different items, simply because they were cheaper. (In case you find yourself in Negril in similar circumstances, the supermarket at the Sunshine Village up on West End Road offers the best deals on soft drinks and tomatoes.)

We even scrimped on entertainment. Most days we walked the five kilometres to the Pickled Parrot, a restaurant-bar that sat on a cliff face overlooking the eerily blue water. Whenever we spotted a waiter coming we'd jump into the water until he left. At night, we'd wander along Long Bay Beach, gazing longingly into the resorts where spring breakers were dancing and singing and having wet T-shirt competitions. Then we'd make our way to the beachside stages where second-rate reggae bands gave second-rate, but free, concerts. As a special treat we'd sometimes share a bottle of Red Stripe between us.

For a really special treat, we'd visit the cheapest Jerk Chicken man in Negril, splashing out and buying a piece of chicken each. The guy cooked the chicken on a homemade barbecue fashioned from an old 44-gallon drum in an awkward spot beside Norman Manley Boulevard. He missed the spring breaker trade – they were all on the beach – so most of his customers were locals, or destitute travellers like the GND and me. Business was often slow, so after he'd cooked our chicken, he'd bring it over to the wooden table and sit with us for a while, talking.

One night his girlfriend turned up and demanded a piece of chicken.

'Have you got the money for it?' he asked.

'Money!' she screeched. 'What you want money for? I your girlfriend!'

He then patiently explained his operating cost, how much

he paid for each piece of chicken, how much profit he made on each piece and how many pieces he'd have to sell to cover the cost of giving her a piece for free.

'You so tight, mon,' she yelled. 'It's like the phone. You never let me use the phone!' She snatched her bag and stormed off, tottering on her high heels. 'Don't you be expecting no booty,' she called back, over her shoulder.

It seems we weren't the only couple in Negril fighting over money. Chastened, the GND agreed to e-mail her father the next day and ask him to lend us some money.

The only Internet cafe we could find was above one of the restaurants on the beach. It was run by an old rasta who had been talked into getting iMacs by a slick guy from New York, on the promise that they wouldn't give him any trouble. Every time we dropped by we found him knee-deep in cables, trying to figure out which one plugged into the computer, the modem and the phone jack. The GND e-mailed her father and we crossed our fingers.

Because we didn't have much money, the rasta would let the GND quickly log on over the next couple of days to check if there was an e-mail from her father for free. Each day we'd quickly scour the inbox for the magic message – Re: The money is in your account! When it finally came, and we had verified it by dragging out a couple of hundred Js from the ATM at the National Commercial Bank, I offered to pay the Internet cafe owner for all the times I had used his computer.

He refused. 'Hey mon,' he said. 'Just do the same to someone in need in your country.'

With our finances back in order and our bills paid, it

was time to head off to Montego Bay. We'd been cutting it fine – our flight to Havana left at 11 – so to get there in time we had to catch the 6 am minivan to Lucea where we would change for a van to Montego Bay. The first part of the journey was fine, a pretty jaunt along the coast, in the morning cool, listening to Beenie Man imploring President Clinton to be 'havin' it the doggy way' with Monica Lewinsky. It was probably the most pleasant journey we'd made in Jamaica. Then we arrived in Lucea and it all went pear shaped.

Lucea was a town that had seen better days. Most of the buildings had broken windows and peeling paint. The bus station, a muddy block opposite the town's petrol station, was hectic and chaotic, and getting onto a minivan going to Montego Bay well nigh impossible. Two left without us, too crowded to fit us in. Whenever we tried to get on one, we were unceremoniously pushed out of the way. 'Get out of the way, whitey!' one guy had said. 'Let black people on first!' said another. I lugged my bag from one van to another, suffering an extended bout of baggage-related Tourette's Syndrome and getting increasingly pissed off.

Finally, when our bags were thrown on top of a van going to Montego Bay, I questioned the price of our fare. I had been watching the conductor and the price he charged us was considerably higher than the price the other passengers were paying.

'Just pay him the money,' said the GND. Now that there was money back in my account she had become quite the spendthrift again. What a short memory she had!

But I refused. I was sick of Jamaicans adding another

50 per cent on top just because of the colour of my skin. After an increasingly heated debate, the guy collecting the money finally agreed to charge us the right rate. As he took our money he muttered 'Cheap Charlie!' under his breath.

That did it. I exploded. Everything that I had been holding in came out in a torrent. I wasn't just abusing the minivan conductor, I was abusing the rastas at the Bob Marley Museum, the barmaid at the Artland Guest House, the boat guy at Negril.

'You guys want respect?' I spat. 'Well, how about respecting us? You want to be treated as human beings? Well how about treating me as a human being and not like a walking wallet?'

The guy just looked at me stunned. 'Are you on crack?' he said.

That stopped me dead. I realised I was wasting my time and got into the van exasperated. The GND gave me the kind of look that said, 'What did you achieve by all that?' and shook her head. I think my cheap-Charlie ways were beginning to annoy her too.

I spent the rest of the way to the airport at Montego Bay, and the entire flight to Havana, silently composing a very harsh letter to the Jamaican Tourist Board. The GND, I'm sure, was wondering if perhaps I really did have a secret drug problem.

CHAPTER TWENTY-FIVE

Cuba

Annoying Habit >>> Jealousy
Culprit >>> Peter

The GND and I arrived in Havana to find Joan Osborne, REM, Fleetwood Mac and Bonnie Raitt there too. Thanks to the phenomenal success of *The Buena Vista Social Club*, Cuba had become something of a panacea for ailing musical careers. They were all in town, defying the wishes of their government by staying at the Hotel Nacional, a fantastic Art Deco monument high on a hill overlooking the Straits of Florida in the old gangster section of Havana called Vedado, and playing with local musicians. Rumour had it that Woody Harrelson was spotted jamming with the house band up in the piano bar as well.

Of course, it isn't strictly illegal for Americans to visit Cuba. United States law allows them to visit the country – they're just not allowed to spend any money while they're there. There are no direct commercial flights between the two countries, however, so any US citizen wanting to improve their musical cred has to get a flight from either Canada or Mexico. Whatever way they came, the fading musicians would have needed an accommodation voucher from the Hotel Nacional to get into the country. Unfortunately, in our rush to get out of Jamaica, the GND and I hadn't got an accommodation voucher from anywhere.

In the end it wasn't really a problem. The friendly immigration guy at José Martí International Airport, looking very spiffy in a neat khaki uniform and sporting a fetching pencil-thin moustache, said we could still enter the country – just as long as we booked a room with the accommodation guy standing at a bench against the wall, handwriting vouchers for Havana hotels. Unfortunately, all the budget hotels in Havana were full and the cheapest room he could offer us was $60 a night. I looked at the GND, dismayed.

'I'm not asking my dad for any more money!' she said, reading my mind.

I remembered a business card that Alison, one of the Australian medical students in Honduras, had given us. It had the address of a family who rented out rooms to travellers, a family she had stayed with when she was here. I wasn't sure that it was strictly legal, but I showed it to the accommodation voucher guy and he nodded his head enthusiastically and took us back over to the immigration guy. He smiled too and let us enter Cuba without a hotel voucher. I was touched. These guys had bent the rules to help us, rather than use them to extract extra money out of us.

'That wouldn't have happened in Jamaica,' said the GND, smiling.

We caught a taxi from the airport to the centre of Havana, a 25-kilometre journey through farmland and light factories. A deliberate government policy of diverting resources throughout the whole of Cuba has limited growth in the capital and saved it from the heavy traffic, rampant commercialisation and extensive slums that plague nearly every other Latin American city. We reached the town centre without realising it was the town centre at all.

The apartment on our business card was in the old part of town, among the labyrinth of lanes and crumbling tenements of La Habana Vieja. The numbering system was Byzantine and confusing, and the driver turned the meter off while he asked people for directions. We found the apartment eventually – it was on the third floor of an old colonial building overlooking the massive Capitolio building (a replica of the US Capitol Building in Washington) – and rang the buzzer. A middle-aged lady with her hair in curlers came out onto a small wrought-iron balcony. On spotting us, she sent her son down to open the huge wooden doors and let us in. He led us up the worn marble staircase and into the flat where his mother had two cold fruit drinks waiting for us.

Her name was Joaquina and she was one of the new breed of entrepreneurs taking advantage of the relaxed regulations that allow Cubans laid off from inefficient state enterprises to start their own businesses. Where they were limited to earning 200 pesos (about $10) a month as a state employee, there was potential to earn much more through self-employment. Some opened small restaurants, limited to 12 chairs and employing only family members, called paladares. Others, like Joaquina, opened their doors and their spare bedrooms to tourists. The scheme had proved so successful that tax revenues from the self-employed sector now accounted for 10 per cent of the national budget income.

After telling us we were free to use the bathroom, Joaquina gave us the bad news that she didn't have any rooms available. A few calls on an old Bakelite phone later, however, and she'd lined up an apartment for us with her old friend Sergio and organised a cyclo – the Cuban version of a rickshaw – to take us there.

Sergio lived in a slightly less salubrious part of the old town, a block or two from the Capitolio rather than overlooking it, and in an apartment block built in the twentieth century rather than the sixteenth. He was in his late thirties and was deeply impressed that we were from Australia. 'We get "Skippy" here,' he said. 'It is good for the children. No violence. No sex. Good morals.'

Once gain, Skip had proved to be Australia's greatest ambassador. I did make a note, however, not to tell Sergio that the GND and I weren't married.

Like most of Havana, the apartment block had seen better days. It was shored up with wooden planks and the lock on the front security door needed a whack before it would unlock. But the apartment itself was clean, bright and cool. It had two bedrooms, a kitchen with a fridge and stove, and a laundry where we could do our washing. There was even an old b&w television in the lounge room we could watch. At $20 a night, all things considered, it was quite a bargain. We said we'd take it.

'It'll be like we're living together,' said the GND, twirling around in the lounge room. 'Imagine, our very own apartment in Havana.'

It was true. We'd been travelling together for close to six months, spending twenty-four hours a day together, often in the company of other smelly backpackers. We'd slept together in hotel rooms every evening and eaten every meal – breakfast, lunch and dinner – in a restaurant. But we hadn't actually lived together – you know, having breakfast at a table reading the newspaper, choosing something to wear from clothes hanging in a wardrobe, or even squeezing the toothpaste in the wrong place. This apartment in Havana gave us the chance to try it out.

The apartment was certainly homely enough. In a lot of ways, the furniture reminded me of the furniture of my childhood. We had a faux wooden laminated dining table. And a two-tone vinyl couch. Even the television set was a reminder of growing up in a pre-colour world. You couldn't just turn it on and expect a picture. You had to plug it in and let it warm up. And when you turned it off, the picture shrank to a tiny dot in the centre of the screen that stayed there for a good ten minutes. If you wanted to change the channel you had to get up from your seat and physically twist the knob. It was my BR (Before Remote) childhood all over again. But instead of my dad using me as a human remote control, it was the GND.

The bedrooms, on the other hand, reminded me of my grandmother's house. The bed was lumpy and covered with a chenille bedspread. The dressing table was fake timber laminate and had a large glass mirror cut in a weird fifties-style shape. The only thing missing was the mock Asian jewellery boxes full of crappy costume jewellery and a glass beside the bed for dentures.

When we went upstairs to Sergio's apartment to pay our 'rent' I began to suspect that the apartment may well have belonged to his mother. She sat in a corner in a rocking chair, rocking with a pissed-off look on her face. Sergio's apartment wasn't any bigger than the one we were staying in, but it housed Sergio, his wife, his two daughters and his mother. From what we could see, Sergio and his wife had one room, the daughters and their grandmother the other. I guess at $20 a night in a country where the average monthly wage is $10 he could afford to upset his mother. It certainly allowed him to splash out on a few luxuries. When we met the whole family in the stairwell the next day, Sergio had had a haircut and his daughters were wearing pretty new dresses.

It doesn't take long to realise why UNESCO made the whole of old Havana a World Heritage site. Founded in 1515, it was one of the most strategically important cities in Spanish America and, left untouched by any major natural disasters and devastating wars of independence, Havana has survived as an almost complete example of a Spanish colonial complex. A lack of hard cash since the revolution of 1959 has meant that the ancient palaces, plazas, colonnades, churches and monasteries have escaped 'renovation'. So instead of the prissy aura of places like Prague and Florence, Old Havana has an authentic feel as if we were stepping back in time.

This disconcerting 'back to the future' feeling is not helped by the number of old American cars on the road. Walking down Máximo Gómez on our first day in Havana, I felt like we had walked into an episode of 'Happy Days', only a Hispanic version, where the Fonz wears a wispy moustache and Mrs C has a penchant for striped Lycra. Every single car that passed us was a relic of American motoring history – a pre-war Chevy here, a 1950 Ford there. It occurred to me that the Automobile Association of America should declare Havana a living museum as well.

Considering that the Cubans have not been able to import spare parts from Detroit since the revolution, the cars were in great condition. In an amazing display of ingenuity, any parts that are needed are reconditioned or made from scratch. The back streets of old Havana are lined with men patching and respraying their cars and under every apartment block there is a workshop where engine blocks are being winched out and reconditioned on wooden benches. A chap was rebuilding a 1948 Bel Air outside our apartment.

Now, I know it's easy to romanticise about a place like La Habana Vieja. And I don't want you to think that I was blind to the problems facing the good folk of Havana. Their homes were falling apart around them. The supply of water and electricity was intermittent at best. And if they wanted to go anywhere they had to line up to get on one of the camel buses, long hump-shaped cabins pulled around town by a prime mover. There were signs of change, though. On every street there were little family-run enterprises selling ice creams, fruit juice or pastries to passersby. Dollar shops were springing up for the new entrepreneurs to spend their hard-earned money on western luxury goods like Coca-Cola and washing powder that actually got whites whiter. Elsewhere, there were street markets selling fruit and vegetables and stuff for santería religious ceremonies like beads, seeds and knives. Unfortunately, the most popular items being sold on the streets of Havana were striped Lycra tops and shorts.

Lycra is never a good look at the best of times, even when you're a lean cyclist making your way through the French Alps. But when you're a Cuban lady in your middle years carrying a few extra pounds, it's a travesty. Yet on the streets of Havana every women over 30 years old and weighing 60 kilograms and upwards insisted on wearing the whole ensemble. Worse, the outfits were striped – vertically – and the lines snaked from neck to knee in a very circuitous manner.

But I digress. On the whole, the GND and I discovered Old Havana to be a place of hidden squares and churches and quiet cobbled corners that have not changed for centuries. It was full of kids in bright red and white uniforms walking along in single file and old ladies sitting on corners sucking on cigars. And it throbbed with the sound of Latin music – from every car, from every shop, from every house. Imagine a city where everyone was

playing the *Buena Vista Social Club* soundtrack at once on
constant rotation and you get an idea of what it's like
walking the streets of Havana.

After Jamaica, we were surprised how friendly the Cubans
were. Everywhere we went people smiled at us and said
'Hola'. One woman, standing on a street corner chatting
to friends, spotted our Lonely Planet guidebook and ran
across the street, dodging a rambling Chevy, to point out
her picture on it. After the attitude of Jamaica it was such
a wonderful change.

'It is so fantastic here,' said the GND. 'Why didn't we
come here sooner?'

◙   ◙   ◙

The GND was tired from walking, so we found a little cafe
opposite a small park to sit and rest called Cafetería Torre
La Vega. Our guidebook had said it was 'perfect for those
on a tight budget', but it turned out to be a charming place
with a high wooden bar and tables and chairs on the
footpath. We sat in the afternoon sun, delighted, sipping
on coffee as good as in Europe and watching life go by in
the small park opposite. A mother sat on an iron bench,
watching her kids playing. Another woman came along and
chatted with her for a while. Opposite the park, on the
stone steps in front of a colonial doorway, two old guys
sat, smoking cigars. One wore a beret, both had thick silver
moustaches. A pair of pretty girls walked by in Lycra crop
tops and tight jeans, and stopped to say hello. They flirted
with the old guys, who nudged each other after the girls
left.

Much has been made of the plight of the Cuban people, particularly by the Cuban exiles in Miami and New York who fled the country after the revolution. They like to paint their countrymen as poor, oppressed people leading sad, miserable lives. But that afternoon I remember thinking that the scene we had observed could have come straight out of a 1950s American Community Values propaganda film. There was a real sense of community here in Cuba, and the sort of family values that Americans remember fondly and often wish they had back again. It was about then that the GND and I decided to give up any idea we had of rushing around the rest of the country and spend the rest of the week in Havana.

It was the people who made Havana such a special place. After Jamaica, where everyone was ripping us off, the kindness and generosity of the Cuban people was overwhelming. On our second night in Havana, we were wandering the old city looking for somewhere to eat when we were approached by two scruffy young guys, street kids. One could speak a semblance of English. He asked us if we were looking for somewhere to eat and when I nodded, motioned for us to follow him.

They led us through crumbling buildings and unlit lanes – scary, but quite the norm in Havana – to a window covered by a grill. Behind it, a family had set up a makeshift kitchen and were doling out meals of beans, rice and chicken in cardboard boxes for the equivalent of 30 cents a meal. It wasn't anything fancy, but it was tasty and filling. Better still, they took pesos, not dollars. If we'd wandered into a tourist restaurant we would have got a meal of a similar quality, but it would have cost us $20. The guys, happy to have helped us, smiled and said good night. I called them back and bought them a meal each. They hadn't expected any reward and beamed with delight. I guess that's what I liked about the place.

I also liked the way the Cubans refused to beg. They were too proud to simply stick their hands out, and instead would come up with inventive ways of getting money from you. The most popular method was to follow you, sketch a picture of you and then sell it to you for 50 cents. I had my portrait surreptitiously drawn as we browsed through the open-air book market at Plaza de Armas and then again near the cathedral. They were never any good. In fact, they were really quite dreadful. But I appreciated the initiative shown and bought both.

The only blight on Havana I could see was the public transport. For the most part the GND and I had been able to avoid it. We spent much of our time in Havana walking, wandering down tiny lanes just to see where they would take us. But after three days of stumbling upon vistas, we decided to make a day trip to Guanabo, one of the nearby beaches on Havana's riviera, and saw first-hand what the long-suffering Cubans have to go through every day.

Our guidebook said that the number 400 bus left for Guanabo from the corner of Calle Gloria and Agramonte near Havana's central train station, and within ten minutes of the GND and me arriving on the designated spot it did. The bus was a relic of the pre-revolution years too, and I was delighted to discover that we didn't have to queue to get on and that there were a few empty seats waiting for us as well. But we had barely settled in before the bus stopped and every other passenger was pouring off and dashing for a bus shelter on the other side of the road. The bus was empty before the GND and I realised that we should have been doing the same thing as well. By the time we reached the other side and joined the queue, the man handing out cardboard chits to intending passengers had run out. To rub salt into our wounds, the very same bus we had just got off did a U-turn and everybody with chits clambered back on again.

It was another hour before the next bus to Guanabo came along again. There was the same mad dash. And the same guy handed out chits again. But this time the GND and I were at the head of the queue and we were able to get a window seat right up front. An hour later we were at Guanabo.

So what was Guanabo like? Well, the sand was white and the water a beautiful aqua blue. But the buildings surrounding it were a little worse for wear. And there seemed to be an inordinate number of European men lying on towels, inactive and looking very, very bored.

On our fourth day in Havana we went to Vedado to change money. Vedado is at the other end of the Malecón, the road that follows the coast along the Straits of Florida. A low wall runs all the way around and it is a favourite spot for couples to sit and watch the sea or gaze at the highrises on the point at Vedado. It was also a popular spot for fishermen and boys throwing stones into the oceans or playing chicken with the waves that crashed onto the rocks, sending a plume of sea spray onto the road and forcing the owners of the old Chevies to check that the windscreen wipers still worked. At each T-intersection or set of lights along the Malecón packs of people would wait. When a car stopped they would approach the driver and ask for a lift. I guess it beat lining up for hours to get on a crowded camel bus.

Vedado is the modern part of Havana. In Cuba, modern means anything built in the fifties, so where the architecture in the old city is pure Spanish colonial, here it is the perfect snapshot of American gangster chic. Which is hardly surprising really. Before the revolution Havana was the playground of Miami's mobsters. Batista, the thuggish Cuban dictator at the time, turned a blind eye to the prostitution and gambling and, in return, millions of dollars were pumped into the Cuban economy, albeit from dubious sources. Wandering the streets of Vedado, crumbling and unpainted, you could almost hear the music, the gunshots and the clink of glasses. It must have been one hell of a town.

The only place you can get a cash advance on a credit card in Cuba is in a bank in the lobby of the Habana Libre, the former Hilton Hotel, where Fidel and his barbudos set up headquarters on the 22nd floor in January 1959. There was a long queue – the computer terminal they used was about as reliable as a city bus – so the GND waited for me in the airconditioned hotel lobby. An hour later, I emerged, ironically with a fistful of US dollars, to find her chatting with Leroy, a lobbyist from Washington.

Leroy was a chubby Afro-American in the jolly Fat Albert mould and had been in Havana in January. He'd had such a good time that he was back, only a couple of months later. 'I'm a single guy so I like a little action,' he said with a wink.

Unfortunately, in the few month since he was here last, Fidel had cleaned the action up. A police crackdown had put a couple of thousand working girls behind bars. 'I went straight to the beach from the plane,' he said. 'Nothing! It was deserted.' He shrugged his shoulders and laughed. He wasn't too fussed. He figured there'd still be a little action around. He'd just have to find it.

'Say, you guys going to the baseball match?' he asked.

Apparently the Baltimore Orioles were playing the Cuban national side in an exhibition match that weekend. It would be the first time a major American team had played in Cuba since the revolution. Not being particularly big baseball fans, it was the first we'd heard about it.

'Man, everyone is here for that,' Leroy said. 'ESPN have shipped in a satellite broadcast van to beam it back live to the States. Every one of the 30 major league teams have sent down a rep to watch it. And apparently, old Fidel's gonna show up. It's gonna be awesome.'

I asked if we needed to buy tickets.

'I don't know, but I'll ask that pretty concierge,' said Leroy, motioning to a stunning black girl with tiger eyes, standing behind the counter in a tailored navy-blue uniform. Soon he was tangled in a flirty conversation with her – maybe he was asking her where the action was now – so we never did find out about the baseball tickets. When we asked Sergio later that night, he seemed to think we could just turn up for the game. Tickets for a match like this, he reasoned, would have to cost at least $2, far too much for your average Cuban.

Our days in Havana soon fell into a bit of a pattern. We'd buy fresh bread and cheese from a bakery near our apartment for breakfast and maybe call into a café for a coffee on the way. We'd visit a museum, like the Museo de la Revolución, where the GND could gaze lovingly at all the Che memorabilia and mouth Fidel's final eulogy to his comrade – 'If we want to express how we would like to be the men of future generations, we should say: We want them to be as Che!' (I know it was illogical, but I felt jealous. I wanted her to admire me in the way she admired Che. But it seemed that all this journey had done was lessen her opinion of me.) Or we'd visit a cigar factory and watch little old men with pictures of Che on their desk roll the very finest cigars in the world.

After lunch at the Torre La Vega, I'd take up the furtive offers whispered conspiratorially from people on the street to come back to their apartments and peruse boxes of counterfeit cigars, on offer for a fraction of the official factory price. Then, at night, we'd go to Havana's China Town, a tiny lane just off Calle Dragones, and enjoy a huge Chinese banquet with ice cold beers for a pittance, all paid for in pesos. Then we'd return to our apartment, perhaps calling first into Hemingway's favourite bar, La Bodeguita del Medio, for a quick mojitov (the big man's favourite drink), to watch a program on sugar cane production and retire. Life was good.

I've got to say the part of the day I looked forward to most was perusing the cigars. Although not a smoker, since coming to Central America I had become quite the cigar aficionado. I knew my Lonsdales from my Churchills, and my Culebras from my Belicosos. And after reading cigar magazines and visiting their websites, I knew which cigars had the richest aromas and the most delightful flavours. I also knew that the best Cuban cigars, and hence the best in the world, were the Cohiba Esplendidos and the Montechristo As. While I couldn't afford them at factory prices – a box of 25 Esplendidos cost $325 at the Cohiba Factory in Havana, over a $1000 back home – a box of counterfeits were going for only $30 on the street.

It wasn't the bargain price that attracted me. To be honest, I suspected that they weren't really Esplendidos anyway, and if they were, they were probably the ones that were poorly rolled or drew badly. It was the intriguing insight you got into how your average Cuban lived. To avoid trouble with the police, the counterfeit cigar sellers didn't carry the cigars on them. They kept them at a safe house, usually a friend's apartment. The buying process involved following the seller down tiny lanes, often on the other side of the street so as not to alert the suspicion of the police, and up creaky staircases or dilapidated lifts to tiny crowded apartments. After locking the door, the cigars were pulled out from under the mattress, or under a pile of clothes in a wardrobe, for viewing, and, if you were an expert like me, for sniffing.

Anywhere else in the world, I would have been suspicious that I was being set up to be rolled. But in Havana, I felt perfectly safe. Not only was the business of negotiating a price conducted in a fair and friendly manner, the lady of the apartment would often provide refreshment. The fact that I was handing over the equivalent of three months' wages for a box of cigars that were probably nicked from the factory anyway, no doubt helped too.

◼   ◼   ◼

It was Sunday, the day of the historic baseball match between Cuba and the Orioles. The match was being held in the Stadium Latinoamericano, a crumbling edifice a couple of suburbs away from our apartment. Rather than risk public transport, the GND and I walked, and we were alarmed to discover that a huge crowd had turned out for the game. We went to the ticket windows to buy a ticket only to find that it was an invitation-only affair – Fidel had handed out tickets to the best factory workers and they had been bused in from all over the province to watch the match.

We joined the line of people entering anyway, and when we reached the gate and the guy taking the tickets, tried slipping him a $5 note. He was an old proud man, and he turned us away with such an incredible look of disdain that I wanted the ground to swallow me up. With my crass gesture I had proved to him that I was the embodiment of the evils of capitalism and in return he gave me a withering look that was full of all the contempt and hatred he held for our way of life.

A large contingent of Orioles fans had come along especially to see the match, so we went around to the gates where they were being let in to see if we could get in there. The entrance here was even tighter – the Americans all had laminated tickets with holograms on them and they clung onto them as if they were about to be robbed by street urchins. We probably could have bribed one of them to give us one, but it would have cost us more than $5.

Just as we were about to give up, we were called over by two young Cuban schoolboys standing beside a tree. They had figured out what we were after and offered us their tickets. There was no way of knowing if they were real – they were just simple slips of paper, something you'd expect to get when you bought a raffle ticket, really – but they only wanted $2 each so we took them anyway. We joined a queue – not the same one as before, I was too ashamed – and surprisingly we were allowed in, despite the fact that, with my loud Hawaiian shirt, I was obviously not Pedro from the local ball-bearing factory and the tickets said 'Personal e intransferible'.

The seats were not numbered so we made our way up into the stand and found a spot, sitting on the wooden slat seats from which paint was peeling. I ventured off to buy the GND an ice cream and a Cuban soft drink. On the way back I noticed that the stadium had a souvenir shop. I thought it'd be cool to get a souvenir of the match. So, it seems, did all the Americans. They were throwing themselves at the window hoping to get a pennant, a mini baseball bat, a poster even, with an unseemly vigour. The stall was run by one little old lady who took one order at a time, calmly writing each purchase into a huge ledger book. She was totally unfazed by the crowd, despite the fact that she was doing more business in that day, no doubt, than at every local match since the revolution. To be honest, she didn't look like she cared whether she sold anything or not, an attitude that sent the Americans into a rage. 'I can't believe this,' one said, clearly appalled. 'No wonder this country is in such a mess!'

I've got to say, I liked her style. The old lady didn't get flabbergasted. It probably didn't matter if she sold anything or not – she had a job, a job for life, probably. And unlike in the competitive US of A, it didn't matter how many pennants she sold, how fast she moved them, or whether she was writing a report on how they could be sold over the Internet, she would still have a job. She wasn't at home each night worrying if she was about to be retrenched because of a corporate downsizing. In solidarity, I stayed in the scrum and bought a pennant and a poster.

I got back to the GND just as the game was about to start. There was a burst of music and the two teams came out onto the ground. There was a commotion among the crowd. Everyone was straining to see a lone figure walking slowly to a dias and microphone set up just in front of the pitcher's mound. In battle fatigues and with the bushy beard, there was no mistaking who it was. It was the big man himself – El Presidente, Señor Fidel Castro.

Now, I know the Americans hate the guy. And there's the line that he's bankrupted his nation, oppressed his people and made an absolute fool of the CIA and their laughable attempts to kill him with exploding cigars. But there was an energy in the crowd that day when he walked out and spoke to them that was electrifying. It wasn't out of fear. It wasn't hatred. They genuinely loved the guy.

Seeing Fidel was the most exciting part of the day. The

Orioles won the baseball match three–two after extra innings. Not that the Cubans cared. Their team had handled themselves well – in fact, except for a tactical blunder in the seventh, they could have won it. They were happy at seeing a quality match, and pleased that their $10-a-month boys had matched a team with a payroll in excess of $80 million. Walking back to our apartment the GND and I passed all the happy workers filing onto the old beat-up buses that had brought them there, the name of the factories they had come from handwritten on signs stuck in the front of the buses.

It was our last night in Havana so I wanted to take the GND out dancing. We were still watching our money, so a big night out like the Club Tropicana, with its Barry Manilow decor and beautiful, pert-breasted dancers, was out of the question. We'd heard about a small club near the Plaza de la Revolucíon called Rincón del Tango, but when we turned up we found out it was closed for the night. Another group of foreigners turned up, including two Argentinean brothers called Jorge and Antonio. They had a Cuban girl with them. She had matchstick-thin legs and she tottered dangerously on ridiculously high heels. She spoke English perfectly and introduced herself as Maria, but told us to call her Flaca, Spanish slang for skinny. She said she knew a small club nearby and beckoned for us to follow.

The club was tiny and seedy, dark and barely lit by flickering neon lights. The lights gave the darkness a green hue and in front of the bar there was a collection of battered tables and chairs. There was a tiny stage, loaded up with drums, bongos, saxes and trumpets, guitars, bass and keyboard. A 15-piece band had squeezed into the space of an inner-city bathroom. The music started and soon everyone was up dancing as if it was a Jennifer Lopez film clip.

The more outgoing of the brothers, Jorge, danced with Flaca. Antonio, the other brother, stayed at the table and tutted with disgust. 'These people are so sexual here,' he said. 'I don't like it.' When his brother started dancing in a manner that could only be played on television late at night. Antonio looked alarmed. 'I think I must be adopted,' he said.

A couple of songs in, Jorge came over and dragged his brother onto the dance floor. He called Antonio 'the pope' and was determined to loosen him up. Antonio, however, wasn't having a bar of it. He shuffled from one foot to another with a bored look on his face. Flaca, annoyed, grabbed hold of him and started rubbing against him, albeit in time with the music and in a manner that suggested that it may well have been a dance move. 'The pope' could dance – he was Latin American, he was born with the rhythm in him – but he didn't want to succumb to Flaca's advances, and steadfastly refused to look her in the eye.

Flaca was equally determined to loosen him up. She caught the eye of the band leader and gave him a signal. The next number they played was sex on a stick, with a chorus that sounded like 'Jiggy, jiggy, jiggy'. Antonio couldn't fight it any longer, and let the music overtake him. He was a good dancer, certainly better than his brother, and together with Flaca he danced up a storm, and an indecent one at that. He returned to the table ashamed. Antonio, the pope, had lapsed. Jorge gave him a slap on the back.

I realised that Antonio never really had a chance. Cuba and its people were infectious. You couldn't help but be won over and swallowed up by their friendliness and lust for life. But I wondered whether it would stay that way when Fidel finally died and the tourist hordes from across the straits descended on the city wanting their Big Macs and Starbuck Megaccinos.

And I wondered how the GND and I would survive once we were back in the 'real world'.

CHAPTER TWENTY-SIX

Yucatán

(Mexico)

Annoying habit >>> Moodiness
Culprit >>> Peter

Although we had spent just over a week in Havana, arriving in Cancún, the resort town on Mexico's Yucatán Peninsula, was quite a culture shock. It was everything Cuba wasn't – bright, brash and tacky – and was full of large white Americans from the frozen northern states looking for a week or two of sand and sun.

What struck me most was how crass it all seemed after Havana. As we made our way through customs we were blitzed by illuminated signs advertising car-hire companies and beach resorts, and we were handed an official 'Cancún passport' by pretty girls in tight T-shirts. The passport was little more than a collection of special promotion vouchers – an Irish bar called Pat O'Briens offered us a free pitcher of sangria, the local Planet Hollywood franchise offered 10 per cent off the bill as did the Hard Rock Cafe, KFC offered nine free chicken nuggets, and every bar, pub and restaurant was offering a complimentary drink.

The rabid advertising didn't relent on the short trip from the airport into town either. The road from the airport was a forest of billboards advertising mobile phones and American Express credit cards. There was even a huge 24-sheeter singing the praises of the local Wet & Wild Amusement Park. In Havana, the closest thing we'd seen to a Wet & Wild was when the pipe in our kitchen burst.

The amazing thing is that 30 years ago there was absolutely nothing where this shrine to rampant consumerism now stands. It was just a tiny fishing village, a deserted sand spit and a hell of a lot of swamp. Then, in the early seventies a bright spark on the Mexican Tourist Board came up with the idea of building a world-class resort here. The result is a little bit of Florida on the Caribbean, with just a touch of Mexican flavour to justify the fact that the hordes who fly in for a week or two to stay in a resort have to pull out their passports.

We didn't stay in Cancún. We couldn't. The spring breakers were still in town driving the prices up and, to be frank, the billboards and the pyramid-shaped hotels that lined the shore frightened me. Instead we caught a bus down the Riviera Maya, the coastal stretch between Cancún and Tulum, to Playa del Carmen, a smaller, more laid-back beach resort 65 kilometres away.

Of course, 'smaller' and 'more laid-back' are relative terms. The GND and I arrived in Playa del Carmen just after dark to find the place overrun with sexually frustrated college students intent on drinking more tequila than is sensible. Worse, all the budget hotels listed in our guidebook were full and we were forced to take a noisy room on a main road run by a transvestite. We wandered back into the town centre and along the pedestrian mall, Avenida Quinta, a strip of neon lights, clothes shops, restaurants and bars called Pancho's and Señor Frog's that boasted three-hour happy hours and the best selection of tequila in town. Disconcertingly, there were also hairbraiders displaying samples of their work on mannequin heads, detached and put on top of broomsticks.

The restaurants along here were too loud or too pricey so we ventured down the side streets towards the beach. Here we found a surprisingly empty Hooters Restaurant, but the GND refused to go in. There was also a small family-run restaurant with tables and chairs on the sand. They were offering a two-for-one deal on beers, so we ordered a couple of Coronas, kicked off our shoes and wriggled our toes in the sand. The sound of the waves crashing on the shore was soothing and drowned out the din of the carousing back on the mall. The GND peered into the darkness, trying to get an idea of what the beach looked like, but gave up when the beers arrived. We clinked the bottles together. Our Central American odyssey was drawing to a close.

We were woken early the next morning by buses revving noisily outside our window, and made our way down to

the beach just as it was coming to life. It was stunning –
seriously, you've never seen a beach like the beach at Playa
del Carmen. The sand is white – incredibly white. And the
water is blue – an unearthly shade of aqua. If you saw a
picture of the beach in a brochure you'd swear it had been
touched up. And because the sand on the beach is made
up of microscopic plankton fossils rather than silica, it stays
cool, even on the hottest days. The tourist board calls it
airconditioned sand. And it is.

The American college students had partied well into the
night, so the beach remained pretty much deserted until
around midday, when they began to stir from their slumber.
The water was as delightful to swim in as it was to look
at, and the weather was perfect. The GND and I stayed
there for most of the morning, only moving when we were
unwittingly entangled in an impromptu Frisbee match
between two frat boys only just stumbling home.

Yet, despite the idyllic setting, there was a noticeable rise
again in the tension between me and the GND. Little things
I did – like change the lyrics to songs – were annoying her.
And I was upset by her insistence that we buy presents for
people back home. I argued that we couldn't afford to.
Despite getting a loan from her father we were still on an
extremely tight budget.

'We can't go back without presents,' the GND insisted.
'What would that look like?'

'It would look like we didn't have much money left,' I
said. 'Are you prepared to go without food just so you can
buy your brother something he'll probably put in a cup-
board?' I was probably being a little unfair. It's just that

my family have been conditioned over the years not to expect anything when I get back from overseas. They know that whenever I go away I always cut my finances as fine as possible. In fact, I think they regard it as a kind of gift when I don't ring up reverse charges from some far-flung corner of the globe to ask them to lend me some money.

We spent most of our time in Playa del Carmen fighting like this. After close to six months of biting our tongues, of watching what we said because of the long road ahead, now the end was in sight and we were sniping like a pair of old pensioners.

'Well, I'm sick of these arguments,' I'd say. 'I'll be glad when we get home and you're out of my life.'

'Fine,' the GND would say. 'I can't wait either!'

Then we'd go and lie on a sugar-white beach and swim in azure blue water, living a life out of a romance novel. You go figure.

We took a day trip down to the ruins at Tulum. Tulum, or the City of Dawn, is a collection of Toltec-inspired buildings on top of a cliff, overlooking a beach as magical as Playa del Carmen's. Our guidebook described it as a 'product of Mayan civilisation in decline', and if it was indeed one of the last great Mayan cities, I'd suggest that the location had something to do with it. I mean, it was breathtaking. If you were an ancient Mayan living there – a perfect white beach and blue waters only a short stroll from your stone hut – why would you bother continuing with a life of conquering and pillaging? They probably developed the same kind of attitude that has kept Australia conspicuously absent from the list of the world's great nations. Why bother expanding an empire when you've got great weather, a great beach and seafood to burn?

Inspired by the location, the GND decided that she wanted to go for a swim, so we made our way to a beach a little further along, lined by a collection of cabañas popular with backpackers. The beach was littered with debris from the sea so we took our time picking a spot. Just as we had settled and were spreading our towels on the sand, one of the male sunbathers stood up and walked into the water. The guy was completely naked, his willy flopping freely as he walked. We had stumbled on a nudist beach.

I've always wondered what the protocol is in these situations, especially when the said nudists stroll straight past you as they did here in Tulum. Are you expected to take your clothes off too? And is it bad form if you don't? We had a quick swim (wearing our swimming costumes), gathered our things and beat a hasty retreat to the highway, where we waved down a bus heading back towards Playa del Carmen.

On the way back to Playa del Carmen we stopped at Xcaret, an eco-archaeological theme park built on an old communal turkey farm. I had been intrigued by the place after seeing a brochure calling it 'Nature's Sacred Paradise' and describing it as 'xotic, xuberant and xciting!'. Of course, the brochure didn't mention that it was built on a pile of turkey shit. It tended to focus on the sparkling blue lagoon, the butterfly pavilion, the zoo and the minor Mayan ruins. Any pesky thoughts of treading in something squidgy were banished by promises of exciting underground river rides, dancing Spanish horses and a Las Vegas-style ancient Mayan ceremony spectacular.

As you can imagine, such world class entertainment does not come cheaply. Entry alone cost $25 dollars each, a five-minute swim with the dolphins an extra $50. And I've got to say that it took me some time to convince the GND that the money would not be better spent on a set of souvenir cacti salt and pepper shakers for her mother. A few minutes after handing over our money it became apparent that it would have been.

Xcaret turned out to be little more than a pretty inlet that had been given the full Disney treatment – albeit with a Mayan 'eco-archaeological' theme – a collection of restaurants, souvenir shops and bars. There was a recreation of a Mayan village where bored locals pretended to weave carpets or make tortillas. The zoo was little more than a jaguar asleep under a tree. And the complimentary underground river ride involved putting on a bright pink life vest and letting a river take you through a series of dull caves to a lagoon full of overweight Americans floating on canary-yellow inner tubes. The only half-decent attraction was the recreation of the ball game played by Mayans in the mock ball court just to the left of the cafeteria. The guys were dressed in traditional costumes and seemed to be the only park employees that put in even the slightest bit of effort. The GND was not impressed and when we got back to Playa Del Carmen she bought a baseball cap for her father, just to spite me.

After close to six months on the road the end of our journey was upon us and we couldn't just wander aimlessly any more. Our flight out of Mexico was only days away and we were still 1172 kilometres from Mexico City. We had to plan the rest of our trip carefully, not only so we could see all the stuff we wanted to see, but also because it was Easter, and most transport options in and out of the Yucatán Peninsula were heavily booked. Public holidays! They're the bane of every free-spirited traveller!

I sat down with our guidebook in our noisy, airless room and figured that if we left early enough we could catch a bus across the vast scrubby plains of the Yucatán to the great Mayan ruins at Chichén Itzá. After half a day there, we could continue on to the old colonial town of Mérida then, a day later, endure a 20-hour bus ride to Mexico City. It was an audacious plan, and one that would see us traversing 1172 kilometres and visiting an ancient ruin and a quaint colonial town in only three days. Worse, every one of those three days was an Easter holiday.

My plan started well enough. We were able to book a couple of seats on a bus as far as Chichén Itzá the night before we left. But the main computer network that linked all the bus companies had crashed, making it impossible to book anything after that. And we would simply have to take our chances after we arrived. If the lines at the Playa del Carmen bus station were anything to go by, we'd need more than our fair share of luck.

Chichén Itzá was a bumpy four-hour bus ride away across a vast scrubby landscape baked hard by an unrelenting sun. It was hot and stuffy on the bus – we'd caught a non-airconditioned one to save money – and the GND and I spent most of the journey bickering. It started when I got on the bus and sat in the window seat.

'You always take the window seat,' said the GND,

annoyed. 'Why can't I have the window seat for a change?'

To be honest, I hadn't really noticed. Throughout the trip I had simply got on buses and sat down. I was convinced that over the course of the six months the GND had sat next to the window – actually, thinking about it, I'm sure it had always been the order we got onto the bus that had determined who got the prized seat – but instead I said that if it bothered her so much she should have said something.

'Well, it does bother me,' she answered. 'And I've just said something.'

I got up and stood in the aisle, making a grand gesture with my hand as the GND settled in beside the window. To be honest, the fighting was getting a little too much. The end of the trip was only days away, but it had got to the stage where I was beginning to wonder if the relationship would last that long.

Chichén Itzá is the most famous and best restored of the Yucatán Peninsula's Mayan sites. In the late tenth century, it was invaded by the Toltecs, who moved down to the peninsula from their central highlands capital of Tula. After getting off the bus, paying our entrance fee, stashing our packs in a baggage room and stepping out into the archaeological zone, I wondered how the Toltecs had coped with the heat. We hadn't felt heat like this since León in Nicaragua. It was a dry, crackling heat that evaporated sweat instantly and made the top of your head hot to the touch.

If the 25-metre pyramid called El Castillo in the centre of the park was anything to go by, they had coped rather well. Not only was it huge and impressive, it was also the Mayan calendar set in stone. During the spring and autumn equinoxes – the GND was annoyed that we'd missed both – sunlight and shadows form a series of triangles on the side of the north staircase that mimic the slithering of a serpent. As well as El Castillo, the folk of Chichén Itzá were also able to throw up the largest ball court in Mexico, a clutch of very attractive temples and a 'Group of One Thousand Columns', just for the heck of it. In the scorching heat that day, the GND and I were barely able to stagger from one impressive stone edifice to another.

In our defence, we had to cope with something that the Mayans and the Toltecs never had to deal with, a huge Easter Saturday crowd. Every family in Mexico, it seemed, had decided that this Easter it was time to get in touch with their Mayan heritage. The entire Chichén Itzá archaeological zone was full of screaming kids and harried, exhausted parents freaked out by how much a day at the ruins was costing once you added the price of admission, drinks, food, ice creams and treatment for heat exhaustion.

Chichén Itzá certainly wouldn't be my first choice for a family day out. It was a huge, open site, with one solitary, scrawny tree in front of El Castillo. Mothers would gather their children together and then dash, en masse, from the shadow of one monolith to another. After coaxing their young families up the steep stairs to the top of the pyramid, mothers would then scurry about, making sure young Juan or Juanita wasn't going too close to the edge. Then, as they lined up in the sun for 40 minutes to go down a staircase into the pyramid, the same mothers would fan their youngsters with a newspaper. After lining up for close to an hour myself (the GND refused to fan me, in case you're wondering), I wondered what the kids made of it all. At an amusement park back home there's at least an exciting ride guaranteed to make you bring up your fairy floss. Here the kids had to be content with a stone statue of a reclining man.

I've read since that Chichén Itzá is guaranteed to 'awe the most jaded of visitors'. Obviously the author hadn't met the likes of the GND and me. That day, in the heat, with the crowds, and in the moods we were in, we were just going through the motions. We ticked off the temples and the ballcourt. We wandered through the 'Group of the Thousand Columns' and took a few photos of the Temple of the Skulls, simply because the carved skulls looked cool. The fact that I didn't get upset when I discovered that Chac-Mool, the famous stone carving of a reclining man that sits high on a temple overlooking El Castillo, was closed for renovations shows just how travel-weary I was that day. After only a couple of hours we collected our packs and waited in the carpark for the next bus to Mérida.

My grand plan allowed for a day or two in Mérida. But when we arrived at the modern bus station, a good four blocks from the Plaza Mayor and the city's massive cathedral, we discovered that the direct buses to Mexico City were booked solid until after our plane left. However, there were a couple of seats available on a bus leaving that evening. If we wanted to get to the capital in time for our flight we'd have to take it.

To be honest, I don't remember much of that trip. I

was exhausted from travelling and from our morning in Chichén Itzá. I know we passed through Campeche and Coatzacoalcos, and Veracruz and Córdoba as well, but on that journey they were just a collection of bus stations where we stocked up on cans of warm Pepsi and limp cheese sandwiches. I can recall quite vividly the return of the topés, the stratospheric speed humps that had been the bane of our early travels in Mexico, but mercifully absent in the Yucatán. (It was just as we entered Villahermosa and I'd finally nodded off to sleep.) And I remember getting annoyed by the GND tossing and turning, trying to get comfortable in the non-reclining seats. Oh, and when she handed back my Walkman after the batteries went flat. But that was about it.

I do remember arriving in Mexico City though. After six months trundling through Central America – climbing volcanoes, being struck dumb by the damage caused by Hurricane Mitch, bickering with the GND, sharing romantic Caribbean beaches with the GND, and eating more beans and rice than any person ever really should – it felt like we were coming home. The bus came into the eastern bus station, out near the airport, so when we caught a taxi back to the Centro Histórico it followed the same route as when we arrived, passing the same shuttered shops and the same lumpy prostitutes. Caught up in the nostalgia of it all, we foolishly decided on impulse to stay at the Hotel Zamora again.

Over those next few days it felt like we were an old married couple going back to the town they had met to relive all the romantic moments of their courtship. We popped into Casa Del Pavo where we shared our first flan. And into Gili Polo where we ate our first rancho-style rotisserie chicken. We propped up the bar in our favourite cantinas and the GND went into everyone of the zapatería (shoe shops) that she had judiciously avoided when we arrived. And when we ate breakfast at Café La Blanca, we were delighted to see that the organ grinders were still there – the same ones. They didn't recognise us when we waved at them – why would they? – but it made our day to see them again.

We were bickering less now. Apart from a minor altercation of just how many pairs of new shoes the GND really need to take back with her to Australia, our relationship seemed to have evolved – finally – to a point where we respected each others' funny little ways or at least knew enough about them to avoid them. We had gone the full Montezuma, not just physically through Central America, but emotionally with each other as well. We had seen both the good and bad, and, in the case of the GND's ongoing attempts to stay off the cigarettes, the ugly too. (Just joking – I was very proud of the way she passed the street vendors now without even commenting.)

Over the course of six months we had shared the same sorts of trials and tribulations that couples go through in twenty years of marriage. We had nursed each other through sickness. We had shared spectacular sunsets and horrific bus rides. And we had heard each other making the kind of noises that most couples don't encounter until the twilight years and they're both using incontinence protection. Sure, we'd had our fights. But hey, I remember my grandparents bickering and they were married for over 50 years. (Although I'm sure Pa never heard Nan do Donald Duck impersonations with her butt.)

Some things hadn't changed. When we caught the metro up to Zona Rosa to check our e-mail, the GND got felt up on the crowded subway carriage again. But this time I caught the guy. I grabbed him by the shoulder and told him in what I thought were no uncertain terms – in pidgin Spanish – that the GND was my girlfriend and that he was a pig. He scurried off, alarmed, and I felt pretty pleased with myself. I had stood up for my woman's honour and put my newly acquired Spanish skills to use. The GND looked at me smiling, shaking her head.

'Cero means zero, you idiot,' she said, with a chuckle. 'Pig is *cerdo*.'

Noticing I was a little crestfallen, she took my arm. 'I'm sure he got the picture,' she said. 'Thank you.'

It looked like we'd be using those companion fares after all.